INTERNATIONAL SERIES OF MONOGRAPHS IN
EXPERIMENTAL PSYCHOLOGY

GENERAL EDITOR: H. J. EYSENCK

Volume 4

PERSONALITY AND AROUSAL

PLATE 1. (By courtesy of the Ministry of Defence.)

Personality and Arousal

*A Psychophysiological Study of
Psychiatric Disorder*

BY

GORDON S. CLARIDGE

*Department of Psychological Medicine,
University of Glasgow*

PERGAMON PRESS

OXFORD · LONDON · EDINBURGH · NEW YORK
TORONTO · SYDNEY · PARIS · BRAUNSCHWEIG

Pergamon Press Ltd., Headington Hill Hall, Oxford
4 & 5 Fitzroy Square, London W.1
Pergamon Press (Scotland) Ltd., 2 & 3 Teviot Place, Edinburgh 1
Pergamon Press Inc., 44–01 21st Street, Long Island City, New York 11101
Pergamon of Canada, Ltd., 6 Adelaide Street East, Toronto, Ontario
Pergamon Press (Aust.) Pty. Ltd., 20–22 Margaret Street, Sydney, N.S.W.
Pergamon Press S.A.R.L., 24 rue des Écoles, Paris 5e
Vieweg & Sohn GmbH, Burgplatz 1, Braunschweig

First edition 1967

Library of Congress Catalog Card No. 67–18148

PRINTED IN GREAT BRITAIN BY A. WHEATON & CO. LTD., EXETER
3192/67

FOR MARION

CONTENTS

PREFACE

THIS book brings together a series of studies of psychiatric disorder undertaken between 1958 and 1962 while I was research assistant to Professor H. J. Eysenck at the Institute of Psychiatry, London. The experiments themselves were almost all carried out, however, in Southampton at the Royal Victoria Military Hospital, Netley, and my acknowledgements here reflect the curious conjoint nature of my appointment in Professor Eysenck's department.

Needless to say, I owe my greatest debt to Professor Eysenck himself for his good-humoured tolerance of his "man at Netley", for all he taught me about personality research, and for allowing me to follow my hunches where they led, often, I suspect, no less sceptical of their outcome than I. I am also grateful to him for letting me read, prior to its publication, the manuscript of his new book *The Biological Basis of Personality*. Some of the ideas expressed there will conflict, some will agree, with those developed here. I personally would find it discouraging if this were otherwise, since at least it can be said of personality that there are now facts and ways of gathering facts that we can argue about.

My other loyalty—to the Royal Victoria Hospital—is expressed in the frontispiece to this book. At a time when the demolition of this historic building is being contemplated there seems no more appropriate way of placing on record my own personal debt to R.V.H., which over many years has made notable contributions to medical care and medical research, often in circumstances less agreeable than those under which I myself was able to work.

Of those associated with the Royal Victoria Hospital I am especially indebted to its former Commanding Officer, Colonel R. G. Davies, and to Brigadier J. McGhie, Director of Army Psychiatry. In addition to giving me permission to test the patients and RAMC personnel under their care, they both actively stimulated the work by encouraging their medical officers to collaborate with me on several research projects. Indeed, much of the research would not have been possible without the co-operation of the hospital medical staff, particularly Drs. R. N. Herrington, M. H. Davies and R. J. Wawman. It is refreshing to record an example of completely amicable collaboration between the psychologist and the psychiatrist which was not only mutually stimulating to us as individuals but which also gave tremendous impetus to the research itself.

Of these three former colleagues I am particularly grateful to my close friend Dr. Herrington for his continued contribution to the research since our days at Netley. Hours of discussion with him in many places since then have left an indelible stamp on the ideas expressed in this book; while the scholarly appendix he has written for it on the pharmacology of barbiturates will act, I hope, as a sobering antidote to some of the more speculative psychologizing indulged in elsewhere in the book.

Thanks are due to Mr. A. E. Hendrickson and Miss Nona Hemsley, both of the Institute of Psychiatry, for carrying out many of the statistical analyses and to Professor Max Hamilton, Department of Psychiatry at Leeds, and the Leeds University Computing Laboratory for additional computational help. Permission to quote extracts from their publications was kindly given by John Wiley & Sons Inc., Basic Books, and the editor and publishers of *Acta Psychologica*.

Of those in Glasgow who assisted me, mention must first be made of Professor T. Ferguson Rodger who, with great forbearance, allowed me to continue writing in the face of more urgent departmental duties. I hope he will regard it as a small measure of my appreciation that this book has issued finally from his department. I would also like to thank Misses A. I. Logan and M. Hagan for their efficient typing of the manuscript and Miss Sheila Pattison, Department of Medical Illustration, Western Infirmary, for her expert preparation of the diagrams. To my other colleagues in the Department of Psychological Medicine I express my sincere gratitude. All of them, in their different ways, helped to ease the birth pangs of publication.

Finally, I wish to acknowledge those early psychophysiologists whose researches at the end of the last century anticipated much that is now being rediscovered in psychiatry. In particular I would like to recall Ch. Féré who, in the preface to his remarkable book, *La Pathologie des Emotions*, prepared his readers with the following

comments, which are still only too appropriate some three-quarters
of a century later:

> The somatic conditions of psychic phenomena, their individual variations,
> normal or pathological, the different modes of expression of pain, are not
> yet known to us save in a manner of little precision. The study which is to
> follow has no pretension to fill the void, but only to bring together the
> documents capable of serving to clear up the question in the light of facts of
> observation and experiment.

GORDON S. CLARIDGE

Department of Psychological Medicine,
University of Glasgow

INTRODUCTION

ATTEMPTS to establish an "experimental psychopathology", based on physiology and scientific psychology, can be traced back to the last decades of the nineteenth century. During that period men like Kraepelin in Germany, Féré in France, and Mosso in Italy, were vigorously pursuing the doctrine that psychological phenomena were manifested in measurable somatic processes. To the modern student of psychophysiology accounts of their remarkable experiments on reaction time, fatigue, drug response, and emotion make fascinating reading. To the casual contemporary observer of their work it might almost have seemed as though the study of mental pathology was soon to achieve the status of a scientific discipline.

Unfortunately, this promising alliance between experimental psychology and medicine was overshadowed by other developments in psychiatry. Kraepelin is now mainly remembered for his contribution to descriptive classification and Féré for his discovery of the psychogalvanic reflex. Certainly the traditions of psychophysiology were continued, scattered throughout the scientific literature, but only in the past fifteen years or so has it re-emerged as a discipline in its own right. Indeed, it is as recently as 1964 that the journal *Psychophysiology* was established to cater for the needs of those mongrel scientists who work in the borderland between the psyche and the soma.

During its period of relative quiescence psychophysiology, through the efforts of writers like Elizabeth Duffy, gave birth to such concepts as "arousal" and "activation". These were largely ignored until later advances in neurophysiology gave them new significance. By this time psychophysiology had lost some of its former links with psychiatry, mainly due to theoretical weaknesses in the field of personality study. Abnormal psychology was dominated by psychodynamic theories of personality, while psychiatry was an uneasy coalition between the organic and the phenomenological.

An important branch of the early movement to apply objective techniques to the study of behaviour lay, of course, in the work of

Russian physiologists at the turn of the century. This had tremendous impact on the general psychology of the West, though it had only sporadic influences on Western psychiatry, despite Pavlov's own concern with the pathophysiology of mental illness.

Three major developments in psychology are now contributing to a revival of interest in establishing a more scientific basis for psychiatry. The first is the application of precise statistical techniques to the measurement of personality. This has allowed important dimensions of personality to be isolated and promises to put psychiatric classification on a quantitative basis. The second is the renewed search for psychophysiological and objective behavioural correlates of descriptive personality characteristics, both in the normal and abnormal fields. The third is the growing realization that the study of individual differences is an essential part of any attempt to understand behaviour in general. The processes responsible for such phenomena as attention, fatigue, perception, and psychopharmacological response are again being seen as the very same processes underlying personality. As the early psychophysiologists themselves realized, the study of the psychiatric patient is especially valuable in this context, since it allows extreme individual variations of response to be investigated at the same time as it contributes to a greater understanding of mental illness.

The important contribution of Professor Eysenck in all three of these research areas scarcely needs emphasizing here and it was his inspiration that led to many of the experiments reported in this book. In 1955 I read, in mimeographed form, an early account of his excitation–inhibition theory of personality. This persuaded me that Eysenck had opened up a line of research from which psychology and psychiatry could once more derive mutual benefit. At about the same time I became interested in Duffy's arousal concept and in its similarity to Eysenck's idea of excitation–inhibition, with its Pavlovian origins. It was clear that arousal theorists had paid less attention than Eysenck to individual differences, though they had maintained closer links with physiology. The experiments described in the following chapters had the general aim of trying to integrate these two theoretical viewpoints by relating some aspects of arousal theory to Eysenck's more systematic analysis of personality. The work has drawn on physiological evidence and used physiological techniques more than Eysenck himself has done. Basically, however, the theoretical orientation is similar and is, I feel, a logical extension of Eysenck's original speculations about psychiatric disorder.

The book describes a series of overlapping studies carried out over a number of years and using a very wide variety of experimental techniques in both neurotic and psychotic patients. During the period of the research a number of working hypotheses were adopted, rejected, and modified as new facts emerged. In planning the layout of the book several alternatives presented themselves. Finally, it was decided to present the results in a form which reflected the chronological development of the theory eventually adopted and outlined in the last two chapters. The remainder of the book is divided roughly into two parts. The first five chapters are concerned with neurosis, especially with the detailed examination of Eysenck's theory of dysthymia–hysteria. Chapters 6 and 7 give an account of some exploratory studies of psychosis looked at from a similar psychophysiological viewpoint.

The main experiments were carried out on all or part of two groups of 123 neurotic and thirty-four normal subjects, almost all of whom were military personnel. For convenience, details of these two main groups will be given here, but an additional sample of civilian neurotics also studied is described in Chapter 2. Details of the psychotic sample are given in Chapter 6.

The neurotic sample was divided into sixty-six dysthymics and fifty-seven hysterico-psychopaths. The sample was predominantly male, the dysthymic group containing only two and the hysterico-psychopathic group only four female patients. One neurotic (female) patient was a civilian but she, being the relative of an army officer, was under military care.

All patients were diagnosed by the psychiatrist in charge of the case. This presented little difficulty with respect to conversion hysteria which was relatively common in this population. In searching for other cases the psychiatrists were given brief descriptions of the kind of patient required, the distinction being made between those individuals showing a marked hysterical or psychopathic personality and those giving clear evidence of somatic anxiety and/or obsessional symptoms. In the latter, dysthymic, group the most common syndrome was, in fact, generalized anxiety with occasional super-added phobic reactions and obsessional traits. No further breakdown of this group was attempted, although the hysterico-psychopathic group could be divided into twenty-three conversion hysterics, twenty-nine hysterical personalities, and five psychopaths.

With one exception, the control group consisted of predominantly male volunteers working at the Royal Victoria Hospital. Most were RAMC personnel, although one was a male civilian storeman attached to the hospital and one a QARANC nursing sister. The only other female subject was tested elsewhere at a later date. She was a university student and therefore fell within the same age range as the relatively young military population from which the group as a whole was drawn.

Data for age, IQ, and weight in the three groups are shown, respectively, in Tables 1, 2, and 3. In all cases intelligence was

TABLE 1. AGE (YRS) IN THREE GROUPS OF SUBJECTS

	Dysthymics	Normals	Hysterico-psychopaths
N	66	34	57
Mean	25·4	23·2	23·1
SD	5·11	5·23	4·44

F-ratio: 3·94, $p < 0·05$

t-tests
Dysthymics vs. Hysterico-psychopaths: 2·54, $p < 0·02$.
Dysthymics vs. Normals: 2·08, $p < 0·05$.
Normals vs. Hysterico-psychopaths: 0·09, N.S.

TABLE 2. IQ IN THREE GROUPS OF SUBJECTS

	Dysthymics	Normals	Hysterico-psychopaths
N	66	34	57
Mean	111·3	112·1	110·4
SD	12·59	11·02	11·51

F-ratio: 0·03, N.S.

TABLE 3. WEIGHT (LB) IN THREE GROUPS OF SUBJECTS

	Dysthymics	Normals	Hysterico-psychopaths
N	66	34	57
Mean	147·7	144·1	151·3
SD	15·62	19·45	19·01

F-ratio: 1·81, N.S.

assessed by means of the Raven's Progressive Matrices and the percentile score converted to its IQ equivalent. It can be seen that the groups were well matched for IQ and weight, but that there was an overall significant difference in age (Table 1). This was due to the fact that dysthymics were, on average, somewhat older than both normals and hysterico-psychopaths. The finding may reflect an age bias in the presentation of dysthymic and hysterical symptoms. Because the groups differed in this way the experimental data were carefully examined for any influence of age. However, no significant correlations were found between age and the experimental measures. Since the age differences were slight and the overall age range relatively narrow, it can probably be safely assumed that this variable had little or no effect on the results.

Finally, some general comments are necessary about the patients taking part in the research. Since they were almost all military personnel they cannot be considered an entirely representative sample of psychiatric patients. Compared with the average civilian hospital population, military psychiatric patients are much more homogeneous with respect to such variables as age, weight, sex, and general physical fitness. This introduces an obvious sampling bias and may appear to limit the extent to which the findings are applicable to the general population. Against this can be set a number of important advantages.

First, use of a military sample makes it possible to select groups that are reasonably similar with respect to a number of variables, for some of which deliberate matching may be difficult. This is true not only of comparisons between different psychiatric syndromes but also of comparisons with normal individuals, since a ready supply of control subjects from a similar background is freely available.

Secondly, military patients are more likely to be free of a variety of physical defects and of the complicating effects of brain damage due to ageing. These factors may have an important influence on some of the tests used in the present research, even though age itself, when confined to a narrow range, did not seem to affect the results reported here.

Thirdly, the appearance of clear-cut cases of hysteria in military populations makes it possible to study a wide range of neurosis. Gross conversion reactions are relatively common in the soldier, whereas it is often claimed that they are now rarely seen in civilian practice. Certainly this was the experience when an attempt was made to validate some of the present findings in a civilian hospital setting, where many dysthymics, but few classical cases of hysteria, were encountered. One reason for this difference between civilian and military practice is that, as will be discussed in more detail in Chapter 5, the military population as a whole seems more predisposed in basic personality to hysterical breakdown. Added to this is the fact that the neurotic soldier, probably more frequently than his civilian counterpart, encounters stress situations from which he can most easily, and perhaps only, escape by developing dramatic hysterical symptoms that call attention to himself.

The fourth, and perhaps most important, advantage of research in a military setting concerns the sample of psychotic patients available. Minor deviations in the behaviour of the soldier are much more easily detected than in civilian life and, if psychosis is suspected or diagnosed, the patient is immediately referred for treatment. It is possible, therefore, to gain access to psychotic patients who are in the early stages of their illnesses and who have received little or no treatment. The largely unknown effects of treatment and chronicity can thus be very carefully controlled.

On the whole, it was considered that the advantages of confining the research initially to military patients considerably outweighed the disadvantages. It makes it easier to isolate important personality parameters which might otherwise be obscured by the many variables that are often difficult to control in studies of the psychiatric patient. It then becomes easier to investigate these variables systematically in subsequent studies of more heterogeneous civilian populations.

CHAPTER 1

THE THEORETICAL BACKGROUND

In 1955 Eysenck published the first version of what was to become probably the most controversial theory of individual differences in contemporary psychology. In two postulates he effectively integrated the essential features of three previous theories of behaviour, those of Pavlov, Hull, and Jung. By doing so he brought within the framework of modern personality theory the hypothesis that individuals differ in the nature of their nervous activity.

According to Teplov (1964), it was as early as the first decade of this century when workers in Pavlov's laboratories first conceived the idea that variations in the strength of the excitatory and inhibitory functions of the nervous system could account for the temperamental differences found among dogs. Pavlov very quickly realized that this concept could be applied to the study of human personality, especially in psychiatric patients (Ivanov–Smolensky, 1954) although it was some years before his views on this topic became fully known to Western readers (Pavlov, 1941).

The general notion of excitation and inhibition as fundamental nervous processes had, however, already found expression in the molar constructs of Hullian learning theory (Hull, 1943). Unlike Russian investigators, Hull paid little attention to individual differences, an omission that Eysenck remedied by formulating the first of his 1955 postulates, based on a combined Pavlov–Hull theory of cortical inhibition. Eysenck proposed that there were differences in the rate at which individuals accumulate reactive inhibition in response to stimulation, inhibition being considered a central, cortical process, rather than a peripheral one, as Hull had suggested.

The second postulate tried to reinterpret the Pavlovian theory of temperamental and nervous types in terms of Western descriptive typologies of personality, particularly that of Jung (1921). Eysenck

1

hypothesized that extraverted individuals were more prone to develop cortical inhibition than introverted individuals. In the Jungian tradition linking normal introversion and extraversion with their abnormal counterparts, it was argued that neurotics would also differ in their proneness to inhibition. Eysenck postulated that cortical inhibition would develop more rapidly in neurotics suffering from hysterico-psychopathic disorders than in those displaying the dysthymic symptoms of anxiety, reactive depression, and obsessionality. Dysthymics and hysterics were thus regarded as criterion or prototype groups for studying the personality correlates of cortical inhibition.

In typically systematic fashion Eysenck had preceded his causal postulates with intensive factor analysis of the descriptive features of personality. On the basis of studies by himself (Eysenck, 1947), and later by Hildebrand (1953), he had provided statistical evidence supporting the Jungian typology and had proposed two personality dimensions of introversion–extraversion and neuroticism to account for the major neurotic disorders. The appearance of the 1955 paper therefore marked the beginning of the second stage in the development of a theory that has tried to relate overt personality characteristics to their underlying causal substrate. It heralded, too, an enormous volume of research in which predictions from the theory have been tested using a wide variety of experimental techniques.

The results of this research led eventually to a formal statement of the hierarchical theory linking the causal or genotypic with the descriptive or phenotypic levels of personality (Eysenck, 1960c). As can be seen in Fig. 1.1, this theory proposes that personality is organized in a stratified manner. At the most fundamental level, that of central nervous function, the excitation–inhibition balance is considered to be a constitutionally determined source of individual differences. This is reflected, at the next immediate level L2, in variations on experimental behavioural measures. The third and fourth stages in the hierarchy consist of more complex observable phenomena, viz. the personality traits of introversion–extraversion (L3) and the social attitudes of tough and tender mindedness (L4). It is assumed that environmental factors begin to exert their main influence at level L3.

It is inevitable that a theory so simple and yet so comprehensive should contain weaknesses and inconsistencies. The perceptive student of Eysenck will not have failed to notice three particular shortcomings of his theory. The first is the relative neglect, within the Eysenckian school itself, of experimental investigations of psychiatric patients. The second is Eysenck's undue concentration on the dimension of extraversion at the expense of other important sources of individual variation, such as neuroticism. The third concerns the relatively loose way in which Eysenck has manipulated the

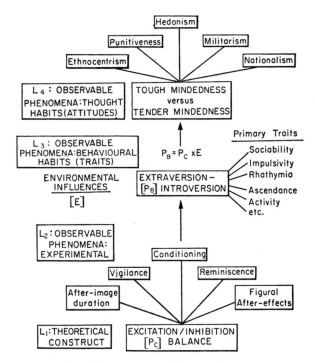

FIG. 1.1. Schematic diagram showing Eysenck's hierarchical theory of personality. (Reproduced by permission of Prof. Eysenck and the Editor, *Int. J. Soc. Psychiatry.*)

concept of excitation–inhibition. These three facts are not unrelated and, although they will be discussed in more detail at various points throughout the book, they require brief comment here in order to provide a background for the experiments to be described and the arguments to be developed later.

As implied in Fig. 1.1, the core of Eysenck's experimental work has consisted of studies of perception, psychomotor performance, and similar techniques in normal individuals rated for extraversion, usually on the Maudsley Personality Inventory (MPI). This is surprising if only because the theory was originally developed partly in order to put psychiatric nosology on a sounder scientific footing. It was introduced, in fact, as "a theory of dysthymia–hysteria". In one of the few excursions into the abnormal field Franks (1956) did demonstrate more rapid eye-blink conditioning in dysthymic neurotics compared with hysterics. This result has been more often used, however, in support of the hierarchical theory of normal introversion–extraversion than as evidence about the aetiology of dysthymia–hysteria.

At the time when the theory was first proposed this narrowing of research interest to normal subjects seemed defensible, because neuroticism, the other major personality dimension isolated in the earlier factor analytic studies, was regarded as orthogonal to extraversion. Being an independent source of individual variation, neuroticism was not expected to influence performance on tests that were selected to measure only extraversion, and therefore inhibition. Similarly, because dysthymics and hysterics were considered to be equally high on neuroticism the differences between them on excitation–inhibition measures could be logically ascribed to the extreme positions they were said to occupy on the extraversion dimension. The use of the neurotic criterion groups simply provided a convenient alternative to the study of normal introverts and extraverts, "dysthymia–hysteria" and "introversion–extraversion" being considered essentially synonymous. In fact, in presenting his theory of anxiety and hysteria Eysenck (1955a) made no formal statement about the possible causal basis of neuroticism. He suggested simply that it may be tentatively regarded as a form of drive related to over-excitability of the sympathetic branch of the autonomic nervous system.

It is now becoming increasingly clear, however, that extraversion and neuroticism are not functionally independent dimensions.[1] Furthermore, their interaction is not confined to the descriptive, L3, level of personality organization, but seems to occur at the more fundamental causal level. The more recent evidence supporting this conclusion will be discussed in a later chapter (Chapter 5). The interaction between the two dimensions was first suggested, however,

[1] This fact has now been formally recognized by Eysenck (1967) in the latest restatement of his theory which is commented upon later in the book (p. 192).

by Claridge (1960) following an investigation of Eysenck's excitation–inhibition hypothesis in normal and psychiatric subjects. In addition to a psychotic group, which will not be considered here, groups of dysthymic, hysteric, and normal subjects were given a large battery of tests covering a wide range of perceptual and perceptual-motor performance. The results substantially confirmed the prediction that the two neurotic criterion groups would lie at opposite ends of a continuum on tests of the L2 type. Compared with dysthymics, hysterics showed significantly poorer auditory vigilance, larger negative time error, and shorter visual after-effects.

A principal components analysis of the data from this experiment was then carried out and four components were isolated. Two of these are of interest here. One was the predicted factor of "extraversion" having, as expected, loadings on the appropriate objective tests, as well as on the E-scale of the MPI. A second factor, which accounted for rather more of the variance than the extraversion component, had moderate or high loadings on a number of "excitation–inhibition" measures, including vigilance decrement, pursuit-rotor performance level, and spiral after-effect. The N-scale of the MPI also had a moderately high loading on this factor, which was tentatively identified as one of "drive". It was concluded that, in neurotics at least, performance was the result of an interaction between the causal process ascribed by Eysenck solely to extraversion and some other general process of drive. The implication here was that the so-called excitation–inhibition balance was really the net result of both personality dimensions postulated by Eysenck.

Adoption of this view necessitated considerable theoretical reorientation and a widening of Eysenck's excitation–inhibition concept, in order to provide a causal model which would account for performance variations among neurotics that were not explained by his 1955 postulates alone. This was done initially by extending Eysenck's theory and reformulating it in terms of the arousal concept. The rationale of this modification becomes clear if the two theoretical viewpoints are compared.

As noted earlier, Eysenck's theory has its roots in behaviourist psychology. Consequently, it has used molar explanatory variables of a Hullian type, suitably modified in order to incorporate important features of Pavlovian theory, out of which behaviourism arose. In the 1955 postulates the major causative role was assigned to reactive inhibition and subsequent attempts to account for the performance differences of introverts and extraverts have usually been made in terms of this variable. Despite this emphasis on inhibition, the influence of Pavlov's writings led Eysenck, from the very beginning, to view the causal substrate of introversion–extraversion as a dynamic balance between excitatory and inhibitory processes in the nervous system. Inhibition and excitation were thought to be reciprocally related, strong inhibition implying weak excitation. The excitation–inhibition balance was, therefore, tilted towards strong inhibition *and* weak excitation in hysterics and extraverts, and towards weak inhibition *and* strong excitation in dysthymics and introverts.

Although Eysenck has seldom quoted excitation as an intervening variable, it could often be used as appropriately as inhibition to explain many of the performance measures he has studied. The opinion that this was so led the present writer to reformulate Eysenck's theory with primary emphasis on excitatory rather than inhibitory nervous processes. This had two advantages. First, it helped to take account of the obvious influence of at least one excitatory variable—drive—on the performance of neurotics (Claridge, *op. cit.*). Secondly, it made it easier to undertake the eventual translation of Eysenck's theory into an equivalent arousal model.

Historically, arousal theories have developed in psychology somewhat independently of the behaviourist movement and arose out of such early physiological studies of emotion as those of Cannon (1929). Both schools are similar, however, in one important respect. Each has tried to give some account, admittedly in different terminology and from different viewpoints, of the energizing or motivational aspects of behaviour.

It is now over thirty years since Duffy (1934) first suggested that the distinction between emotion and motivation was superfluous and that emotion and the intensity, as distinct from the directional, aspect of drive could be placed under a common heading of physiological arousal or activation. Since then a number of other workers, notably Malmo (1958, 1959), Hebb (1955), and Lindsley (1951), have adopted a similar theoretical position, suggesting, like Duffy, that variations in arousal occur along a continuum the lower end of which is represented in sleep. Increases in arousal are paralleled by increasing vigilance and alertness and eventually, at the upper end, by emotional excitement. It is suggested by arousal theorists that changes along this continuum are reflected centrally in the EEG and peripherally in various somatic functions, such as muscle tension, skin resistance, respiration, heart rate, and blood pressure.

Because the original formulation of the arousal concept antedated more recent work on the neurophysiology of awareness and attention, it was not until the functions of the ascending reticular activating system were fully realized (Moruzzi and Magoun, 1949) that a neural basis for arousal could be suggested. Since then psychologists have been quick to seize upon the implications of contemporary neurophysiology for their own discipline (Samuel, 1959) and most arousal theorists have suggested links between the continuum of behavioural arousal and the appropriate central nervous mechanisms.

The considerable evidence supporting the arousal hypothesis has been extensively reviewed by Duffy (1962) who devotes a section of her book to individual differences, with special reference to the functional personality disorders. She concludes that the weight of evidence supports the view that psychiatric patients differ from normal subjects on various physiological measures that appear to reflect arousal level. Duffy notes, however, that the results have sometimes been conflicting, due partly to sampling differences between studies and partly to the heterogeneity of the psychiatric groups investigated.

The problem of heterogeneity in samples of psychiatric patients has, regrettably, been ignored by many workers, who have been content to regard the neuroses and psychoses as homogeneous conditions. This is possibly because a systematic theory of abnormal personality has hitherto been lacking or, as in the case of Eysenck's theory, discounted, especially by clinically oriented psychophysiologists in the field. Arousal theorists themselves have paid little formal attention to individual differences at all, much of the evidence quoted by Duffy, for example, coming from indirect sources. The integration of arousal theory and Eysenck's cogent analysis of personality therefore promised to be a powerful vehicle for exploring the psychophysiology of the psychiatric patient who had not previously been studied in such detail from this point of view. It also offered an opportunity of resolving some of the difficulties inherent in Eysenck's general theory of individual differences, since his account of normal personality is inextricably linked with the causal explanation of psychiatric disorder.

THE AROUSAL INTERPRETATION OF EYSENCK'S THEORY: A WORKING HYPOTHESIS

When Eysenck's theoretical position was re-examined some six years ago it became clear that there were two points at which a link with arousal theory might be possible, since both the dimensions of introversion–extraversion and neuroticism had some features in common with the concept of physiological activation. The excitation–inhibition balance underlying introversion–extraversion could, for example, have been interpreted as an arousal continuum, the extremes of which were occupied by hysterics at the low end and dysthymics at the high end. It has already been noted how many of the performance correlates of excitation–inhibition could be ascribed to variations in excitation, rather than inhibition. Interpreted in this way "cortical excitation" would be synonymous with "arousal", Eysenck (1963) himself having subsequently suggested that the ascending facilitatory properties of the reticular system may form the physiological basis of the psychological concept of excitatory potential.

Unfortunately, it could have been argued with equal, if not greater, conviction that the arousal counterpart in Eysenck's theory was the dimension of neuroticism. Several facts would have supported this interpretation. First, as we have seen, Claridge's (1960) experiment demonstrated that neuroticism, contributing to a drive factor, accounted for some of the association between performance and personality. Secondly, neuroticism was known to correlate with measures of anxiety (Eysenck, 1959a), while both drive (Hebb, *op. cit.*) and anxiety (Malmo, 1957) had for some time been regarded as behavioural manifestations of reticular arousal. Thirdly, and perhaps most important of all, was the assumption made early on by Eysenck (1955a) himself that neuroticism is associated with instability of the autonomic nervous system.

There was already ample evidence that neurosis is accompanied by somatic dysfunction, a fact demonstrated using both groups of autonomic measures (Wenger, 1948) and single indices such as muscle tension (Malmo *et al.*, 1951; Malmo and Smith, 1955), blood pressure (Malmo and Shagass, 1952) and, more recently, pupillary response (Rubin, 1964). There had, however, been few previous studies in which the whole range of neurosis was studied, most investigators confining their attention to anxiety states and/or mixed neurotics. In one of the rare exceptions to this van der Merwe (1948) demonstrated that on one parameter of autonomic activity, emotional tension, anxiety states and hysterics were ranged on either side of normal, with hysterics showing parasympathetic predominance. This finding confirmed the common clinical observation that hysteria is characterized by a relative lack of manifest anxiety—the so-called "belle indifference". It also suggested that variations in autonomic arousal, rather than cortical excitation, could account for the fact that dysthymics and hysterics occupied opposite ends of a continuum on performance measures.

By itself, neither of these two arousal interpretations of Eysenck's theory could be regarded as entirely satisfactory. Each ignored the considerable evidence (Eysenck, 1960a) that at least two descriptive dimensions, and probably two causal processes, were necessary to account for the neuroses. At the beginning of the present research it was decided, therefore, to adopt the following working hypothesis that could be modified as new facts emerged. On the basis of the existing evidence it was proposed simply that a behavioural dimension running from dysthymia to hysteria could be recognized, the underlying concomitant of which was a continuum of arousability. No assumptions were made about the relationship of this causal continuum to either of Eysenck's personality dimensions, the main research technique used initially being to compare various psychophysiological measures of arousal in a population consisting mainly of neurotic patients. By so doing it was hoped to elucidate some of the psychophysiological processes underlying dysthymia–hysteria. These could then be related to measures at the other levels of personality recognized in Eysenck's hierarchical theory. The latter phases of the research were expected to reveal points at which the working hypothesis might need modifying. It will be noticed that the hypothesis postulated a continuum of "arousability", rather than "arousal", and some comment is necessary about the theoretical distinction that should be made between these two terms. Properly speaking, arousability refers to the maximum degree to which the individual can be aroused by stimulation. Arousal level, on the other hand, refers to his prevailing state of activation at a particular time. This may or may not reflect his maximum potential for arousal, although it was assumed here that activation measures taken under standard stimulus conditions would bear a consistent relationship to arousability. The latter, following Eysenck's assumptions about excitation–inhibition, was regarded as a stable biological characteristic of the individual.

It was recognized, of course, that in the intact organism no direct measure of the activating properties of the nervous system is possible. Any psychophysiological index inevitably represents the end-result of a complex interaction between arousing and inhibitory influences. The status of inhibition, both as a molar construct and as a neuro-physiological process, was too well-established for this fact to be ignored (Diamond *et al.*, 1963). However, for the reasons stated earlier, it seemed most parsimonious at the outset to place primary emphasis on excitation or arousal and to explore the explanatory limits of these concepts before invoking other constructs such as inhibition.

Having decided upon an arousal model of dysthymia–hysteria it was necessary to test the working hypothesis using a suitable psychophysiological measure. As noted previously, arousal theorists themselves have relied almost entirely on somatic, autonomic, and EEG indices. To begin with, this approach was rejected in favour of a technique that made use of the known variability among individuals in their tolerance of depressant drugs, viz. the sedation threshold. Theoretically, the use of the sedation threshold had four strategic advantages. First, it promised to be a better direct measure of central nervous excitability than peripheral autonomic indices. Secondly, current work on the physiological action of sedative drugs provided some rationale for its use. Thirdly, it formed a direct link with an existing part of Eysenck's theory which has tried to account for the personality correlates of drug susceptibility. Finally, there was already evidence that psychiatric patients differed markedly in their tolerance of depressant drugs. In the next chapter we shall discuss some of these points in more detail and describe the use of the sedation threshold as a measure of arousability in dysthymia–hysteria.

CHAPTER 2

AROUSABILITY AND THE SEDATION THRESHOLD

INTRODUCTION

Some Theoretical Considerations

It has long been known that individuals vary in drug tolerance and long been suspected that these variations are related to personality. With regard, specifically, to depressant drugs it is popularly believed that the introvert is resistant to the effects of alcohol, while many clinicians have noted the difficulty experienced in sedating the very anxious or excited patient. A number of workers, notably McDougall (1929), Pavlov (1934), and Sheldon and Stevens (1942), have proposed hypotheses to account for these personality correlates of drug tolerance; while most recently Eysenck (1957) followed his individual differences postulates by formally stating a drug postulate linking introversion–extraversion and drug action via the excitation–inhibition concept. According to this postulate, depressant drugs shift the excitation–inhibition balance towards the low excitation/high inhibition end, thus increasing cortical inhibition. Because, according to Eysenck, the introvert and dysthymic neurotic have a naturally low level of cortical inhibition they should resist the effects of such drugs more than the extravert and hysterical neurotic whose natural level of cortical inhibition is said to be already high. Eysenck suggests that the opposite relationship should hold with respect to stimulant drugs. This part of the drug postulate has recently been examined by Giberti *et al.* (1965) using their technique of "stimulation threshold" for methamphetamine, a method which they had shown previously would discriminate effectively between neurotic and psychotic depression (Giberti and Rossi, 1962). The present discussion is, however, confined to depressants and to the barbiturates in particular.

Trouton and Eysenck (1960) have distinguished two research designs for investigating the drug postulate. In the first, a fixed oral dose of drug is given to a random sample of individuals and a test made of the change in performance of the group as a whole on measures of excitation–inhibition. The second design involves the administration by injection of variable quantities of a drug to selected individuals of different personality type. The amount required to reach a chosen criterion of drug effect should vary with personality and provide a quantitative index of individual differences in drug tolerance. This design underlies the technique of sedation threshold, first described by Shagass (1954) and defined by him as the point at which an inflexion occurs in the amplitude curve of barbiturate-induced fast frontal activity in the EEG. This inflexion point is said to coincide with the onset of slurred speech, a behavioural sign of anaesthesia that Shagass has used as an additional criterion for the sedation threshold.

Translation of Eysenck's drug postulate into its equivalent arousal model presents little difficulty, at least with respect to barbiturates. Changes along the continuum of behavioural arousal are clearly reflected in the gradual clouding of consciousness, decline in responsiveness, and eventual induction of sleep following progressive administration of these drugs. The gross behavioural signs are paralleled by an eventual decrease in autonomic reactivity, particularly GSR (Just, 1952; Burch and Greiner, 1960). Similar changes have also been reported using other measures of autonomic function including peripheral vasomotor response (Ackner, 1956) and blood pressure (Martin and Davies, 1965). In interpreting these findings it is, of course, necessary to take account of the peripheral action of such drugs as amylobarbitone, which may produce changes in autonomic, particularly cardiovascular, activity that are unrelated to central arousal mechanisms (Goodman and Gilman, 1955). Nevertheless, it does seem safe to conclude that the barbiturates produce a shift down the arousal continuum as defined by most arousal theorists. This conclusion is further strengthened by neurophysiological evidence, since it is known that the barbiturates have a marked action on the reticular formation (Domino, 1962; Killam, 1962).[1]

[1] Although physiological evidence does provide some rationale for using behavioural drug techniques to study arousal in the intact human, it must be remembered that the pharmacological action of the barbiturates is extremely complex and the tolerance of these drugs is certainly influenced by many specific neurochemical factors that cannot be easily translated at present into molar terminology (see Appendix).

Evidence for a relationship between personality and drug tolerance, assessed by the sedation threshold technique, has appeared in a
series of papers by Shagass and his co-workers. The results have
consistently supported the view that increased barbiturate tolerance,
and therefore high sedation thresholds, tend to characterize patients
in whom a high level of arousal can be inferred. Positive correlations have been reported between sedation threshold and tension
(Shagass, 1954), manifest anxiety (Shagass and Naiman, 1956), and
introversion (Shagass and Kerenyi, 1958a). Furthermore, in a
comprehensive study of 750 patients Shagass and Jones (1958)
demonstrated significant differences in the mean sedation thresholds
of several diagnostic categories. Confining ourselves for the moment
to their findings in the neuroses, these authors reported significantly
higher thresholds in dysthymics than in hysterics. Within the
dysthymic group anxiety states showed the highest thresholds,
followed by patients suffering from neurotic depression and obsessive–
compulsive symptoms, in that order.

Shagass and Jones concluded from their results that variations in
barbiturate tolerance were related to a continuum of manifest
anxiety, on the one hand, and to the personality dimension of
introversion–extraversion, on the other. In presenting this dual
interpretation of their findings, the authors seemed to be describing
a behavioural dimension which closely resembles that of dysthymia–
hysteria. There was already evidence, therefore, that the sedation
threshold might be a suitable experimental tool for preliminary
exploration of the arousal concept applied to Eysenck's theory.
Before undertaking such an investigation it was necessary, however,
for reasons to be discussed below, to modify Shagass' original
method of assessing the sedation threshold.

Problems of Technique

The appearance of Shagass' 1954 paper prompted a number of
other workers to try and repeat his findings. Conflicting opinions
emerged about the accuracy of the sedation threshold technique
itself and, probably as a result of this, about its value as a diagnostic
tool. Most critical were Ackner and Pampiglione (1958) who
dismissed it as valueless on both counts. Boudreau (1958) agreed
with these workers in finding a high rejection rate of subjects due to
the difficulty of defining a recognizable end-point in the EEG
changes induced by barbiturates. Others (Seager, 1960b; Bradley

and Jeavons, 1957) were more successful with a modification of Shagass' original technique and Nymgaard (1959) also reported positive findings with the EEG method. Using the slurred speech criterion Laverty (1958) successfully differentiated introverted and extraverted neurotics, while Kawi (1958) found a significant correlation between clinically judged anxiety and sedation threshold for both amylobarbitone sodium and ethyl alcohol. On the other hand, Thorpe and Barker (1957) concluded that the onset of slurred speech is an unreliable indicator of sedation threshold.

In the search for a more accurate, and sometimes simpler, index of barbiturate tolerance a number of modified procedures have been adopted, with varying success. Fink (1958), for example, used lateral gaze nystagmus as a criterion for the onset of barbiturate anaesthesia, while the present author (unpublished study) explored, with some success, the possibility of using deterioration in simple reaction time to auditory and faradic stimuli as an index of sedation threshold. A quite different approach was employed by Perez-Reyes *et al.* (1962) who described what they have called the "GSR-inhibition threshold", defined as the point at which the GSR to auditory stimuli is eliminated by Pentothal. According to Perez-Reyes the GSR-inhibition threshold and the EEG-determined sedation threshold do not coincide, although both are reached long before the onset of sleep. The latter has itself been used as a measure of barbiturate susceptibility by Shagass and Kerenyi (1958b) who described what they called the "sleep threshold", defined in terms of unresponsiveness to verbal stimuli. The sleep threshold is said to correlate significantly with the sedation threshold (Shagass and Kerenyi, 1959) and with the GSR-inhibition threshold (Perez-Reyes and Cochrane, 1964), and to be a simple reliable test for diagnostic use.

A major difficulty in the measurement of the sedation threshold is the selection of a parameter of behaviour that is sensitive to the effects of barbiturates, but which is sufficiently stable and uninfluenced by extraneous factors to make the detection of an end-point possible. Most critics of Shagass' EEG method have reported fluctuations in the amplitude curve of fast frontal activity; while slurred speech is too crude an index for agreement to be reached on its exact point of onset. The latter criticism also applies, although perhaps to a lesser extent, to the sleep threshold which carries the additional drawback that it requires the administration of a greater quantity of drug than other methods of determining barbiturate tolerance.

The GSR-inhibition technique of Perez-Reyes overcomes some of these difficulties in that it uses a rather simpler physiological index than the EEG. A possible complicating feature is the spontaneous habituation of the GSR in some poorly aroused subjects during drug administration; although Rose (personal communication) claims to have met this difficulty by substituting faradic for the auditory stimuli used by Perez-Reyes. The use of any autonomic measure shares with the EEG technique the added disadvantage that it requires relatively complex apparatus operated under highly controlled conditions. This limits the value of the sedation threshold as a diagnostic tool, a limitation which, because of the massive effects of intravenous barbiturates, may not be offset by any greater precision in measurement.

A further criticism that can be levelled at all previous work on the sedation threshold is the universal use of a discontinuous injection procedure. Without exception, whatever the criterion of threshold employed, Shagass' original procedure has been followed of injecting the drug in a step-wise fashion, that is in "bursts" usually every 40 seconds or so. This practice seems quite illogical in view of the need to maintain, up to the chosen end-point, as smooth a change as possible in the level of consciousness. Some of the difficulties met by other workers in detecting an end-point may have been overcome had they adopted a procedure of infusing the drug continuously, thus eliminating one source of fluctuation in the chosen parameter.

As well as modifications to the sedation threshold procedure itself, there has also been some change since Shagass' early studies in the choice of drug used. Apart from Kawi's (*op. cit.*) special investigation of ethyl alcohol, the most common variation has been the preference for shorter acting barbiturates, such as thiopentone, instead of amylobarbitone sodium which Shagass (1954) used originally. Much of the recent work on barbiturate tolerance is based on thiopentone (Nymgaard, *op. cit.*; Perez-Reyes *et al.*, *op. cit.*; Shagass *et al.*, 1959), although in one of his most recent experiments Shagass reverted to the use of amylobarbitone (Krishnamoorti and Shagass, 1964).

Although their use is normally thought to carry more hazard, the ultra short-acting barbiturates have usually been preferred for practical reasons, because they present fewer management problems during the post-test period. On theoretical grounds they may have certain disadvantages, however. As Dr. Herrington discusses in

B

detail in the Appendix, there is some controversy about the tissue distribution of the thiobarbiturates during slow injection. The role played by body fat, for example, is less certain than is the case with the slower-acting barbiturates. This may introduce an unknown source of error into the measurement of sedation threshold, which is usually expressed in terms of total body weight. It is now clear, even where amylobarbitone is used, that lean body mass probably provides a better correction factor than total body weight. Few sedation threshold studies have paid attention to this particular problem, although Rose (personal communication) recently found no correlation between the GSR-inhibition threshold, using thiopentone, and two measures of relative body fat.

The status of the sedation threshold has often been judged on its merits as a diagnostic tool and the negative findings that have sometimes been reported have detracted somewhat from its potential value as a psychophysiological research technique. Methodological difficulties have added to the doubts that many clinicians have expressed about the test, but alternative threshold procedures are now beginning to re-establish its place in psychiatric research. It was with this hope, during the period of greatest pessimism about the sedation threshold, that the particular modification to be described here was devised.

The Digit-doubling Technique

In deciding upon an alternative to Shagass' sedation threshold technique a number of requirements had to be met. The first was the practical one that, because of the limitations imposed by the facilities available, the procedure should be simple and require little apparatus. This restricted the choice to behavioural, rather than physiological, parameters. On the other hand, it was felt that, if a satisfactory but simple technique could be devised, then its ultimate value as a practical diagnostic tool in a clinical setting would be considerably increased. A second requirement was that the method should provide continuous monitoring of the subject's level of consciousness up to the threshold, thus ensuring the accurate detection of an end-point. Thirdly, it was necessary to adopt, for the reasons given above, a continuous infusion rather than a step-wise injection procedure for administering the drug.

The method finally devised and first described by Claridge and Herrington (1960) consisted of assessing the effects of intravenous amylobarbitone sodium on a simple task of doubling digits. The exact procedure was to present to the subject a tape-recorded series of random digits played at the rate of one digit every 2 seconds. The subject was required to respond by doubling the digits while receiving a continuous intravenous infusion of amylobarbitone sodium, administered at the rate of 100 mg/min, the solution being prepared so that 2 cm^3 contained 100 mg. The digits were grouped on a score sheet in blocks of five and during the test the number of errors per block was noted, an error being regarded as an incorrect doubling response, the repetition of a digit, or a complete failure to respond. The injection was continued until errors exceeded 50 per cent in two consecutive blocks of digits. The sedation threshold was then taken as the point midway between the last two blocks with less than 50 per cent error and the first two blocks with more than 50 per cent error. The amount of drug administered up to that point could then be determined accurately from a chart relating blocks, and hence time, to drug received. This dosage was then corrected for the body weight of the subject, giving the sedation threshold in the conventional form of mg/kg. In view of the comments made in the previous section it would have been desirable to correct for lean body mass only. Unfortunately the possible importance of this modification was not realized at the time when the experiments reported here were undertaken. The effects on sedation threshold of variations in body fat are currently being explored, however. To control for diurnal variation, the standard procedure adopted in almost all cases tested was to assess the sedation threshold during the morning, following a light breakfast. No patient was on drugs at the time of testing.

Experience with this technique over several years has shown it to be an entirely satisfactory method of determining sedation threshold. Clear-cut end-points can be detected in the majority of cases and the procedure is a simple, practical one that can be carried out quickly with minimum disturbance to the patient. Since it was originally described the method has been criticized by Martin and Davies (1962) on the grounds that fluctuations in consciousness do occur, making it difficult to determine a suitable end-point. It should be pointed out, however, that these authors adopted a step-wise injection procedure. It is hardly surprising, therefore, that they met the difficulties they describe. Krishnamoorti and Shagass (1964), on the other hand, used the digit-doubling method quite successfully in conjunction with a step-wise injection technique, although they did report, as might have been expected, slight irregularities in the response curves of most subjects. The only workers to replicate the method exactly supported our own conclusions (Moffat and Levine, 1964). Their results confirmed the importance of using a continuous infusion technique for administering the drug.

With regard to the test–retest reliability of the method, only indirect evidence is available since it was not possible to repeat sedation threshold measurements on a sufficiently large number of patients. The stability of the sedation threshold assessed on an EEG criterion is, however, fairly well-established. Shagass and Naiman (1956) have demonstrated a high test–retest correlation for this method, while Nymgaard (1959) reported little change in the threshold on repeat testing, even after drugs. Shagass and his colleagues noted variations in sedation threshold (Shagass *et al.*, 1957) and sleep threshold (Shagass *et al.*, 1959) which reflected the clinical status of the patient, although they reported high test–retest reliability in the absence of marked affective change. Seager (1960a), after reviewing work on the sedation threshold, also concluded that the measure is remarkably constant, provided no significant improvement occurs in the clinical condition of the patient. The only test so far of the reliability of the digit-doubling method has been carried out on a rather atypical sample of patients, a small group of fifteen early psychotics tested before and after treatment by Herrington and Claridge (1965). Treatment produced marked changes in the thresholds and clinical state of these patients but, despite this, the test–retest correlation was still significant although not high, r being $0 \cdot 59$, $p < 0 \cdot 05$. The appropriate study still remains to be done in order to establish the exact test–retest reliability of the digit-doubling technique. There seems no reason to expect, however, that it should differ markedly from other methods of determining the sedation threshold.

A further advantage of the method described here is that, on average, a smaller drug dosage is required to reach the end-point than in the case of the only other simple technique, the sleep threshold, with which it has been shown (Krishnamoorti and Shagass, *op. cit.*) to be highly correlated. These authors reported even lower average values than our own and attribute this to their slower rate of injection. Both injection rates tend, of course, to produce higher absolute threshold values than when an EEG or GSR-inhibition technique is used. The intercorrelations between these various methods suggest, however, that they all measure a fundamentally similar underlying process and that they sample the level of awareness at different points along the arousal continuum.

In their original report of the digit-doubling technique Claridge and Herrington (1960) described its use in a preliminary study of neurotic patients. The findings substantially supported those of Shagass and Jones (*op. cit.*) that dysthymic patients show significantly higher sedation thresholds than hysterical neurotics. Since that early study data on much larger groups of subjects have been collected. The rest of this chapter is devoted to the detailed presentation of this data and an examination of the hypothesis that variations along the behavioural continuum of dysthymia–hysteria are paralleled by individual differences in the sedation threshold.

SEDATION THRESHOLD IN NEUROTIC AND NORMAL SUBJECTS

The Subjects

The composition of the neurotic and normal samples studied has already been described in detail in the Introduction, since sedation thresholds were obtained on all the subjects referred to there, viz. sixty-six dysthymics, fifty-seven hysterico-psychopaths, and thirty-four normal subjects. It will be recalled from the appropriate tables (p. xvi) that the groups were relatively homogeneous with respect to age, IQ, and weight. The subjects also fell into a very narrow range of physical fitness and body build, a fact which partly protected the group results, if not individual values, against possible error due to gross variations in fatty tissue.

In addition to this predominantly military sample, a group of forty-five civilian neurotic patients was subsequently collected. Forty of these patients were diagnosed as dysthymics and five as hysterics. In the case of civilian patients, individual sedation threshold data will be presented here for the dysthymics only. The scores for the five hysterics will be included when the military and civilian neurotic samples are considered as a combined group. Most of these civilian patients took part in a validating study of the sedation threshold reported by Claridge *et al.* (1964), although seven dysthymic patients were tested elsewhere.[1]

---

[1] The author is grateful to Dr. Herrington for supplying the data on these patients.

As might be expected, civilian patients were much more hetero-geneous than the military groups, especially with respect to age, sex, and diagnosis. Compared with a mean age of 25·4 yr SD 5·11 for military dysthymics, civilian dysthymics had a mean age of 42·1 yr SD 11·82. While almost all military patients were male, the sexes were more evenly divided in the civilian group, nineteen being male and twenty-one female. Similarly, whereas the diagnosis of anxiety state predominated among military dysthymics, civilians covered the whole range of dysthymic disorders, seventeen being diagnosed as chronic anxiety states, seven as obsessionals, and sixteen as reactive depressives.

Results

Considering the main sample of military patients first, it can be seen from Table 1 that there was an overall significant difference in the mean sedation thresholds of the three groups. Dysthymics

TABLE 1. SEDATION THRESHOLD (MG/KG) IN THREE MILITARY GROUPS

	Dysthymics	Normals	Hysterico-psychopaths
N	66	34	57
Mean	9·34	7·36	6·66
SD	1·77	2·32	1·68

F-ratio: 32·46, $p < 0·001$

t-tests
Dysthymics vs. Hysterico-psychopaths: 7·80, $p < 0·001$
Dysthymics vs. Normals: 4·45, $p < 0·001$
Normals vs. Hysterico-psychopaths: 1·70, N.S.

showed significantly higher thresholds than both hysterico-psycho-paths and normal subjects, only the comparison between the latter two groups failing to reach significance. This similarity between the control group and hysterico-psychopaths is of interest because, as noted in the Introduction, the normal sample was drawn from a population which was biased towards greater hysterical predisposi-tion than the general population. There will be occasion to refer to this point again later (Chapter 5, p. 102 ff.).

Breakdown of dysthymia and hysterico-psychopathy into its various subgroups is shown in Tables 2 and 3, respectively. In the case of dysthymia this could only be done for the civilian group,

because of the preponderance of anxiety states in military dysthymics. The reverse was true for hysterico-psychopathy since too
few civilian hysterics had been tested.

TABLE 2. SEDATION THRESHOLD (MG/KG) IN THREE SUBGROUPS OF
DYSTHYMIA

	Civilian dysthymics				Military dysthy-mics
	Chronic anxiety states	Obsessional neurotics	Reactive depressives	Total group	
N	17	7	16	40	66
Mean	11·00	10·26	9·10	10·14	9·34
SD	2·42	2·32	2·49	2·46	1·77

TABLE 3. SEDATION THRESHOLD (MG/KG) IN THREE SUBGROUPS OF
HYSTERICO-PSYCHOPATHY

	Conversion hysterics	Hysterical personalities	Psychopaths
N	23	29	5
Mean	6·73	6·81	5·69
SD	2·13	1·23	1·21

F-ratio: 0·953, N.S.

Considering dysthymia first, two points should be noted in Table 2.
The first is the very close similarity in the mean sedation thresholds
of military dysthymics and civilian dysthymics as a whole. The
second is the resemblance of chronic anxiety states, obsessional
neurotics, and reactive depressives. Neither the difference between
the military and civilian groups nor that between the various
subgroups of dysthymia was significant, the overall F-ratio being
1·61 (df 3/102).

Turning to hysterico-psychopathy, again its various subdivisions
showed no significant differences in mean sedation threshold,
conversion hysterics, hysterical personalities, and psychopaths
closely resembling one another (Table 3). The rather greater standard

deviation found among conversion hysterics should be noted, however. Inspection of the individual scores revealed that this was due
to the inclusion in this group of a small number of patients suffering
from amnesia. Some of these patients had relatively high sedation
thresholds within the dysthymic range, a finding that may have
some clinical implications. Claridge and Herrington (1963b), for
example, speculated that amnesia may differ from other conversion
symptoms in representing a more generalized reaction to severe
stress, resulting in a loss of awareness due to extreme overarousal.
This perhaps contrasts with the localized "inhibitory" symptoms
more usually found in conversion hysteria. Finally, Fig. 2.1 shows
the frequency distributions of sedation threshold for all civilian
and military subjects tested, considered in their three main groups,
dysthymics, normals, and hysterico-psychopaths. The last group

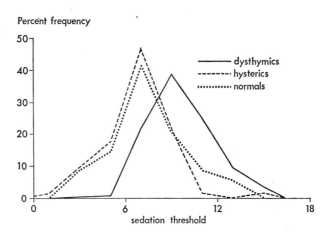

FIG. 2.1. Frequency distributions for sedation threshold in dysthymics,
hysterico-psychopaths, and normal subjects.

includes the five civilian hysterics referred to earlier, making a
total of 168 neurotics in all, viz. 106 dysthymics and sixty-two
hysterico-psychopaths. The close similarity between normal subjects and hysterico-psychopaths is clearly seen, both with respect
to mean and range of threshold. The other feature of note is the
considerable overlap between the two major neurotic groups, despite
the significant difference in their mean sedation threshold scores.
This suggests a continuously variable parameter of barbiturate

tolerance, running from extreme dysthymia, through normality, to extreme hysterico-psychopathy.

DISCUSSION AND CONCLUSIONS

The results reported here clearly support those of Shagass in almost every respect. Dysthymics as a whole have significantly greater resistance to barbiturate anaesthesia than hysterico-psychopaths and, within each of these diagnostic groups, no significant differences can be demonstrated between patients assigned to various subcategories. With regard to the sedation threshold, at least, it seems justifiable to accept Eysenck's classification of the neuroses into two major groups of dysthymia and hysteria.[1] These two conditions clearly represent, however, only the extremes of a continuum of barbiturate tolerance running throughout the neurotic and normal samples. Although, for reasons discussed earlier, the mean threshold of the normal group was shifted towards the low end, the range of values found covered almost the whole of that for neurotics, i.e. from 2·84 to 12·86 mg/kg.

It has been argued that the sedation threshold is a measure of arousability. If this is accepted, then the results substantially confirm the working hypothesis put forward in the previous chapter. A behavioural dimension can be recognized, running from dysthymia to hysteria, having as its underlying concomitant a causal continuum of arousability. The apparent stability of the sedation threshold in the absence of marked clinical change suggests that it measures a relatively unvarying biological characteristic of the individual.

Having demonstrated these personality correlates of sedation threshold and the suitability of the technique as a measure of arousability, the next stage in the research was to try and forge a more direct link with orthodox arousal theory. The latter, it will be recalled, has concentrated on autonomic and EEG indices of arousal, research on the sedation threshold having proceeded somewhat independently. However, on theoretical grounds some relationship would be expected between the sedation threshold and the more usual physiological measures of arousal. Evidence relating to this hypothesis will be described in the following chapter.

---

[1] For the sake of brevity we shall revert from here on to the use of the term "hysteria" to cover "hysterico-psychopathy".

SUMMARY

The rationale for using the sedation threshold as a measure of arousability was discussed and some of the recent evidence using different sedation threshold techniques was reviewed. Sedation thresholds, using the digit-doubling technique, were assessed in sixty-six dysthymics, fifty-seven hysterics, and thirty-four normal subjects. Confirming results obtained previously on smaller samples, dysthymics were found to have significantly higher sedation thresholds than both normals and hysterics. The failure of the normal group to differ significantly from hysterics was theoretically consistent with the bias towards extraversion in the control subjects. Comparison with the sedation thresholds of an additional group of civilian dysthymic patients revealed no difference between these patients and the main group of military dysthymics. Further, breakdown of dysthymia and hysteria into their various subgroups indicated that there was no difference in the mean sedation thresholds of obsessional neurotics, anxiety states, and reactive depressives, on the one hand, and conversion hysterics, hysterical personalities, and psychopaths on the other. It was concluded that a very wide distribution of barbiturate tolerance could be demonstrated which paralleled variations in personality type.

CHAPTER 3

AUTONOMIC AND EEG CORRELATES
OF AROUSAL

SOME THEORETICAL CONSIDERATIONS

It was noted in an earlier chapter that, although there have been many studies of autonomic function in the neurotic patient, little attempt has been made to integrate the findings with a systematic theory of personality. In the case of arousal theorists working in the psychiatric field, attention has been confined mainly to giving an account, in physiological terms, of psychological concepts like "anxiety", which has been viewed as a state of heightened activation (Malmo, 1957). As well as being associated with increased autonomic, specifically sympathetic, activity, anxiety is also accompanied by desynchronization of the EEG, leading to a reduction in alpha rhythm and the appearance of faster rhythms normally found in states of high arousal (Lindsley, 1951). In view of the relationship demonstrated between anxiety and barbiturate tolerance (Shagass and Naiman, 1956), an investigation of the autonomic and EEG correlates of the sedation threshold therefore became a logical sequence to the experiments reported in the previous chapter.

At the time when these experiments were undertaken there had been little attempt to relate the sedation threshold to other psychophysiological measures. Shagass, of course, had used EEG changes to assess the sedation threshold itself, while studies had been reported on the effects of barbiturates on autonomic responses such as GSR (Burch and Greiner, 1960). These have since been investigated more thoroughly by Lader (1964) and exploited as an alternative method of measuring sedation threshold (Perez-Reyes et al., 1962). Little attention had been paid at that time, however, to the psychophysiological correlates of sedation threshold viewed as an index of personality variation. This is possibly because the procedure had not penetrated arousal theory, with its psychological rather than psychiatric orientation.

The sedation threshold was, in fact, devised originally as an empirical diagnostic tool for psychiatry. It is of interest, therefore, that one of the few early attempts to correlate it with a measure of autonomic response involved a similar diagnostic technique, the blood pressure response to Mecholyl, a parasympathomimetic drug. In the experiment referred to, quoted by Shagass and Jones (1958), Sloane found no relationship between sedation threshold and various indices of blood pressure change on the Mecholyl test. Seager (1960a) later confirmed this negative finding on a mixed group of psychiatric patients.

Extension of the present research to the study of autonomic and EEG parameters of arousal was therefore guided at the outset almost entirely by theoretical considerations. Despite Sloane's negative result, it seemed worth pursuing the hypothesis that a common process of arousability was responsible both for sedation threshold and for other, autonomic and cortical, indices of activation in the nervous system. If this could be demonstrated, the working hypothesis linking the arousal concept with Eysenck's theory would be considerably strengthened. The causal basis of dysthymia–hysteria could then be stated more explicitly in psychophysiological terms.

It was anticipated that, if there was a relationship between sedation threshold and other indices of arousal, then the association might be revealed with respect either to measures of the ongoing level of activity or to measures of the reactivity to stimulation, or to both. Little distinction has actually been made between these two parameters of arousal, Duffy (1962) regarding them both as manifestations of a general process of activation. They are known, in any case, to be inextricably related, a fact which led Wilder in the early thirties to formulate the "law of initial values". In one of his most recent papers Wilder (1957) has summarized the implications of this law for research in psychiatry. The law of initial values states that the magnitude of response in a given physiological system will vary inversely with the level of functioning in the system when the stimulus is applied. The principle expresses the homeostatic nature of the autonomic nervous system, although there is some evidence that it may not be linear over the whole range of autonomic activity (Freeman and Katzoff, 1942).

The interdependence of level and reactivity measures is especially complicated when the relationship among a group of subjects, rather than within a particular individual, is being considered. This is because the so-called "basal" level of each subject in the group will partly reflect his autonomic reaction to the experimental situation. This will be a function of arousability. Various workers have suggested statistical solutions to correct for the dependence of change scores on pre-stimulus level (Lacey, 1956; Benjamin, 1963; Heath and Oken, 1962) although these may not be entirely satisfactory if a very wide range of arousal is being investigated.

It was not possible at the outset to predict, therefore, precisely which parameters of physiological function would be most highly correlated with sedation threshold, if indeed a relationship existed. It seemed most likely, however, that the crucial measures would be those that maximized individual differences in arousability, viz. measures of reactivity or levels under stress, rather than basal scores. For this reason particular attention was paid to techniques that produced fairly pronounced autonomic effects, such as those using pharmacological stressors. In this respect the work differed from much of that reported in the psychological literature, although it did reflect the interdisciplinary nature of the research. Pharmacological tests have often been explored as diagnostic procedures in psychiatry (Cyvin *et al.*, 1956), although rarely, if at all, by psychologists within the context of a theoretical framework such as that proposed here. Their use provided a unique opportunity of bridging the gap between abnormal psychology and experimental psychiatry.

In addition to the autonomic and EEG correlates of sedation threshold, two other aspects of the data will be considered here. The first is the correlation between the different autonomic measures taken during the various experiments. The second is the relationship between the autonomic and EEG measures. In both cases some degree of intercorrelation would be expected, if the hypothesis of arousability as a stable biological characteristic is tenable. A number of complicating factors have to be borne in mind, however.

The first is that of "response specificity", a concept introduced to take account of the fact that individuals show idiosyncratic patterns of autonomic response, some showing their greatest reactivity in terms of blood pressure, others in terms of skin conductance, and so on (Lacey, 1950; Lacey and Lacey, 1958). Response specificity would be expected to reduce the size of correlations between different autonomic measures of arousal, although probably only to a certain degree. As Lacey *et al.* (1953) themselves pointed out, while all subjects do not show an equal change in all autonomic systems, nevertheless there is an overall, usually sympathetic, response to imposed stress, thus making some degree of interindividual correlation likely. Similarly, Broadhurst and Eysenck (1965), after an investigation of physiological activity in the rat, concluded that response specificity is a limiting concept, rather than one that entirely invalidates the view of emotionality as a general factor of personality. The use here of a psychiatric sample, presumed to cover a wide range of arousability, was also expected to favour positive correlations between autonomic measures and help to overcome the limiting effects of response specificity.

A more serious difficulty concerns the relationship between autonomic and EEG measures of arousal. At least one worker (Sternbach, 1960) has reported a zero correlation between alpha index and a composite measure of autonomic response; while Darrow *et al.* (1946) suggested that the association between autonomic and EEG activity may depend on the existing arousal level, the sign of the correlation during the resting state being opposite to that found under conditions of cortical excitation. Similarly, Stennett (1957) described a curvilinear relationship between palmar conductance and alpha amplitude, the latter rising initially and then falling with increasing autonomic arousal. The evidence suggests that positive correlations between cortical and autonomic indices are more likely where arousal level is moderately high. There may, however, be an increasing tendency for a reversal in sign to occur with greater relaxation. The size and sign of correlations within groups of individuals may depend, therefore, on the level of arousal that predominates in the group at the time of testing.

A third source of variability, tending to militate against high correlations, arose out of the design of the investigation itself. With two exceptions, all of the measures concerned were taken on different occasions, sometimes weeks or even months apart. This contrasts with much of the work reported in the literature, where attention has often been concentrated on simultaneous monitoring of various physiological systems. The lengthy intervals between measurements did, however, make it possible to determine their stability over time and to decide how far arousability could be validly regarded as a relatively fixed biological characteristic of personality.

DESCRIPTION OF THE DATA

Most of the experiments relating sedation threshold to autonomic response have already been published elsewhere and these results will only be summarized here. However, the opportunity is taken of bringing all of these findings together and of considering in rather more detail the interrelationship between the various autonomic and EEG measures. The data available for analysis consisted of four EEG parameters, measures of the blood pressure response to three physical stressors, and two autonomic indices monitored simultaneously during the performance of a vigilance task. In describing the measures below it is convenient to subdivide them in terms of the separate experiments from which they were derived, giving under each heading the particular parameters considered here. In each case a brief introduction and description of the experimental procedure will be given, although for more complete details the interested reader is referred to the original papers cited.

The experimental subjects formed part of the military sample of neurotic and normal individuals described in the Introduction and in the previous chapter. Since they took part in what was, in effect, a series of separate investigations, not all measures were taken on all subjects, but in most cases there was sufficient overlap between experiments to make cross-correlation possible. In the case of the neurotic samples there was a variation in the proportion of different diagnostic groups represented. This was not considered important since the investigation was primarily concerned with the continuous variation from dysthymia to hysteria, rather than with the differences between arbitrary psychiatric categories. The association between psychophysiological status and the descriptive continuum of dysthymia–hysteria had already been well-established in the sedation threshold studies.

Cold Pressor Test

The response of the blood pressure to immersion of a limb in cold water has long been regarded as a standard test of cardiovascular reactivity (Hines and Brown, 1936). Exposure to cold has both local and remote effects (Keele and Neil, 1961). The immediate effects include contraction of the arterioles causing an increase in peripheral resistance; while reflex stimulation of the hypothalamus by afferent impulses from the cooled area also occurs. This results in a rise in both the systolic and diastolic blood pressures. In addition to the effects of cold itself, other influences probably contribute to the blood pressure change. It has been suggested, for example, that response to the cold pressor test is proportional to the degree of pain experienced (Wolff, 1951). The test probably measures, therefore, a complex arousal reaction having both physiological and psychological components.

A number of workers (e.g. Igersheimer, 1953) have used the standard cold pressor test as a measure of sympathetic reactivity in psychiatric patients, particularly psychotics, and some of this evidence will be reviewed later (Chapter 7). Theron (1948) included cold water stress in a detailed investigation of emotional stability in normal subjects. He studied its effects on peripheral vasomotor reaction, rather than blood pressure, and derived two factor measures from his data which were weighted on the cold pressor response. It was on the basis of these factor measures that van der Merwe (*op. cit.*) subsequently differentiated neurotics of the dysthymic and hysteric type.

Because of the simplicity of the cold pressor test Claridge *et al.* (1963) chose to use it in a preliminary study of the autonomic correlates of sedation threshold. In that experiment the subject was asked to keep his hand in a cold water bath kept at a minimum temperature of 4°C. Three pre-stressor blood pressure readings were taken at 1-minute intervals and, after immersion of the hand, every half-minute for a further 3 minutes. The following four measures from that experiment will be considered here:

> *Basal Systolic BP.* The mean of the two readings prior to stress.
> *Basal Diastolic BP.* Calculated as for basal systolic pressure.
> *Systolic BP Change.* The area, in arbitrary units, under the plotted post-stress BP readings, areas of rise being taken as positive and areas of fall as negative.
> *Diastolic BP Change.* Calculated as for change in systolic pressure.

In calculating both scores of blood pressure change areas of fall were subtracted from areas of rise, the resulting, usually positive, value being taken as a measure of sympathetic reactivity.

Mecholyl Test

Mecholyl (acetyl-beta-methycholine chloride) is an acetylcholine-like substance having a parasympathomimetic action on the cardio-vascular system. Its usual effect is to cause increased peripheral vasodilatation and decreased cardiac output, resulting in a fall in blood pressure. Considerable individual variation occurs in the extent of blood pressure drop and in the rate at which the blood pressure is restored to normal through reflex homeostatic mechanisms.

Although a number of workers (Myersan *et al.*, 1937; Gold, 1943; Altman *et al.*, 1943) had previously used the Mecholyl response as a measure of autonomic reactivity in psychiatric patients, the test is usually associated with the name of Funkenstein, who described what has since become known as the Funkenstein test (Funkenstein *et al.*, 1948). In its complete form the Funkenstein test consists of two parts in which the blood pressure response to both Mecholyl and adrenaline is measured. Most workers have concentrated, however, on the effects of Mecholyl and the procedure will be referred to here as the Mecholyl test.

In their original report Funkenstein and his colleagues distinguished seven types of reaction to Mecholyl, classified in terms of the relative drop and kind of recovery shown by the blood pressure following injection. Since then a number of modifications to the procedure and scoring of the test have been described (see Feinberg, 1958). Perhaps the most familiar is the modification used by Gellhorn (1953), who reduced the number of reaction types to three and suggested that response to Mecholyl provides a direct measure of posterior hypothalamic (sympathetic) reactivity.

The practical application of the Mecholyl test has concentrated on its diagnostic value in depression and its ability to predict the outcome of ECT. Studies in this area will be considered in Chapter 7, but in the meantime it should be noted that Rose (1962), after reviewing the literature on the Mecholyl test, concluded that as a diagnostic or prognostic tool it is of little clinical value. This is certainly due partly to the test's poor reliability when arbitrary classifications in terms of reaction type are used. Rose suggested that reliability is good in those studies where a quantified scoring system is substituted, such as maximum drop in blood pressure or area under the baseline blood pressure. Most workers using the test in recent years have, in fact, adopted such a quantitative scoring system. In one of the latest investigations of the Mecholyl test Ingram and Brovins (1966) introduced a number of new modifications both to the procedure and to the scoring method. Using a drug dosage corrected for body weight and an intravenous route of injection, they demonstrated extremely high test–retest correlations for a number of carefully derived measures of blood pressure response.

Despite its poor reputation as a diagnostic procedure, the Mecholyl test was considered by Wawman *et al.* (1963) to have some promise as a research technique and it was used by them as part of the investigation described here. Briefly, the procedure involved a 20-minute rest period, during which blood pressure was recorded every 3 minutes. Further readings were then taken at 1-minute intervals following a subcutaneous injection of 25 mg of Mecholyl. The four measures from that experiment included here were as follows:

> *Basal Systolic BP.* The mean of the last three pre-injection readings.
> *Basal Diastolic BP.* Calculated as for basal systolic pressure.
> *Mean Systolic BP Change.* The mean of the minute systolic readings taken during the post-injection period minus the basal systolic pressure.
> *Mean Diastolic BP Change.* Calculated as for the systolic change.

Interpretation of the change scores was such that more positive, or less negative, values were assumed to reflect greater sympathetic reactivity.

Rogitine Test

Compared with other substances acting on the autonomic nervous system, such as adrenaline, Mecholyl, and atropine, little use has been made in psychiatry of tests involving sympatholytic drugs. In devising such a test Davies *et al.* (1963) argued that a more direct measure of sympathetic reactivity should be obtained by studying the effects of an adrenergic blocking agent, rather than those of a parasympathomimetic drug. The drug chosen was Rogitine (phentolamine) which antagonizes the pressor effect of the sympathetic amines, causing a fall in blood pressure. The main clinical use of

Rogitine had previously been in the diagnosis of phaeochromo-cytoma, its effects in relation to personality in non-medical cases not having been studied. Variations in blood pressure response to the drug had, however, been noted with small doses in hypertensive (Gifford *et al.*, 1951) and larger doses in normotensive (Heinzel *et al.*, 1952) individuals. As might be expected, the extent of blood pressure fall and rate of recovery roughly paralleled the changes produced by Mecholyl.

The procedure used by Davies *et al.* (*op. cit.*) and summarized briefly here was to take systolic blood pressure readings every 3 minutes during an initial resting period of 30 minutes. Rogitine was then injected intravenously at a dosage corrected for body weight in the proportion 0·2 mg/kg. After injection the blood pressure was taken at half-minute intervals for at least 2 minutes and then at 1-minute intervals for the next 3 minutes, or until the blood pressure had reached a steady level. The measures derived from the experiment were as follows:

> *Basal Systolic BP.* The mean of the two lowest readings during the 30-minute pre-injection period.
>
> *Maximum Systolic BP Change.* The greatest absolute change in pressure from the pre-injection level. Some of these scores were positive and some negative.

As with the Mecholyl test it was expected that greater sympathetic reactivity would be reflected in more positive, or less negative, blood pressure change scores.

Heart Rate and Skin Conductance

These measures were obtained from an investigation of an auditory vigilance task during which heart rate and skin resistance were monitored continuously for a period of 30 minutes. The vigilance task itself and its relationship with autonomic response are considered in Chapter 4, the present discussion being confined to the physiological measures.

Heart rate was recorded on a standard electrocardiograph and details of the procedure can be found in Claridge and Herrington (1963b) who have also described some preliminary findings obtained with this measure. In a subsequent, previously unpublished, experiment the measurement of skin resistance was added and the data used here included the latter as well as all the heart rate material eventually collected.

Skin resistance was recorded on a linear response psychogalvano-meter, using palm-to-palm siting of 1 in. polished brass electrodes, applied dry. The subject's resistance level was monitored from a meter at 1-minute intervals during the vigilance task and the readings eventually converted to conductance units.

Both the heart rate and skin conductance scores were analyzed by fitting linear regression lines to the data for each subject. For this purpose the 30-minute recording period was divided into six 5-minute intervals and the appropriate regression coefficients calculated on the six scores so obtained. The measures used here were the intercept coefficients, representing the level of heart rate and skin conductance present during vigilance performance. These were assumed to reflect arousal level under mild psychological stress.

EEG Measures

The data used here formed part of an experimental study of the EEG correlates of the spiral after-effect (Claridge and Herrington, 1963a). EEG records were taken on a standard electroencephalo-graph and exact details of the procedure, including electrode placement, are given in the original paper. Four measures were derived from each subject's record, as follows:

Alpha index. Per cent time during which alpha rhythm was present, as assessed over ten randomly selected 10-second samples of the subject's resting, eyes-closed, record.

Alpha frequency. The mean frequency of alpha rhythm averaged over ten 1-second samples of the resting record.

Alpha amplitude. The mean peak-to-peak amplitude of the alpha waves averaged over the same ten 1-second samples of record used in determining alpha frequency.

Alpha blocking time. The time, in seconds, for alpha to return after eye-closure following previous inspection, for 1 minute, of a rotating spiral. Of several criteria for alpha return examined, that used here was based on the point at which alpha index had returned to that found in the resting record. In all cases a correction was made for normal alpha latency on eye-closure, a measure of this being subtracted from the spiral-induced blocking time.

In interpreting these measures the assumption was made that heightened arousal would be reflected in low alpha index, fast alpha frequency, reduced amplitude of alpha rhythm, and a long alpha blocking time.

PHYSIOLOGICAL CORRELATES OF SEDATION THRESHOLD

Results

Autonomic measures. Table 1 summarizes the correlations between sedation threshold and the various measures of autonomic activity. The table is arranged in two halves, Table 1a containing all the measures of reactivity and Table 1b measures of pre-stress blood pressure level. The heart rate and skin conductance scores are included in Table 1a, since these were assumed to reflect arousal level under stress.

Comparing the two halves of the table, it can be seen that significant relationships with sedation threshold were confined to measures of reactivity or stress arousal level, little association being found with basal scores. Sedation threshold correlated significantly and positively with heart rate and with the systolic blood pressure response to both Rogitine and Mecholyl. The last two results indicate that subjects with high sedation thresholds showed a more rapid recovery of blood pressure after stress, indicating greater sympathetic reactivity in these individuals. The effect was seen most clearly in the case of Rogitine, as illustrated in Figs. 3.1 and 3.2. Figure 3.1 shows individual blood pressure curves for four subjects who typified the kind and range of responses found on the Rogitine test. It can be seen that reactions ranged from a profound fall in blood pressure to a marked overshoot beyond the resting baseline level. These varied responses parallel the individual sedation threshold values also shown in the figure. Figure 3.2 demonstrates the orderly change, with increasing threshold, from negative to positive reactivity scores on the test. This was true for both normal and neurotic members of the sample.

Considering the remainder of Table 1a, it can be seen that sedation threshold was not related to the change in diastolic pressure in response to Mecholyl, a finding that will be commented upon later. As predicted, the cold pressor measures correlated positively with sedation threshold but not, however, significantly. When the

TABLE 1. CORRELATIONS OF SEDATION THRESHOLD WITH VARIOUS AUTONOMIC MEASURES

(a) *Measures of reactivity or level under stress*

	Heart rate level	Rogitine test Max. Syst. BP Change	Mecholyl test		Cold pressor test		Skin conductance level
			Mean Syst. BP Change	Mean Diast. BP Change	Systolic BP Change	Diastolic BP Change	
r	+0·44	+0·50	+0·47	−0·03	+0·16	+0·26	+0·12
N	64	35	34	34	45	45	35
	(40 neurotics + 24 normals)	(21 neurotics + 14 normals)	(27 neurotics + 7 normals)		(32 neurotics + 13 normals)		(21 neurotics + 14 normals)
p	0·001	0·01	0·01	N.S.	N.S.	N.S.	N.S.

(b) *Pre-stress measures*

	Rogitine test Basal Systolic BP	Mecholyl test		Cold pressor test	
		Basal Systolic BP	Basal Diastolic BP	Basal Systolic BP	Basal Diastolic BP
r	+0·26	+0·03	+0·20	+0·04	+0·13
N	35	34	34	45	45
p	N.S.	N.S.	N.S.	N.S.	N.S.

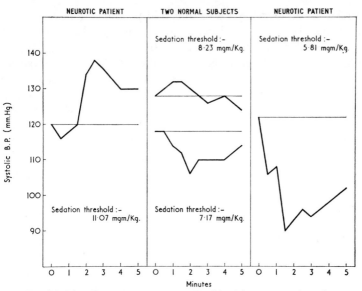

FIG. 3.1. Blood pressure response to Rogitine of two neurotic and two normal subjects. (Reproduced by permission of the Editor *Brit. J. Psychiat.*)

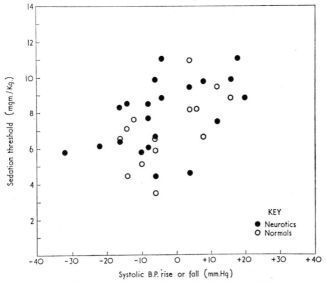

FIG. 3.2. Relationship between sedation threshold and blood pressure response to Rogitine. (Reproduced by permission of the Editor *Brit. J. Psychiat.*)

correlation between basal level and cold pressor response was par-tialled out, the value for r in the case of the diastolic pressure rose to $+0 \cdot 33$, which was significant at the $0 \cdot 05$ level. Partialling out the influence of basal level in the case of the systolic response had no effect on its correlation with sedation threshold. Finally, there was no correlation between skin conductance level and sedation threshold, although when normal subjects were considered alone the correlation was positive, as predicted, but just failed to reach significance ($r = +0 \cdot 42$, $N = 14$). In the twenty-one neurotics forming the rest of the sample, the equivalent correlation was slightly negative, r being $-0 \cdot 21$. This difference between neurotics and normal subjects was not repeated on the cardiovascular mea-sures, which tended to show parallel results in both groups, as illustrated in Fig. 3.2.

EEG measures. None of the EEG measures showed a significant rectilinear relationship with sedation threshold. In a combined group of forty-six neurotic and normal subjects the value for r was exactly zero in the case of both alpha frequency and alpha amplitude, and $+0 \cdot 22$ in the case of alpha blocking time. On a rather larger group of fifty-four subjects in whom alpha index could be calculated the product moment correlation between this measure and sedation threshold was $-0 \cdot 12$.

However, when these data were plotted graphically it was found that sedation threshold and alpha index were related in a curvilinear fashion, the departure from linearity being significant at the $0 \cdot 01$ level. As can be seen in Fig. 3.3, both high and low alpha index values were associated with a low sedation threshold, the optimum sedation threshold falling at about 50 per cent time alpha. This tendency was found in both neurotic and normal subjects.

Discussion

The results provide acceptable evidence that individual differences in sedation threshold are, as predicted, consistently related to variations in sympathetic reactivity. Significant relationships were confined, however, to cardiovascular measures, especially heart rate and the blood pressure response to the two autonomic drugs. Results for the cold pressor test were less clear-cut, although the contaminating effects of pre-stress level emphasizes the need for an adequate resting period in procedures of this kind. Longer and more controlled rest periods were used in the Mecholyl and Rogitine studies, where corrections for basal level were not necessary.

The skin conductance findings were disappointing and did not parallel those for the cardiovascular measures. This may have been due to the inadequate recording technique and limited facilities available at the time. An alternative reason is that the wrong para-meter was chosen for investigation. A recent study by Lader and Wing (1964), for example, has demonstrated a close relationship

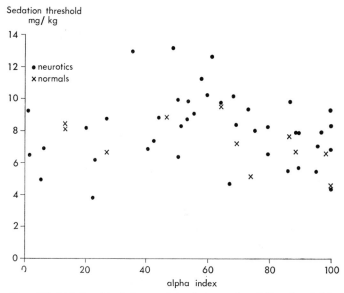

FIG. 3.3. Relationship between alpha index and sedation threshold, illustrating curvilinear nature of regression.

between anxiety and habituation rate of the GSR, a measure that may provide a better index of arousability than skin conductance level. Unfortunately, it was not possible to derive measures of either spontaneous GSR's or habituation rate from the skin conductance data, although attention should be paid to these parameters in future investigations.

The restriction of significant relationships to measures of reactivity rather than basal level of autonomic activity confirmed the expecta-tion that the sedation threshold would correlate most highly with indices that maximized differences in arousability. It is of interest, too, that the closest association with sedation threshold was found in the Rogitine experiment. In many respects this study was technically superior to the others in the series. It involved a direct and relatively profound autonomic stress induced by intravenous injection, which Altschule (1953) maintained was the only defensible route of drug administration for accurate work in this field.

Although a superficially negative result, the lack of association between sedation threshold and the Mecholyl diastolic response may have been due to the complex action of this drug. It could be accounted for in terms of the differential effects of adrenaline and noradrenaline on the cardiovascular system (Keele and Neil, 1961). It is possible, for example, that hyperreactors to the drug responded with an intense sympathetic discharge involving secretion of adrenaline from the adrenal medulla. Since, unlike noradrenaline, adrenaline produces an overall decrease in peripheral resistance, the diastolic blood pressure falls under its influence. This effect would be added to the hypotension produced by Mecholyl itself. Thus, both hyper- and hyporeactors would be characterized by slow recovery of the diastolic blood pressure, resulting in a failure of this measure to correlate with the sedation threshold. The finding warns against a simple interpretation of complex autonomic tests of this kind.

In the case of the EEG measures, certainly the most interesting result was the curvilinear relationship between sedation threshold and alpha index. This suggests that the mechanisms underlying sedation threshold do not exactly parallel those responsible for cortical measures of arousal. Both appear to co-vary in the same direction only up to a moderate level of cortical activity, beyond which point increasing activation is associated with a gradual decrease in barbiturate tolerance. The significance of this finding will be discussed further in a later chapter. In the meantime, it can be concluded that the association between sedation threshold and other physiological measures seems to be confined mainly to indices of autonomic, rather than cortical, arousal.

INTERCORRELATION OF AUTONOMIC MEASURES

Results

Table 2 shows the correlations between the various measures of blood pressure change obtained from the cold pressor, Mecholyl, and

TABLE 2. CORRELATIONS BETWEEN VARIOUS MEASURES OF BLOOD PRESSURE CHANGE[1]

	Rogitine Max. Syst. BP Change	Cold pressor Syst. BP Change	Cold pressor Diast. BP Change	Mecholyl Mean Syst. BP Change	Mecholyl Mean Diast. BP Change
Rogitine Max. Syst. BP Change	—	+0.50 $p < 0.01$	+0.53 $p < 0.01$	+0.58 N.s.	+0.11 N.s.
Cold pressor Syst. BP Change	26 (13 Ne + 13 No.)	—	+0.61 $p < 0.001$	+0.54 $p < 0.01$	−0.05 N.s.
Cold pressor Diast. BP Change	26 (13 Ne + 13 No.)	46 (33 Ne + 13 No.)	—	+0.50 $p < 0.05$	−0.17 N.s.
Mecholyl Mean Syst. BP Change	7 No.	26 (18 Ne + 8 No.)	26 (18 Ne + 8 No.)	—	+0.18 N.s.
Mecholyl Mean Diast. BP Change	7 No.	26 (18 Ne + 8 No.)	26 (18 Ne + 8 No.)	34 (27 Ne + 7 No.)	—

[1] Since the size of samples and the proportion of neurotics (Ne) and normals (No) in each varied this information is, for clarity, given in the corresponding cells on the left side of the matrix.

Rogitine tests. Ignoring, for the moment, the extreme right-hand column, it can be seen that all other correlations were positive and averaged about 0·50. Except for the Rogitine/Mecholyl comparison, which was based on a very small number of subjects, the correlations were all significant at various levels of confidence. The complete failure of the Mecholyl diastolic response to correlate with the other blood pressure measures, including the systolic response on the same test, parallels its lack of association with the sedation threshold and may provide some support for the explanation given of that result.

Table 3 shows the comparable correlations for measures of pre-stress blood pressure from the three tests. While of less interest theoretically, these results do provide some estimate of the test–retest reliability of the basal blood pressure readings. These, it will be remembered, were taken on different occasions, often by different observers, over a relatively long period of time. It should also be noted that they were recorded after varying lengths of rest and thus represented different estimates of basal level. As would be expected, the lowest and non-significant correlations were those between systolic and diastolic blood pressure from different tests. All correlations were positive, although none was high. The finding presumably reflects the variety of conditions under which the measurements were taken.

When correlations were computed on the change scores for neurotic and normal subjects taken separately, no difference was found in the direction, and little in the size, of r for the two groups. If a difference were found it tended, as expected, to be in the direction of higher correlations in neurotic patients, where the range of arousal was naturally greater.

Comparison of the blood pressure measures with the heart rate and skin conductance data revealed no significant relationships. The five correlations between heart rate and the blood pressure change measures ranged from $-0·23$ to $+0·37$; while the equivalent correlations for skin conductance ranged from $-0·48$ to $+0·15$. In the case of the resting blood pressure the range of r was from $+0·02$ to $-0·45$ for heart rate and from zero to $+0·12$ for skin conductance.

A small significant positive correlation was found between skin conductance and heart rate, the only two measures taken simultaneously. The value for r was $+0·35$ ($p < 0·05$) in a combined

TABLE 3. CORRELATIONS BETWEEN VARIOUS MEASURES OF PRE-STRESS BLOOD PRESSURE[1]

	Rogitine Basal Syst. BP	Cold pressor Basal Syst. BP	Cold pressor Basal Diast. BP	Mecholyl Basal Syst. BP	Mecholyl Basal Diast. BP
Rogitine Basal Syst. BP	—	+0·41 $p < 0.05$	+0·39 $p < 0.1$	+0·51 n.s.	+0·39 n.s.
Cold pressor Basal Syst. BP	26 (13 Ne + 13 No.)	—	+0·47 $p < 0.001$	+0·52 $p < 0.01$	+0·29 n.s.
Cold pressor Basal Diast. BP	26 (13 Ne + 13 No.)	46 (33 Ne + 13 No.)	—	+0·30 n.s.	+0·31 n.s.
Mecholyl Basal Syst. BP	7 No.	26 (18 Ne + 8 No.)	26 (18 Ne + 8 No.)	—	+0·65 $p < 0.001$
Mecholyl Basal Diast. BP	7 No.	26 (18 Ne + 8 No.)	26 (18 Ne + 8 No.)	34 (27 Ne + 7 No.)	—

[1] As in Table 2 sample sizes are given on the left side of the matrix.

group of thirty-four neurotic and normal subjects. When neurotics and normals were considered separately, the correlation was found to be positive in both groups, but much higher in neurotics ($r = +0.65$, N $= 21$, $p < 0.01$) than in normal subjects ($r = +0.11$, N $= 14$, N.S.).

Discussion

The main conclusion that can be drawn from these results is that the predicted positive relationships were found either (a) where measures of the reactivity of the same autonomic system (e.g. blood pressure) were intercorrelated, even though such measures were taken on quite different occasions and involved different stressors; or (b) where measures of different autonomic systems monitored on the same occasion were correlated. The failure of significant correlations to emerge otherwise is not too surprising in view of the variety of stressors used, the diurnal instability of the functions involved, and the possible intrusion of response specificity.

In view of the findings reported in the previous section, it is of some interest that the most consistent results again appeared on tests using severe physical stress. It is possible that such techniques provide a more accurate method of assessing individual differences in autonomic arousability, since they are less subject to the effects of subtle psychological changes which otherwise influence arousal level. This conclusion is supported by the close relationship found between sedation threshold and tests of autonomic reactivity using pharmacological stress. In general the results do suggest that a common process of arousability may be responsible for variations in autonomic reactivity, although clearly many specific factors operate to reduce the size of correlations between different measures. Furthermore, significant relationships using autonomic measures may only appear where, as in a neurotic sample, a wide range of arousability is studied.

CORRELATION OF AUTONOMIC AND EEG MEASURES

Results

Alpha index. Of twelve correlations calculated with alpha index six were entirely non-significant, the values for r ranging from -0.11 to $+0.19$. In samples where both neurotic and normal subjects were included no substantial differences were found in the size of correlations for the two subgroups taken separately. The remaining six correlations are shown in Table 4, where it can be seen that two just failed to reach an acceptable level of significance, while heart rate and two measures of systolic blood pressure change correlated substantially with alpha index. With one exception, all of the correlations were in the predicted direction, increased sympathetic reactivity being associated with reduced incidence of alpha rhythm. The exception to this finding occurred in the case of the diastolic response to Mecholyl, where a significant positive correlation was found. However, the unusual behaviour of this measure in a previous part of the research will be recalled.

In the case of the heart rate and cold pressor data referred to in Table 4, correlations with alpha index were calculated for neurotic and normal subjects separately. Values for r were not substantially different with respect to heart rate, r being -0.71 (N = 10, $p < 0.05$) in normals and -0.44 (N = 30, $p < 0.02$) in neurotics. The correlation between cold pressor diastolic change and alpha index was again higher in normals ($r = -0.55$, N = 11, p < 0.1) than in neurotics ($r = -0.22$, N = 13, N.S.). The greatest difference between neurotics and normals was found in the case of the cold pressor systolic blood pressure change. Here the correlation with alpha index was entirely non-significant in neurotics, r being -0.07 (N = 13). In normal subjects the correlation was -0.82 (N = 11), which was significant at the 0.01 level.

Plotting the data for these three autonomic measures against alpha index for the combined groups of neurotics and normals revealed a moderate departure from linearity of regression. This was most marked with respect to cold pressor systolic change, where in a few individuals with activated (low alpha) EEG records a fall, rather than the usual rise, in blood pressure occurred in response to the cold pressor stress.

Alpha blocking time. Results here were entirely non-significant, the range of twelve correlations being from -0.48 to $+0.08$. The pattern of correlations was found to be very similar in both neurotic and normal subjects and no evidence of curvilinearity of regression emerged.

Alpha frequency. Findings here were similar to those for the previous measure, twelve correlations ranging from -0.40 to $+0.32$, none of these values being significant. The distribution of

TABLE 4. CORRELATIONS OF ALPHA INDEX WITH VARIOUS AUTONOMIC MEASURES

	Heart rate level	Rogitine test Basal Syst. BP	Rogitine test Max. Syst. BP Change	Cold pressor test Systolic BP Change	Cold pressor test Diastolic BP Change	Mecholyl test Mean Syst. BP Change
r	−0·53 40	−0·53 11	−0·73 11	−0·73 24	−0·35 24	+0·43 22
N	(30 neurotics + 10 normals)	(Normals)		(13 neurotics + 11 normals)		(17 neurotics + 5 normals)
p	0·001	0·1	0·02	0·001	n.s.	0·05

correlations again appeared to be entirely random, with no evidence of departure from linearity of regression or of a difference between neurotic and normal subjects.

Alpha amplitude. Eight out of twelve correlations with this measure were non-significant, the range of values for r being from -0.26 to $+0.22$. Of the remaining four correlations, one was of doubtful reliability, being based on only nine subjects, while two were of opposite sign to that predicted. Both skin conductance and cold pressor basal systolic blood pressure correlated positively with alpha amplitude, the respective values for r being $+0.48$ (N = 19, $p < 0.05$) and $+0.42$ (N = 21, $p < 0.05$). Thus, high autonomic arousal was in both cases associated with *increased* alpha amplitude. In the predicted direction, however, was a negative correlation between alpha amplitude and cold pressor diastolic blood pressure change, the value for r being -0.46 (N = 21, $p < 0.05$). In no case was a significant departure from linearity of regression found.

Discussion

The evidence from this part of the study was clearly equivocal, two measures—alpha blocking time and alpha frequency—showing no relationship with the autonomic indices. In the case of alpha amplitude two reversals of prediction made the results difficult to interpret and the four significant correlations could have arisen by chance.

The findings for alpha index were somewhat more encouraging and suggest that this may be one of the more suitable parameters of EEG activity worth further investigation. Although there was a high proportion of non-significant correlations it is perhaps not entirely chance that the significant relationships that did emerge involved measures previously found to be promising indices of arousability, viz. heart rate and Rogitine blood pressure response. The curvilinear relationships found between alpha index and some autonomic measures are reminiscent of the result reported earlier with respect to sedation threshold. They parallel, too, Stennett's (*op. cit.*) similar finding using skin conductance and alpha amplitude. The main conclusion that can be drawn here is that autonomic measures tend to follow the sedation threshold in showing a rather complex relationship with EEG parameters. To this extent the two sets of results are consistent with each other in so far as they suggest that the mechanisms responsible for cortical arousal may not be

c

identical with those determining autonomic reactivity and sedation threshold.

In this chapter an attempt has been made to elucidate further some of the causal physiological processes underlying dysthymia–hysteria. Although the results as a whole suggest that this behavioural continuum may be multiply determined by several nervous processes, an important source of individual variation can be identified as arousability, measured in terms of the sedation threshold and its autonomic correlates. The transition from dysthymia through normality to hysteria can be visualized, at a psychophysiological level, as a continuum running from high barbiturate tolerance and strong sympathetic reactivity, at one end, to low tolerance of sedatives and weak responsiveness of the sympathetic nervous system, at the other end. A way of linking contemporary views on arousal to Eysenck's personality theory has therefore been suggested.

The results presented also confirm the conclusions recently reached by Gellhorn and Loofbourrow (1963), who hypothesized that central arousal due to sympathetic discharge from the posterior hypo-thalamus may be a common determinant of the sedation threshold and Mecholyl tests. After reviewing the relevant physiological and psychiatric evidence, these authors made a number of suggestions for future research and predicted positive correlations between the sedation threshold and measures of sympathetic reactivity such as the Mecholyl and cold pressor tests. Thus, Gellhorn and his col-league provided, albeit in retrospect, further rationale for under-taking the experiments reported here.

The pattern of correlations between sedation threshold and autonomic activity confirms that it is theoretically important to distinguish between arousal and arousability. The distinction helps to account for the consistently high correlations between measures of reactivity and sedation threshold and the latter's uniformly low correlation with measures of basal level of autonomic activity. Of course, even under so-called basal conditions individual differences should still exist, due to the differential arousing effect of the situation under which resting measurements are taken. These will not reflect arousability so accurately, however, because of the deliberate attempt that is made, during the pre-stress period, to narrow individual differences and produce comparable basal levels. The application of relatively severe, especially pharmacological, stress would be expected to maximize individual differences, so that measures of autonomic activity taken under these conditions will reflect variations in the potentiality for arousal. It is of interest that similar effects can be demonstrated with the fairly mild psychological stress induced by the performance of a vigilance task.

In conclusion, although it may be anticipated that further analysis will reveal additional sources of individual variation, for the moment it is possible to accept the working hypothesis suggested in Chapter 1 that differences in the behaviour of dysthymics and hysterics are partly due to their respective positions along a causal continuum of central nervous arousability. The next stage in the discussion is to consider how far these arousal differences can account for behaviour on performance tests of the kind normally studied by Eysenck and his colleagues. This problem will be examined in the next chapter.

SUMMARY

On the basis of previous evidence it was predicted that variations in sedation threshold would be related to other, autonomic and EEG, indices of arousal. The results of a number of investigations of this hypothesis in neurotic and normal subjects were summarized. On a variety of measures, especially the blood pressure response to phentolamine, sympathetic reactivity was found to be greatest in patients with high sedation thresholds, although sedation threshold was unrelated to basal measures of autonomic response. A significantly curvilinear relationship between sedation threshold and alpha index was reported, a low threshold being associated with both a high and a low alpha index. A moderate degree of intercorrelation was found between the various autonomic measures. The latter, however, tended either to be unrelated to the EEG measures or to show some evidence of curvilinearity of regression. It was concluded that, taking account of the complexity of the physiological parameters under investigation, there was acceptable evidence linking autonomic mechanisms with the sedation threshold and supporting the view that variations in arousability could account for individual differences along the behavioural continuum of dysthymia–hysteria.

CHAPTER 4

DYSTHYMIA–HYSTERIA
AND PSYCHOLOGICAL PERFORMANCE

AROUSAL, DRIVE, AND EXCITATION–INHIBITION

So far in this book we have been concerned with establishing some of the physiological correlates of dysthymia–hysteria. At the next level in the hierarchy of behaviour it is possible to recognize another class of phenomena which properly belong to the field of experimental psychology. Both theories from which the present research was derived have postulated a causal link between nervous mechanisms and overt performance. In the case of arousal theory, this has been achieved by recasting the arousal concept in its rather more molar form and identifying it with "drive". The viewpoint of arousal theorists has been well summarized by Duffy (1962) who concludes:

> The degree of activation of the individual appears to affect the speed, intensity, and co-ordination of responses, and thus to affect the quality of performance. In general, the optimal degree of activation appears to be a moderate degree, with the curve expressing the relationship between activation and performance taking the form of an inverted U. However, the effect of any given degree of activation upon performance appears to vary with a number of factors, including the nature of the task to be performed and certain characteristics of the individual.

Eysenck's different theoretical position and greater concern with individual variation have led him to consider slightly different parameters of behaviour, although the general areas covered by his studies have been similar to those investigated by arousal theorists, namely those of attention, perception, and psychomotor performance. The method most commonly used to test Eysenck's personality theory has been to examine the relationship between questionnaire measures of extraversion, and performance on a wide variety of experimental tasks. These have included conditioning (Franks, 1957), figural after-effects (Eysenck, 1955b), time judgement (Eysenck,

1959b; Lynn, 1961) and various aspects of pursuit-rotor performance (Star, 1957). As well as giving rise to numerous scientific
papers, the results of some of this research have been brought
together in book form (Eysenck, 1957b, 1960b).

As discussed in Chapter 1, although Eysenck has postulated
individual differences in both excitation and inhibition, he has
preferred to manipulate inhibition as the primary variable affecting
performance. Following his 1955 postulates, he has proposed that
differences in the performance of extraverts and introverts are due
to the greater rate at which extraverts develop cortical inhibition,
which is said to have a decremental effect on behaviour. Differences
between hysterics and dysthymics have been explained in the same
way, since it has generally been assumed that dysthymia–hysteria
and introversion–extraversion are synonymous, at least at the
experimental behavioural level. Translation of Eysenck's causal
theory into its arousal equivalent clearly has implications for his
account of psychological performance. Individual differences in
performance on some tasks could readily be explained in terms of a
variation in arousal or drive level, rather than cortical inhibition.
This is particularly true of the comparison between dysthymics and
hysterics who, as shown in the two previous chapters, exhibit wide
variations in arousability. Claridge (1960), in fact, demonstrated
that drive was an important variable affecting the performance of
neurotics, a finding which, of course, led to the arousability hypothesis formulated in Chapter 1. It has also been argued elsewhere
(Claridge, 1961) that variations in drive may provide a more parsimonious explanation of some of the performance differences
described by Eysenck. This would include behaviour on such
measures as the speed or level of performance, which activation
theorists quite reasonably consider to be dependent on arousal or
drive. In the case of some parameters of performance, therefore, it
seems unnecessary to invoke inhibition to account for individual
differences, especially as the arousal concomitants of dysthymia–
hysteria appear to be well-established.

When we turn to other parameters of behaviour, however,
Eysenck's model seems superior to that of the arousal theorists,
who cannot easily handle such experimental phenomena as the
decline in vigilance or psychomotor speed over time, or reminiscence, the spontaneous increment in performance that occurs
following an interpolated rest in massed practice. It seems more

likely that these phenomena reflect the activity of some kind of inhibitory process and Eysenck has naturally paid particular attention to performance measures which implicate inhibition as a primary cause of individual variation.

When the performance correlates of dysthymia–hysteria were examined in the present research it was clearly important, therefore, to recognize the possible limitations, at this level of behaviour, of a simple arousal model of personality. It was realized that performance was almost certainly the result of a complex interaction between both arousing and inhibitory influences and the aim of the research was to try and determine the relative importance of these two variables. Before considering the detailed evidence, however, it is necessary to comment on some of the more recent developments in Eysenck's theory, which has now been extended to account for the influence of drive on performance.

Eysenck visualizes drive as a process which interacts with inhibition in such a way that, when performing under conditions of high drive, the individual will be able to tolerate greater amounts of cortical inhibition. The effects of inhibition on performance will therefore be altered if there is a simultaneous variation in drive level. In order to test this hypothesis, Eysenck and his colleagues have undertaken a large programme of research on motivation (Eysenck, 1964b). The experiments have all been carried out on normal subjects in whom drive was manipulated by comparing two groups of industrial apprentices working under different incentive conditions. It was demonstrated that the groups were similar in extraversion (Eysenck and Warwick, 1964b) and therefore assumed that differences in the proneness to inhibition were due to variations in drive.

These motivational studies have been concerned with situational drive, as distinct from what Feldman (1964) has called the "chronic" notion of drive, i.e. drive viewed as a basic and relatively permanent characteristic of the personality. However, in one paper Eysenck (1962c) has suggested how variations in chronic drive may affect performance. Drive in this sense is identified with neuroticism and the argument relating drive and inhibition is similar to that used in the general motivational studies. Thus, it is proposed that a high degree of neuroticism will lead to a greater tolerance of cortical inhibition. It is important to note that this modification to Eysenck's personality theory leaves his causal explanation of extraversion essentially unaltered, since it is assumed that normal introverts and extraverts, and presumably therefore dysthymics and hysterics, do not differ in drive level. Theoretically, the neurotic criterion groups should be equally high in drive, while normal samples will be randomly distributed on neuroticism. Eysenck (1962c) suggests that it is necessary in performance studies to match subjects for neuroticism; otherwise the predicted relationship between extraversion and inhibition may fail to appear, or may be distorted by simultaneous variations in drive.

An attempt to link this learning theory concept of drive with the psychophysiology of arousal was made by Eysenck and Warwick (1964a), who demonstrated some differences in the skin resistance of high and low drive subjects used in the motivational experiments. This finding would also lend some support to the hypothesis linking chronic drive with neuroticism. Generally speaking, however, Eysenck's account of drive carries some difficulties when looked at from an arousal viewpoint since, as discussed in Chapter 1, arousal, and therefore drive, could be identified with the causal substrate of either neuroticism or extraversion. Because of the similarity between the concepts of arousal and cortical excitation it could be argued that their common behavioural counterpart is drive. This view would be supported by Eysenck's own suggestion that reticular activation may form the neurophysiological basis of cortical excitation (Eysenck, 1963). If drive is assigned solely to neuroticism, then there may be little need to postulate an excitatory component to excitation–inhibition at all, unless it is assumed to have some different property from drive.

Clearly much of the confusion here is semantic and due to the varied usage of such conceptually similar terms as "drive", "excitation", and "arousal", all of which refer, in different terminology, to the positive activating features of nervous function, as distinct from its negative inhibitory properties. In planning the present series of experiments the arousability hypothesis proposed in Chapter 1 again seemed to be the simplest one to adopt as a working theoretical framework. With the support of the evidence described in the two previous chapters, dysthymics and hysterics were assumed to differ in arousability or, to use Feldman's (*op. cit.*) term, in their chronic drive level. Hypotheses for the various experiments to be described were formulated on the basis of this arousal model, where available evidence indicated that drive was probably an important determinant of performance. In the case of measures where inhibition seemed likely to be a mediating variable, the null hypothesis was tested. The theoretical position adopted therefore differed from that of Eysenck only with respect to the greater emphasis placed on excitatory, as distinct from inhibitory, nervous mechanisms. This was an inevitable result of translating Eysenck's causal model into the terminology of arousal theory, which has taken little account of inhibitory processes in psychological performance.

PLAN OF INVESTIGATION

With one or two exceptions to be mentioned later, the performance data described here were collected on various subsamples of the military groups of neurotic and normal subjects described earlier. Eight tests were chosen for investigation, all of them being representative of those studied by Eysenck himself. In addition to the Archimedes spiral after-effect, they included tests of vigilance and time perception, and five psychomotor tasks. The last mentioned were serial reaction time, under both paced and unpaced conditions, the Tsai–Partington number tracing test, a symbol substitution task, and a modified version of the Stroop test. In the case of a few of these tests, some data have already been published elsewhere and the results presented here are for the expanded samples now available. Where a test has been described previously, details of the experimental procedure will be found in the paper cited.

Measures from each test will be discussed from two points of view: first, in terms of group differences between dysthymics, normals, and hysterics; and secondly, in their relation to psychophysiological measures of arousal. The latter aspect of the data will, with a few exceptions, be confined to the sedation threshold, since only here had a sufficient amount of data been collected to make correlational analysis possible. One exception occurred in the case of the two autonomic measures recorded simultaneously during vigilance performance. Otherwise, correlations computed between autonomic or EEG and performance variables were considered to be of doubtful reliability and difficult to interpret. A very large number of correlations was computed, but few were significant. Attenuation was undoubtedly due partly to the fact that the measures were taken on different occasions and it has already been noted what effect this has on correlations even between measures of the same autonomic function. It was hardly likely, therefore, that any substantial association would be found between autonomic measures and performance variables taken days, weeks, or months apart. Even correlations that were statistically significant were computed on small samples and could have arisen by chance. Unless stated otherwise it can be assumed that correlations between performance and measures of arousal, other than sedation threshold, were either non-significant, or of too doubtful reliability to be considered worth recording.

Although the general prediction was made that arousability and performance would be positively related, the possibility was borne in mind throughout that inverted-U relationships might be found. Indeed, on certain tests theoretical considerations led to the prediction that curvilinear relationships between performance and arousability would appear. Pairs of variables on which correlations were calculated were always plotted for inspection and, if necessary, tested statistically for non-linearity of regression.

In discussing the tests individually, attention will be focused mainly upon measures of performance level and/or performance decline. Reminiscence scores were also collected, however, from all five psychomotor tasks and from one experiment using the Archimedes spiral. Reminiscence is of special theoretical interest because of the important place it has occupied in Eysenck's investigation of inhibition. In view of this, all of the reminiscence data will be brought together in a separate section at the end of the chapter.

EXPERIMENTAL FINDINGS

Archimedes Spiral After-effect (SAE)

The illusion of apparent movement induced by fixation of a previously rotated spiral has been of interest to psychologists for many years and Holland (1965) has recently reviewed the considerable literature on the test. In a clinical setting the Archimedes spiral after-effect, or SAE, has been most often used to investigate brain damage, usually with equivocal results. Some authors (Holland and Beech, 1958) have reported reduced and others (Spinack and Levine, 1959) increased after-effects in organic patients. Following the publication of Eysenck's causal postulates, the personality correlates of the SAE became of interest and Eysenck's (1957b) prediction that dysthymics should report longer after-effects than hysterics was confirmed in two previous studies by the present writer (Claridge, 1960; Claridge and Herrington, 1960). The association between personality and the SAE in normal subjects seems to be much more tenuous, Holland (1962) finding no relationship with extraversion in a factor analytic study of a large quantity of data from industrial apprentices. Results for this test therefore follow a trend commonly noted in research on Eysenck's theory, namely an association with personality in the neurotic criterion groups, but not in normal subjects differentiated in terms of questionnaire scores.

Physiological correlates of the SAE have been examined in a number of studies. A significant positive correlation with sedation threshold in a small group of neurotic and normal subjects was reported by Claridge and Herrington (*op. cit.*) and this finding has since been confirmed by Krishnamoorti and Shagass (1964). In another experiment Claridge and Herrington (1963a) investigated the EEG correlates of the SAE. They found it to be significantly correlated with both resting alpha index and alpha blocking time induced by previous fixation of the spiral. Thus, longer subjective after-effects were reported by subjects showing evidence of higher resting cortical arousal and greater physiological responsiveness to visual stimulation. Similarly, a significant correlation has been reported between SAE and alpha block following light fixation (Agathon and Lelord, 1961; Agathon, 1964).

Finally, in a series of studies referred to in the previous chapter the relationship of the SAE to various blood pressure measures was described. Claridge *et al.* (1963) reported a significant association between the test and both systolic and diastolic resting blood pressure. No correlation was found with blood pressure change after cold pressor stress. This lack of association with reactivity measures was confirmed for both Mecholyl by Wawman *et al.* (1963) and for Rogitine by Davies *et al.* (1963). The latter authors also replicated the significant correlation between SAE and resting blood pressure. They concluded, after factor analysing their data, that the spiral after-effect may reflect a somewhat different aspect of nervous activity from that measured by other arousal indices.

The data presented here are for much larger samples than those reported on previously. The main sample was, in fact, identical with that described for sedation threshold in Chapter 2; that is to say, it consisted of sixty-six dysthymics, fifty-seven hysterics, and thirty-four normal subjects. As with the sedation threshold, additional data will be presented here for the group of forty civilian dysthymic patients described in Chapter 2.

To obtain a measure of the SAE the experimental procedure followed was to use a four-throw Archimedes spiral rotating at 120 rpm to give an expanding effect during rotation and hence a contracting after-effect. Trials consisted of two 1-minute fixation periods, with a 1-minute rest between trials. The mean, in seconds, of the two after-effects obtained was taken as a measure of the subject's SAE.

Group differences. Table 1 shows the main SAE results for the military samples. It can be seen that, paralleling the sedation threshold findings, there was a highly significant difference between

TABLE 1. SPIRAL AFTER-EFFECT (SEC) IN THREE MILITARY GROUPS

	Dysthymics	Normals	Hysterics
N	66	34	57
Mean	18·90	12·71	11·37
SD	5·91	5·48	5·37

F-ratio: 29·672, $p < 0.001$

t-tests
Dysthymics vs. Hysterics: 7·331, $p < 0.001$
Dysthymics vs. Normals: 5·158, $p < 0.001$
Hysterics vs. Normals: 1·089, N.S.

the three groups, dysthymics reporting significantly longer after-effects than both hysterics and normals. As with sedation threshold, the difference between hysterics and normals was not significant. This was again probably due to the bias towards hysterical predisposition found in our normal sample (see Introduction).

Table 2 shows the means for the civilian sample of forty dysthymic patients and its three subgroups of chronic anxiety state, obsessional neurosis, and reactive depression. It can be seen that there was little difference either between military and civilian dysthymics as a whole, or between the three subtypes of civilian dysthymia. Overall comparison with analysis of variance revealed

TABLE 2. SPIRAL AFTER-EFFECT (SEC) IN THREE SUBGROUPS OF DYSTHYMIA

	Civilian dysthymics				Military dysthymics
	Chronic anxiety states	Obsessional neurotics	Reactive depressives	Total group	
N	17	7	16	40	66
Mean	19·89	22·00	20·82	20·63	18·90
SD	7·18	4·63	2·49	6·24	5·91

a non-significant value for F of 0·275 (df 3/102). The difference in the range of scores within these three subgroups of dysthymia should be noted, however, the standard deviation for anxiety states being three times larger than that for neurotic depressives.

Breakdown of the military sample of hysterics revealed, as shown in Table 3, that there was a close similarity in the SAE performance of conversion hysterics, hysterical personalities, and psychopaths. It will be recalled that there were too few civilian hysterics to make

TABLE 3. SPIRAL AFTER-EFFECT (SEC) IN THREE SUBGROUPS OF HYSTERIA

	Conversion hysterics	Hysterical personalities	Psychopaths
N	23	29	5
Mean	10·78	10·63	12·20
SD	4·67	4·73	5·63

F-ratio: 0·218, N.S.

comparison with military neurotics possible. However, the five civilian patients falling into that category are included in Fig. 4.1, which shows the frequency distributions of SAE in normal subjects and in all civilian and military neurotics tested, viz. 106 dysthymics and sixty-two hysterics. It can be seen that the group comparisons exactly paralleled those for sedation threshold. Despite the overall significant difference between groups, there was considerable overlap between them suggesting a continuous variation from low to high SAE. The shift towards low, rather than high, SAE in the present normal sample should again be noted.

In summary, the results substantially confirm, on relatively large samples, the prediction that dysthymics will experience significantly longer spiral after-effects than hysterics. No differences can be demonstrated between the various subgroups of dysthymia and hysteria, thus providing further support for Eysenck's classification of the major neurotic disorders.

Further analysis. In view of the similarity between the group findings for the spiral after-effect and the sedation threshold, it is not surprising that the two tests should be found to be positively correlated. In fact, the correlation between SAE and sedation threshold in the full group of 168 neurotics was +0·33, which was significant beyond the 0·001 level of confidence. Further examination of the data revealed, however, that the relationship between the two tests was not linear, as anticipated originally. As can be seen in Fig. 4.2, while there was a linear increase in sedation threshold up to an SAE value of between 25 and 30 seconds, beyond this point sedation threshold began to decline. This departure from linearity of regression was found on analysis of variance to be highly significant beyond the 0·001 level of confidence.

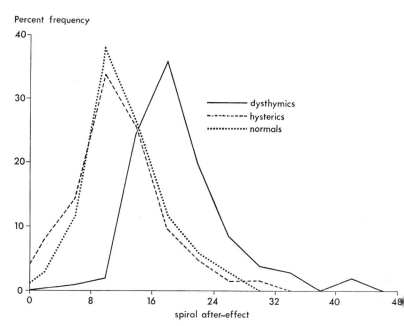

FIG. 4.1. Frequency distributions for spiral after-effect in dysthymics, hysterics, and normal subjects.

The finding that the association between threshold and SAE may not be a simple one was also supported by results on normal subjects. On smaller sub-samples tested previously correlations had ranged from small positive to large negative values. In the total group of thirty-four subjects included here the correlation was found to be −0·03, or virtually zero. Thus, although the sedation threshold and spiral after-effect do co-vary in the same direction, this seems to be confined to neurotic patients and only here over a certain, albeit fairly wide, range of values.

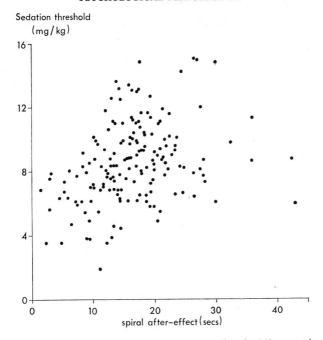

Fig. 4.2. Sedation threshold and spiral after-effect in 168 neurotics, illustrating curvilinear nature of regression.

Time Judgement

In his original investigation of dysthymia–hysteria Claridge (1960) reported a relationship between personality and the estimation of time intervals. When asked to reproduce a series of standard time intervals of short duration, hysterics showed a greater tendency to under-reproduce the intervals than did dysthymics. Both neurotic groups showed greater error of judgement than normal subjects, a finding that was against prediction, although in the normal group a significant correlation with extraversion was found. This was in the expected direction, extraverts showing greater tendency to under-reproduce than introverts. The latter finding has since been confirmed by Eysenck (1959b) and Lynn (1961). Iwawaki (1960) also found that error in time estimation correlated significantly with rhathymia and social introversion, although not with thinking intro-version as measured by the Yatebe–Guilford Personality Inventory. Orme (1962) used rather longer time intervals than those in most other studies and found no relationship between the time perception of normal subjects and either of the MPI scales. In a psychiatric population he reported differences between hysterics and psychopaths, on the one hand, and neurotic and psychotic depressives, on the other.

A possible physiological correlate of time perception was suggested long ago by Hoagland (1933) who demonstrated disturbances of time estimation following increases in body temperature. Changes consistent with Hoagland's findings have recently been reported by Baddeley (1964), who investigated the effects on time perception of reducing the body temperature. No correlation between time estimation and pulse rate was found, although Hawkes *et al.* (1961) did find a significant relationship between these two variables. These results suggest that individual differences in time perception might arise on a basis of variations in arousal level.

The method used here for measuring time judgement followed that described originally by Llewellyn-Thomas (1959). It is essentially a positive feedback technique in which the subject makes a judgement of a standard time interval and is then presented with his judgement as a new standard for the next trial. This procedure is then repeated over a number of trials, thus maximizing individual differences. In the particular version used here the standard time interval presented at the start of the test was 30 seconds, the experimenter defining the beginning and end of this period by tapping on the table with a pencil. The subject was required to tap a third time when he thought the same amount of time had elapsed following the experimenter's second tap. This interval was then presented to the subject as the next standard to be judged and so on for a total of ten trials.

The subjects for the experiment were thirty dysthymics, twenty-three hysterics, and seventeen normal subjects. On the basis of the previous findings it was expected that hysterics would show greater and more rapidly increasing under-reproduction of time intervals compared with dysthymics. In view of their unexpected behaviour in the earlier experiment it was not possible, however, to make a confident prediction about the performance of the normal group.

Results. Figure 4.3 illustrates the trend in performance for the three groups over the ten trials of the experiment. It can be seen that, although dysthymics and hysterics were clearly separated at most stages, the direction of error was similar for both groups. Furthermore, the trend of error was towards increasing over-reproduction, particularly in hysterics. Normal subjects, on the other hand, showed little divergence in error of estimation, but a small constant under-reproduction of the intervals. A two-way analysis of variance carried out on the data revealed that neither the difference between the groups nor the difference between trials was significant, both F-ratios falling below unity. Correlations between error in time perception—i.e. 30 seconds minus the response on the last trial— and sedation threshold were not significant for either normal or

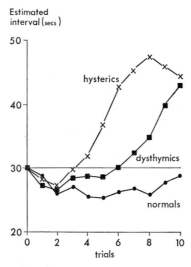

FIG. 4.3. Time-judgement curves in dysthymics, hysterics, and normal subjects, showing trend of error starting with a standard interval of 30 seconds.

neutral subjects. The values for *r* were, respectively, −0·29 (N=17) and 0·15 (N=53). No evidence for curvilinearity of regression was found when the data were plotted.

Results for this test were clearly against prediction, the only similarities with the previous findings being that both neurotic groups tended to show somewhat greater error than normal subjects and hysterics to show greater error than dysthymics. The direction of error in neurotics was opposite to that found in the previous experiment, so that the results seemed to be test-specific. There was no evidence that error of time judgement bore any systematic relationship with chronic arousal level as measured by the sedation threshold.

Auditory Vigilance

Vigilance tasks provide a particularly suitable method of testing a psychophysiological theory of individual differences. The decrement that occurs in attention during a prolonged visual or auditory "watch" under monotonous conditions accords well with the known dependence of arousal level on the maintenance of an adequately varied sensory input (Hebb, 1958). Since the early classic experiments of Mackworth (1950), interest in this field of enquiry has increased and several theories have been put forward to explain vigilance performance (Broadbent, 1963). Considerable individual differences in resistance to the monotony of vigilance tasks have been noted by almost all workers. In a recent symposium on the topic, Buckner (1963) noted the difficulty of accounting for such variation; though in the same symposium, and elsewhere, Bakan described the superior vigilance of introverts compared with extraverts (Bakan *et al.*, 1963; Bakan, 1959). Experiments with psychiatric patients in this field seem rare, although Claridge (1960) demonstrated that dysthymics were significantly better than hysterics on an auditory vigilance task.

In a subsequent experiment Claridge and Herrington (1963b), again using psychiatric patients, demonstrated significant relationships between performance and both sedation threshold and heart rate recorded during vigilance. A number of other workers have also reported an association, in normal subjects, between vigilance performance and concomitantly recorded autonomic measures. Ross *et al.* (1959) monitored skin conductance during a clockwatching task of the Mackworth type and found some evidence that efficiency of signal detection was related to physiological arousal. There was, however, considerable individual variation in the kind of skin conductance change shown during the test. More recently Surwillo and Quilter (1965) demonstrated a relationship between vigilance performance and frequency of spontaneous changes in skin potential. Corcoran (1964), who was primarily interested in arousal changes resulting from sleep loss, reported a parallel decline in heart rate and vigilance and concluded that both probably reflected a change in arousal level.

The data presented here consist of all of the results gathered to date on the auditory vigilance task described in detail elsewhere (Claridge, 1960). The test was a modification of that devised by

Bakan (*op. cit.*), consisting of a 30-minute tape-recording of random digits read out at the rate of one per second. Interspersed in the series were a number of "signals" consisting of three consecutive odd digits. Signals occurred with an average frequency of one per minute, the total number of signals to be detected thus being thirty.

Fifty-seven dysthymics, forty-eight hysterics, and fifty-five normal subjects completed the task.[1] On a proportion of this total sample heart rate or heart rate and skin resistance were monitored simultaneously during vigilance performance. Those subjects in whom heart rate alone was measured were divided into twenty-five dysthymics, sixteen hysterics, and twenty-four normal subjects. Both physiological variables were measured in thirteen dysthymics, eight hysterics, and fourteen normal subjects.

Details of the recording procedure for the physiological measures were given in the previous chapter. As described there, analysis of the data was carried out by fitting linear regression lines to the scores for each individual, skin resistance readings being converted to measures of conductance. In addition to a measure of total signals detected, the same method of analysis was used for the vigilance scores. The procedure used was again to divide the 30-minute test into six 5-minute periods. The linear regressions were therefore based on six scores, each of which represented the number of signals detected in a 5-minute period. The main purpose of using this form of analysis for vigilance performance was to obtain a measure of the rate of decline of vigilance over time. In the case of the physiological indices both level and rate of decline were of interest.

On the basis of previous evidence, it was predicted that dysthymics would show superior vigilance to hysterics and that the level of vigilance performance would correlate positively with physiological measures of arousal. No confident prediction could be made, however, about measures of decline in vigilance over time or their relationship with either the autonomic indices or the sedation threshold.

Group differences. Considering the measure of total vigilance score first, it can be seen from Table 4 that results for the larger sample now available continued the trend found earlier. Dysthymics

[1] To increase the size of the samples the vigilance scores for subjects tested by Claridge (1960) were added to the data collected since that experiment. These additional subjects were taken from the same military population and are described in the original paper.

TABLE 4. VIGILANCE SCORE (TOTAL SIGNALS DETECTED) IN THREE GROUPS

	Dysthymics	Normals	Hysterics
N	57	55	48
Mean	23·2	21·0	14·9
SD	6·37	5·31	6·19

F-ratio: 27·222, $p < 0·001$

t-tests
Dysthymics vs. Hysterics: 7·117, $p < 0·001$
Dysthymics vs. Normals: 1·960, $p < 0·05$
Hysterics vs. Normals: 5·193, $p < 0·001$

showed significantly superior vigilance to both normals and
hysterics, who in turn differed significantly from each other. The
trend in performance throughout the task is illustrated in Fig. 4.4,
where it can be seen that the three groups were separated at all
stages, although the difference between hysterics and normals was

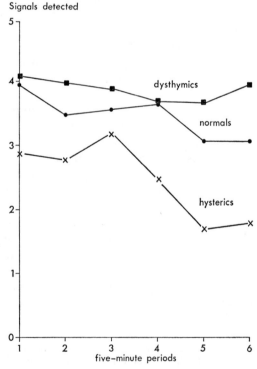

FIG. 4.4. Auditory vigilance curves for dysthymics, hysterics, and
normal subjects.

considerably greater than that between normals and dysthymics. Hysterics showed the most rapid fall-off in vigilance, a trend that is reflected in the regression coefficients given in Table 5. The slope of

TABLE 5. RATE OF VIGILANCE DECLINE IN THREE GROUPS

	Dysthymics	Normals	Hysterics
N	57	55	48
Mean	−0·07	−0·17	−0·28
SD	0·88	0·11	0·36

F-ratio: 5·014, $p < 0·01$

$$\left\{\begin{array}{ll}\text{Dysthymics vs. Hysterics:} & 3·321, p < 0·001 \\ \text{Dysthymics vs. Normals:} & 1·640, \text{N.S.} \\ \text{Hysterics vs. Normals:} & 1·718, \text{N.S.}\end{array}\right.$$

vigilance decrement was in fact significantly greater in hysterics than in dysthymics, although other group comparisons were not significant.

Turning to the autonomic measures recorded during the task, the heart rate and skin conductance data are illustrated in Figs. 4.5 and 4.6 respectively. On both measures dysthymics showed a higher

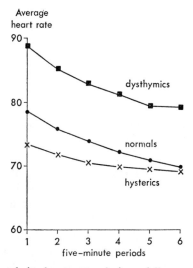

FIG. 4.5. Trend in heart rate during vigilance performance in dysthymics, hysterics, and normal subjects.

average level of sympathetic arousal throughout vigilance than both normals and hysterics. These last two groups were just separated in heart rate at all stages of the task, but this was not true of skin conductance. Here normal subjects had a higher skin conductance

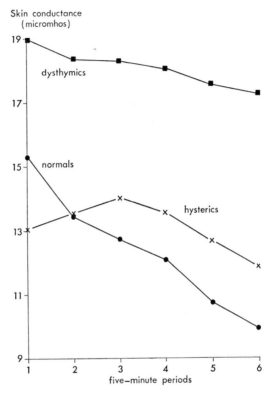

Fig. 4.6. Trend in skin conductance during vigilance performance in dysthymics, hysterics, and normal subjects.

level at the beginning, but declined more rapidly than hysterics, who showed a slight rise in conductance followed by a fall.

The regression coefficients for both slope and level of these two autonomic measures are shown in Tables 6 and 7 respectively. Considering heart rate first, it can be seen from Table 6a that there was a significant overall difference in level and only the comparison between hysterics and normals failed to reach significance. There was also a significant overall difference in rate of decline in heart

TABLE 6. VIGILANCE—HEART RATE LEVEL AND RATE OF DECLINE
(BEATS PER MIN) IN THREE GROUPS

	Dysthymics	Normals	Hysterics
N	25	24	16
	(a) *Level*		
Mean	88·5	79·3	73·7
SD	14·42	16·43	12·51

F-ratio: 5·077, $p < 0·01$

t-tests
Dysthymics vs. Hysterics: 3·077, $p < 0·01$
Dysthymics vs. Normals: 2·194, $p < 0·05$
Hysterics vs. Normals: 1·145, N.S.

(b) *Rate of decline*

Mean	−1·83	−1·68	−0·85
SD	1·26	0·99	1·16

F-ratio: 3·713, $p < 0·05$

t-tests
Dysthymics vs. Hysterics: 2·610, $p < 0·02$
Dysthymics vs. Normals: 0·448, N.S.
Hysterics vs. Normals: 2·195, $p < 0·05$

TABLE 7. VIGILANCE—SKIN CONDUCTANCE LEVEL AND RATE OF DECLINE
(MICROMHOS) IN THREE GROUPS

	Dysthymics	Normals	Hysterics
N	13	14	8
	(a) *Level*		
Mean	18·36	15·87	14·89
SD	13·68	19·32	8·97

F-ratio: 0·137, N.S.

(b) *Rate of decline*

Mean	−0·34	−1·00	−0·23
SD	0·80	1·65	0·45

F-ratio: 1·434, N.S.

rate (Table 6b), although the order of magnitude was opposite to that for level. In fact, as might be predicted from the "law of initial values", rate of decline was very much a function of initial level, a significant correlation being found between the two regression coefficients ($r = -0 \cdot 64$, N = 65, $p < 0 \cdot 001$). As can be seen from Table 7, the group differences in skin conductance were not statistically significant, either with respect to initial level or rate of decline. Like heart rate, however, these two measures were significantly correlated, r being $-0 \cdot 63$ (N = 35, $p < 0 \cdot 001$).

In summary, the group findings confirmed the prediction that dysthymics and hysterics would differ in their respective levels of vigilance and autonomic arousal, though possibly because of the small sample the difference failed to reach significance in the case of skin conductance. Changes in autonomic function during the task were clearly a function very largely of the initial level of arousal, though this was not true of vigilance, where hysterics showed a progressively greater decrement in performance over time than the other two groups.

Further analysis. The main result from the earlier study was maintained on the larger sample of subjects used here. Sedation threshold correlated positively and significantly with total vigilance score in forty-two neurotics, r being $+0 \cdot 44$ ($p < 0 \cdot 01$). In twenty-five normal subjects the comparable value for r was $+0 \cdot 33$ which was in the expected direction, but failed to reach significance. In the case of vigilance decline, opposite results were found in the two groups. In normal subjects sedation threshold correlated significantly and positively with the regression coefficient for slope, r being $+0 \cdot 48$ (N = 25, $p < 0 \cdot 05$): that is to say, decline in vigilance was slower in subjects with high sedation thresholds. In neurotics the correlation was $-0 \cdot 24$ (N = 42), which was not significant.

Analysis of the relationship between vigilance and the autonomic measures yielded only one result of interest and this of borderline significance. In neurotics there was a slight tendency for those with higher initial heart rates to detect more signals, the correlation between initial heart rate and total vigilance score being $+0 \cdot 29$ (N = 41, $p < 0 \cdot 1$). Initial skin conductance level showed no relationship with vigilance score, either in the patient or in the normal samples. Confirming the results of the previous study, there was no association between decline in vigilance and decline in the autonomic indices.

Thus, although there was an average parallel decline in both vigilance and autonomic activity the processes underlying each of these are clearly not related in a simple fashion. One reason for this may have been that other influences, not associated with "psychological" arousal, may have contributed to the decline in autonomic response. Particularly in the case of heart rate, these may have included such factors as physical inactivity, lying down on a bed, and so on. The finding may also illustrate the dependence of vigilance on the state of *chronic* drive, which seemed to be most accurately measured by the sedation threshold. As shown in the previous chapter, the autonomic correlates of chronic drive, or arousability, seem to be confined to measures taken under stress, including vigilance. Under more basal conditions autonomic measures appear less and less to reflect chronic drive state and in this respect it is interesting to note a recent finding reported by Claridge and Herrington (1963b). They demonstrated that although there were marked differences in the waking heart rate of dysthymics and hysterics, these were virtually eliminated during sleep. The mean sleeping pulse rates for the groups differed by only 2·2 beats/min, compared with a difference of 16·3 beats/min, at the beginning of the vigilance task described here. The result illustrates the distinction that needs to be made between arousability as a relatively fixed personality characteristic and the state of transient arousal monitored by autonomic indices.

Serial Reaction Time (unpaced)

As a simple test of psychomotor speed, serial reaction time has advantages over more complex tasks, like the pursuit-rotor, since performance is relatively uncomplicated by learning factors. Perfect or near-perfect performance is possible from the beginning of practice and, as argued elsewhere (Claridge, 1961), the individual's drive level should be reflected in his speed at the beginning of the task, i.e. before other variables, such as inhibition, have begun to influence behaviour. This assumption was not, in fact, confirmed by Willett (1964) with respect to experimentally induced drive, although marked differences in the performance level of dysthymics and hysterics were reported by Claridge (*op. cit.*). In the latter study the subsequent decline that occurred in the performance of all subjects was interpreted as being due to the accumulation of inhibition; although measures of fall-off on this task are known to be very largely determined by the initial level (Venables, 1959; Claridge, *op. cit.*).

Another phenomenon characteristic of psychomotor tasks is the appearance of involuntary rest pauses or "blocks" (Bills, 1931; Broadbent, 1958). These blocks are sometimes accompanied by errors of response and they have been quoted by Kimble (1949) and Eysenck (1956) as forming the basis of conditioned inhibition which leads to permanent performance decrement. In his study of neurotics Claridge (*op. cit.*) found no significant difference in the error score of dysthymics and hysterics. The fact that the related phenomenon of "blocks" may be associated with fluctuations in arousal is suggested by the finding of Bjerner (1950), who analysed some of the physiological correlates of serial reaction time. He demonstrated that during involuntary rest pauses there is a temporary slowing of the heart rate and the appearance of slow waves in the EEG.

On the basis of the foregoing, the only predictions that could be made with any certainty were that dysthymics would be superior in performance level to hysterics and that the measure of initial speed would correlate positively with the sedation threshold. It was also expected that rate of fall-off in performance would be a function of initial level.

Details of the apparatus and experimental procedure used are given in the author's paper cited above. Briefly, the task was a five-choice serial reaction time test, consisting of a display panel containing five lights set in a row. Immediately below each light and in the horizontal plane was a metal tab like a piano key. In operation, the subject was asked to press the key corresponding to the light that was on at any one time. This response extinguished that light and illuminated another light to which a further response was made, and so on. The sequence of stimuli was random over a series of fifty, except that no light was illuminated twice in succession. The testing schedule used was a 10-minute practice period, followed by 5 minutes rest and further practice for 1 minute to obtain a reminiscence score.

In order to calculate measures of initial speed and rate of fall-off, linear regression lines were fitted to the correct response scores for each individual, these being based on the scores for each minute during the first 5 minutes of the test. Analysis of fall-off was confined to this period because, on the particular apparatus used, it was found that, during the second 5 minutes of practice, a gradual rise in speed occurred in many subjects. This was thought to be due to the restriction on the randomness of stimuli, the sequence of which the subjects eventually began to learn. The measure of errors taken was the total number of incorrect responses made during the full 10-minute practice period. Reminiscence was measured by subtracting the score for the last minute of pre-rest practice from the post-rest score.

The results presented here are for a somewhat expanded sample than that reported on previously. The sample was made up of seventeen dysthymics, nineteen hysterics, and thirty-three normal subjects.

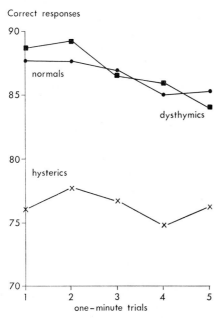

FIG. 4.7. Performance of dysthymics, hysterics, and normal subjects over first 5 minutes of unpaced serial reaction time task.

Group differences. As can be seen in Fig. 4.7 and Table 8, both dysthymics and normals had a significantly faster initial response rate than hysterics, although the first two groups were closely similar. Table 9 shows the mean rate of decline for the three groups as represented by the appropriate regression coefficient. It is clear that the order of magnitude of decline paralleled that for performance level, dysthymics showing greater fall-off than hysterics, with normal subjects again occupying an intermediate position. The overall difference between the groups was not significant, although there was, as expected, a significant correlation between level and fall-off, r being -0.54 ($N = 69$, $p < 0.001$). No significant difference was found in the mean number of errors for each group (Table 10), although the trend was for a slightly greater frequency of errors in hysterics compared with other subjects.

TABLE 8. SERIAL REACTION TIME (UNPACED)

Initial performance level (responses per min) in three groups

	Dysthymics	Normals	Hysterics
N	17	33	19
Mean	90·4	88·6	77·4
SD	14·60	13·35	11·97

F-ratio: 5·350, $p < 0.01$

t-tests
Dysthymics vs. Hysterics: 2·889, $p < 0.01$
Dysthymics vs. Normals: 0·447, N.S.
Hysterics vs. Normals: 2·887, $p < 0.01$

TABLE 9. SERIAL REACTION TIME (UNPACED)

Rate of decline in three groups

	Dysthymics	Normals	Hysterics
N	17	33	19
Mean	−1·16	−0·66	−0·47
SD	1·91	1·49	1·76

F-ratio: 0·775, N.S.

TABLE 10. SERIAL REACTION TIME (UNPACED)

Error score in three groups

	Dysthymics	Normals	Hysterics
N	17	33	19
Mean	11·0	11·5	16·8
SD	10·39	11·18	20·13

F-raito: 0·969, N.S.

Further analysis. The main prediction here that starting speed would be greater in subjects with high sedation thresholds was confirmed for neurotics, but not for normal subjects. In thirty-six patients the correlation between the regression coefficient for level and sedation threshold was $+0.39$ ($p < 0.02$) and in thirty-three normal subjects $+0.12$ (N.S.). In neither group was there any significant association between sedation threshold and rate of decline in response, the correlation being slightly negative (-0.27) in neurotics and zero in normals.

The most consistent findings appeared with respect to the error score. In both neurotic and normal subjects significant negative correlations were found between errors and sedation threshold, those with higher arousal recording fewer incorrect responses. The correlation in neurotics was -0.46 (N = 36, $p < 0.01$) and in normals -0.34 (N = 33, $p < 0.05$).

In most respects, therefore, the results for serial reaction time confirmed the prediction that individuals with high chronic arousal would perform at a faster rate than those with low arousal. When judged against sedation threshold highly aroused subjects also made fewer errors, although the relationship between errors and arousal was not reflected in the group differences on this measure. As found previously, the relationship between initial speed and subsequent rate of decline appeared to follow a "law of initial values", greater decline being found in those subjects who started at a faster response rate.

Symbol Substitution Test

This simple psychomotor test has been used by Eysenck to investigate the effects of experimentally induced drive on performance level and reminiscence. It was of interest, therefore, to compare results with those obtained using subjects differing in chronic drive level. Eysenck and Willett (1962b) found, in fact, that their high and low drive groups did not differ in performance level. In line with the present analysis of dysthymia–hysteria, however, it was predicted that there would be differences between these two types of patient, and an overall relationship with sedation threshold. The samples for this experiment were rather small, there being only eight dysthymics, ten hysterics, and ten normal subjects.

The task was a symbol substitution test of the usual kind. Twenty letters and their symbols were placed at the top of each of a number of consecutive pages. These were followed by lines of letters beneath each of which was a space for the appropriate symbol to be entered. The subject was asked to perform for 5 minutes under massed practice, trials being distinguished by having him place a tick at the point he had reached after each 30-second period. There were thus ten trials in all. A rest of 5 minutes was then given, followed by a further short period of practice for 1 minute (i.e. two trials) in order to obtain a reminiscence measure. The latter was taken as the mean of the last two pre-rest trials subtracted from the mean of the two post-rest trials.

Results. Figure 4.8 shows the trends in performance for the three groups over the ten trials of the experiment. It can be seen that the

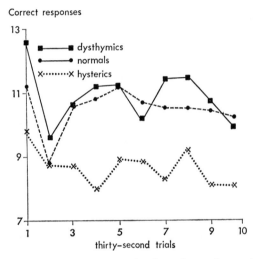

FIG. 4.8. Performance of dysthymics, hysterics, and normal subjects over ten trials of symbol substitution test.

performance level of dysthymics was superior to that of hysterics at all stages of the task, although there was considerable overlap between dysthymics and normal subjects. As shown in Table 11, the overall difference between the three groups was not significant. The somewhat equivocal group findings with this test were repeated in its relationship with sedation threshold. In eighteen neurotic patients sedation threshold correlated $+0.40$ with total score, a value which was significant at the 10 per cent level only. In normal

TABLE 11. SYMBOL SUBSTITUTION TEST

Correct score in three groups

	Dysthymics	Normals	Hysterics
N	8	10	10
Mean	10·9	10·6	8·7
SD	3·09	1·70	1·67

F-ratio: 2·391, N.S.

subjects a zero correlation was found between the two measures. Possibly because of the small samples involved, no firm conclusion could be reached about the relationship between arousal and symbol substitution performance. The trend of the results was, however, in the predicted direction.

Serial Reaction Time (paced)

The assumption made so far has been that dysthymics, because of their higher level of chronic drive, will perform better than hysterics and normals on simple vigilance and psychomotor tasks. It has been noted, however, that under certain conditions heightened arousal may actually lead to a deterioration in performance, because of the latter's curvilinear relationship with arousal (Hebb, 1955). An earlier expression of this now familiar inverted-U phenomenon was the Yerkes–Dodson law (Yerkes and Dodson, 1908). This maintains that for each task there is an optimal drive and that the more complex the task the lower this optimum level will be. There are, therefore, two methods of testing the principle: increasing the drive level during performance of a simple task or increasing the complexity of the task. The method described in this section was of the latter kind. It was predicted that, if a serial reaction time task were paced at a speed that was stressful for the individual, then dysthymics, being already highly aroused, would be taken beyond the optimum drive level for efficient performance. They should, therefore, be inferior in performance to normals and resemble hysterics, who should perform poorly because of their low drive level. It was also predicted that there would be a curvilinear relationship between sedation threshold and performance, when the whole range of arousability from dysthymia to hysteria was considered. These hypotheses were tested on twenty-four dysthymics, seventeen hysterics, and fifteen normal subjects.

The apparatus used was the same as that described in a previous section for unpaced operation. It was so modified that the stimuli were presented independently of the subject's response. The same random presentation was retained and the subject was again asked to press the key in front of the light that was on at any one time. Whether or not he pressed the correct key the light was extinguished after half a second and another light illuminated. The rate of presentation of stimuli was, therefore, 120 per minute, a pacing speed that most individuals reported as being quite stressful. The schedule used was a period of 5 minutes practice, followed by 10 minutes rest and a further period of practice for 1 minute to obtain a reminiscence score. The measure of reminiscence used was the post-rest score minus the score for the last minute of the pre-rest practice period.

Results. The scores for the three groups of subjects are plotted in Fig. 4.9, while Table 12 shows the group means for a measure of the total number of correct responses made during the 5 minutes practice period. It can be seen that, as predicted, on this more stressful version of the test dysthymics failed to show their superiority in performance under unpaced conditions. In fact, they produced significantly fewer correct responses than more moderately aroused normal subjects and, as predicted, did not differ significantly from hysterics.

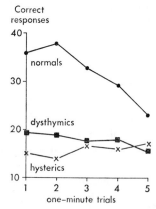

Fig. 4.9. Performance of dysthymics, hysterics, and normal subjects on paced serial reaction time.

TABLE 12. SERIAL REACTION TIME (PACED)
Score (total correct responses) in three groups

	Dysthymics	Normals	Hysterics
N	24	15	17
Mean	89·2	158·2	78·1
SD	70·20	100·73	32·41

F-ratio: 5·580, $p < 0·01$

t-tests
{ Dysthymics vs. Hysterics: 1·501, N.S.
Dysthymics vs. Normals: 8·985, $p < 0·001$
Hysterics vs. Normals: 9·697, $p < 0·001$

Plotting the total correct score against sedation threshold in the combined neurotic and normal groups did not, however, reveal the expected curvilinear relationship between arousal and performance on this test. There was, in fact, no significant association between performance and sedation threshold. In forty-one neurotic patients the linear correlation was +0·21 and in fifteen normal subjects —0·25. Thus, the expectation that the stress of pacing serial reaction time would cause the performance of highly aroused subjects to deteriorate was borne out only with respect to the group differences on the test.

Tsai–Partington Numbers Test

This is a simple perceptual-motor test described by Ammons (1955) and used by Eysenck and Willett (1962a) to test Easterbrook's "cue utilization" theory of attention. Easterbook (1959) has proposed that the utilization of cues in performance gets less as arousal increases, a hypothesis similar to that of Callaway and his co-workers, who have suggested that a focusing or narrowing of attention occurs under high arousal, so that the subject becomes less sensitive to extraneous or distracting stimuli (Callaway and Dembo, 1958).

The Tsai–Partington test requires the subject to join numbers distributed randomly on sheets of paper and the task was interpreted by Eysenck and Willett (*op. cit.*) as one of cue utilization, on the grounds that visual location of the appropriate numbers constitutes the essential element of performance. They demonstrated, as predicted from the Callaway–Easterbrook hypothesis, that normal subjects

D

working under high experimentally induced drive were inferior to low drive subjects. It should follow from this that dysthymics would perform worse than hysterics on the test, with normals intermediate between these two groups. A negative correlation between performance and sedation threshold would be expected. These hypotheses were tested on three samples of eleven dysthymics, eleven hysterics, and twelve normal subjects.

The test consisted of sheets of paper clipped together. On each, page numbers were located at random, the subject being instructed to trace a line from 1 to 2 to 3 and so on through consecutive numbers. He was allowed to perform for 30 seconds, at the end of which time he was told to turn over and start again on the next sheet. Ten such periods of practice were given, each being regarded as a trial. A 5-minute rest was then given, followed by a further two 30-second trials. The score on each trial was the last number correctly reached and the measure of performance level taken for the pre-rest period was the average score over the ten trials. Reminiscence was calculated by subtracting the mean of the last two pre-rest scores from the mean of the scores on the two post-rest trials.

Results. Figure 4.10 and Table 13 reveal that group differences in performance level were quite opposite to prediction. Hysterics were, in fact, inferior to dysthymics, although the differences between the

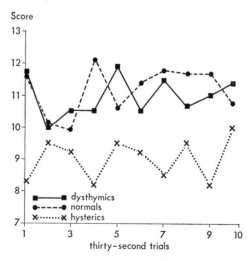

FIG. 4.10. Performance of dysthymics, hysterics, and normal subjects over ten trials of Tsai–Partington numbers test.

TABLE 13. TSAI–PARTINGTON NUMBERS TEST

Correct score in three groups

	Dysthymics	Normals	Hysterics
N	11	12	11
Mean	11·0	11·1	8·9
SD	2·09	1·91	2·66

F-ratio: 3·029, N.S.

three groups were not significant. No relationship between performance and sedation threshold was found, the correlations being zero or near-zero in both neurotic and normal subjects.

Using individuals assumed to differ in chronic arousal level there seems, therefore, to be no evidence on this task to support the cue utilization hypothesis. Instead, the trends of the group data, although not the correlations with sedation threshold, are more in line with those for other simple psychomotor tasks, namely a tendency for high arousal to lead to slightly faster performance.

Colour-word (Stroop) Test

The colour-word interference test was first introduced by Stroop (1935) whose name, however, has been associated with various subsequent modifications of the original version. The basic procedure is similar in all versions, the subject being required to name the colours of the ink of colour-words where the colour and the word are incongruous: for example, the word "red" printed in green ink. A complete review of the history and present status of this test has recently been published by Jensen and Rohwer (1966), who traced its origins back to the end of the last century. As shown by the very large number of references cited by these authors, the original Stroop test, or modifications of it, has been used in many diverse fields of psychological research. In this brief introduction to the test, only those studies that are considered relevant can be mentioned, although the interested reader is referred to Jensen and Rohwer's comprehensive review.

Because of the wide range of research problems to which the Stroop test has been applied, there are a number of theoretical viewpoints from which predictions about its relationship with personality could be derived. The most pertinent here is that which suggests a link between Stroop performance and arousal. Some previous work relating drive to the Stroop test has specifically examined the cue utilization and narrowed attention hypotheses referred to in the previous section. The assumption made in that work has been that heightened arousal will improve performance, because it should follow from the Callaway–Easterbrook hypothesis that increasing arousal will free the subject from the distraction normally causing difficulty in the naming of colour-words. Agnew and Agnew (1963) reported results in line with this prediction. They manipulated drive by electric shock, the threat of shock, and telling subjects that their intelligence was being tested. They found an improvement in performance under high drive conditions, at least on the first testing. These results were corroborated by Callaway (1959) who tested his narrowed attention hypothesis using drugs to alter arousal level. He demonstrated that a depressant drug (amobarbital) increased, and a stimulant drug (methamphetamine) decreased, interference on the Stroop test. Other drug studies have either reported no effect on the test (Quarton and Talland, 1962), or confirmed that depressants will impair performance (Ostfeld and Aruguete, 1962).

Some caution is necessary in applying the results of these studies to the present research which was concerned with chronic, rather than experimentally induced, drive. It has already been noted, with respect to the Tsai–Partington test, that the two methods of manipulating drive may lead to opposite findings. Furthermore, the particular version of the Stroop test used here was relatively stressful and in some ways resembled the paced serial reaction time test described earlier. Using a wide range of chronic arousal, it could be argued with equal ease that high arousal might actually lead to a deterioration in performance on this rather complex task. Unfortunately, the only major investigations of psychiatric patients on the Stroop test have been carried out from a theoretical viewpoint that is difficult to interpret, as Jensen and Rohwer (*op. cit.*) agree. The studies referred to are those by Smith and his colleagues (Smith and Nyman, 1962; Nyman and Smith, 1960). The experiments reported by these workers provided little basis for making precise predictions about the outcome of the present investigation. In view of the uncertainty about the applicability of the Callaway–Easterbrook hypothesis to the Stroop performance of neurotics, it was decided to test the

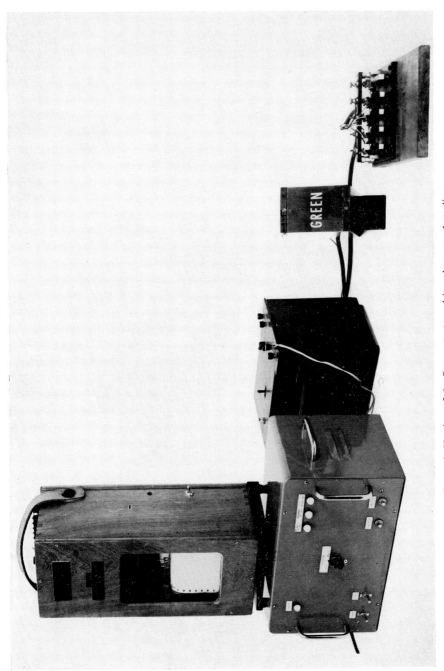

PLATE 2. Version of the Stroop test used in colour-word studies.

null hypothesis. The subjects taking part in the experiment were fourteen dysthymics, eight hysterics, and sixteen normal subjects.

The test material for all previous versions of the Stroop test has consisted of a series of cards containing patches of coloured ink and colour-words printed in incongruous colours. The modification of the test used here departed considerably from this and in some ways can only be loosely regarded as a version of the original Stroop test. Nevertheless, the principles involved in performance were basically similar.

A photograph of the apparatus is shown in Plate 2 and a block diagram in Fig. 4.11. The display box had a screen 4 × 3 in. on which

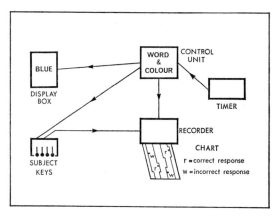

Fig. 4.11. Block diagram showing details of colour-word apparatus (for explanation see text).

could be shown one of the words RED, GREEN, BLUE or YELLOW in any one of these colours, except that denoted by the word displayed. An impulse fed to the control unit from the timer operated a bank of three uni-selectors and changed the display to one of twelve different colour-word combinations. These visual stimuli were programmed in a random order in a series of 150 presentations. The subject's keys were coloured red, blue, yellow, and green. The task involved pressing the key appropriate to the stimulus displayed. Depending on the instructions given to the subject a correct response was one made either to the word displayed or to the colour of the display. A change-over switch on the control unit enabled the particular mode used to be selected. A four-channel recorder indicated the stimulus presented (word or colour) and the key that was operated in response. A Palmer timer provided impulses at rates ranging from ten per second to one per minute.

In the present experiment the rate of presentation of stimuli was standardized at one per second. The experimental procedure was divided into two halves, carried out on different days. On the first day the subject was required to work under the colour condition, i.e. he was asked to respond to the colours in which the words were displayed and to ignore the meaning of the words. After a short period of practice to familiarize himself with the apparatus, the subject performed for 5 minutes and was then given a rest for 10 minutes. He then practised for a further 2 minutes. On the second day the whole schedule was repeated under the other experimental condition, the subject being told to respond to the colour-name and to ignore the colour of the display.

The individual records under both conditions were scored by counting the number of correct and incorrect responses during each minute of performance. Each of these was summed to give four basic measures: total scores of colour-correct, colour-incorrect, word-correct, and word-incorrect. In addition, a measure of the relative difficulty of the two conditions was obtained by subtracting the word-correct total score from the colour-correct total score. Finally, for each condition an index of reminiscence was calculated by subtracting the mean of the two post-rest minute scores from the last pre-rest minute score.

Results. The group trends in correct response for both halves of the experiment are shown in Fig. 4.12. It can be seen that under both conditions normal subjects tended to be superior to the other two groups. The only change in order of performance occurred between the two neurotic groups, dysthymics being superior to hysterics under the colour condition, while the opposite was true in the second half of the test. In both cases, however, the group presumed to be most highly aroused, viz. dysthymics, appeared to be more impaired than normal subjects. Despite the average trends in performance, few of the group differences were statistically significant, possibly because of the small samples involved. Group mean scores for correct and incorrect responses under each condition are shown respectively in Tables 14 and 15, where it can be seen that only in the case of the word-correct score was there a significant overall difference between the groups. This was due to the significant tendency for dysthymics to perform very badly compared with normals. Finally, Table 16 shows the measure of relative difficulty of the two halves of the test. As can also be seen in Fig. 4.12, only dysthymics performed worse under the word condition than under the colour condition. The group differences on this measure were not, however, statistically significant.

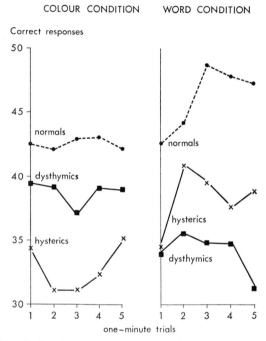

FIG. 4.12. Performance of dysthymics, hysterics, and normal subjects on Stroop test, under colour condition and word condition.

Examination of the relationship between sedation threshold and Stroop performance revealed disappointing results. A curvilinear relationship between arousal and performance might have been expected from the group findings. However, plotting sedation threshold against all possible scores from the test failed to confirm this, while product moment correlations in both normal and neurotic groups were uniformly low and non-significant. Conclusions about the results must, therefore, be tentative, partly because of the small samples used. There is little support for the hypothesis that heightened arousal will improve Stroop performance. The trend, with respect to the group differences at least, is rather towards support of the Yerkes–Dodson principle applied to complex psychomotor performance, dysthymics being more affected by the distracting stimuli than normals. The relatively greater impairment of the

TABLE 14. STROOP TEST (COLOUR CONDITION)

Correct and incorrect responses for three groups

	Dysthymics	Normals	Hysterics
N	14	16	8
	(a) *Total correct score*		
Mean	197·6	211·8	164·2
SD	50·55	50·35	38·61

F-ratio: 2·380, N.S.

	Dysthymics	Normals	Hysterics
	(b) *Total incorrect score*		
Mean	48·9	64·7	74·0
SD	30·12	23·71	45·97

F-ratio: 1·636, N.S.

TABLE 15. STROOP TEST (WORD CONDITION)

Mean correct and incorrect responses for three groups

	Dysthymics	Normals	Hysterics
N	14	16	8
	(a) *Total correct score*		
Mean	170·1	230·6	190·9
SD	44·93	58·16	61·22

F-ratio: 4·371, $p < 0.05$

t-tests { Dysthymics vs. Hysterics: 0·804, N.S.
Dysthymics vs. Normals: 2·917, $p < 0.01$
Hysterics vs. Normals: 1·618, N.S.

	Dysthymics	Normals	Hysterics
	(b) *Total incorrect score*		
Mean	62·1	48·6	55·5
SD	36·38	32·31	21·32

F-ratio: 0·615, N.S.

TABLE 16. STROOP TEST

Difference in three groups between colour-correct and word-correct scores

	Dysthymics	Normals	Hysterics
N	14	16	8
Mean	27·4	−18·8	−26·6
SD	54·80	55·14	83·11

F-ratio: 2·642, N.S.

former under the word condition would be in line with this interpretation and might be explained by the supposedly greater conditionability of dysthymics. Thus, a stronger habit of colour-responding may have been established in these patients during the first half of the test, a "set" which interfered with the change to word-responding required in the second half.

Reminiscence Measures

Since the beginning of this century the classical learning phenomenon of reminiscence has been the subject of considerable experimentation and a number of theories have been proposed to account for the improvement in performance that occurs after a rest is taken following a period of massed practice (McGeoch and Irion, 1952). One of these theories implicates reactive inhibition and proposes that during massed practice an unduly large amount of inhibition accumulates and temporarily depresses performance. The introduction of a rest allows this inhibition to dissipate, thus causing a spontaneous increment in performance level. In the original formulation of his causal theory Eysenck used this explanation to account for individual differences in reminiscence and postulated that, because of their greater tendency to develop inhibition, extraverts and hysterics should show more reminiscence than introverts and dysthymics. The relationship between personality and reminiscence has, in fact, proved to be more complex than this, a finding which has led Eysenck to modify his original hypothesis. Recently, for example, he has suggested that reminiscence may be multiply determined and has proposed a theory based on both inhibition and consolidation of the memory trace (Eysenck, 1964a). Furthermore, the previous predictions relating reminiscence to personality have been modified to take account of the influence of drive (Eysenck, 1962c).

As noted earlier, drive is thought by Eysenck to increase the tolerance of inhibition, so that, other things being equal, reminiscence should be greater in subjects who operate under high drive during the period of massed practice before a rest is introduced. Since chronic drive is identified with neuroticism, simultaneous variations in both neuroticism and extraversion will lead to a complex interaction between these two dimensions. Thus, an introvert who is also neurotic may show more reminiscence than a non-neurotic extravert, even though the former individual is expected to accumulate inhibition slowly.

The evidence relating drive—in Eysenck's sense—to inhibition is, in fact, somewhat equivocal. The prediction that high situational drive will lead to greater reminiscence was confirmed on the pursuit-rotor (Eysenck and Maxwell, 1961; Willett and Eysenck, 1962), although the opposite result was obtained with a symbol substitution task (Eysenck and Willett, 1962b). No difference was found by Willett (1964) in the reminiscence scores of high and low drive subjects after massed practice on serial reaction time. Equally conflicting findings emerged when drive was equated with natural variations in neuroticism among normal subjects. Eysenck (1956a) reported a positive correlation between the N-scale of the MPI and reminiscence, while other studies have found the opposite (Star, 1957). In a factor analytic study of pursuit-rotor performance Eysenck (1960e) described a factor having positive loadings on a number of reminiscence measures and a high negative loading on neuroticism. In that experiment, therefore, neuroticism tended to reduce reminiscence, a finding supporting Star's results. In three experiments reported by the present author little support was found for the hypothesis that dysthymics and hysterics would differ in reminiscence. No differences were found between these two groups either on the pursuit-rotor (Claridge, 1960) or on serial reaction time (Claridge and Herrington, 1960). In a second study of serial reaction time Claridge (1961) found differences only when reminiscence scores were corrected for performance level. In all three of these experiments the main differences between dysthymics and hysterics were on measures of performance level, a finding, of course, supported by the results reported earlier in this chapter.

The lack of consistency in the results of previous work on reminiscence and normal personality made it difficult to formulate any precise predictions for the present research; though our own earlier work with neurotics suggested that dysthymics and hysterics would not differ in reminiscence. It was decided, therefore, to test the null hypothesis.

The tests from which psychomotor reminiscence measures were gathered, and the manner in which the scores themselves were calculated, have already been described in the previous sections. An additional measure of reminiscence was obtained from an experiment using the Archimedes spiral. The procedure followed here was that described by Eysenck and Eysenck (1960). Twelve 30-second trials were given under massed conditions, the disc being rotated immediately the end of each after-effect had been reported. This schedule was followed by a 3-minute rest and two further trials were then given. The measure of reminiscence taken was the first post-rest SAE minus the last pre-rest SAE. The subjects taking part in this experiment consisted of twenty-nine dysthymics, seventeen hysterics, and sixteen normal subjects.

In analysing the results attention was paid to two aspects of the data: first, group differences in reminiscence and its relationship to sedation threshold and, secondly, the intercorrelation between reminiscence measures taken from different tests.

Results. The group findings for the seven reminiscence scores are brought together in Table 17, where it can be seen that only on one measure was there a significant difference between dysthymics, hysterics, and normal subjects. This occurred in the case of the word-condition of the Stroop test, where the order of magnitude of reminiscence was opposite to that predicted from Eysenck's theory, i.e. dysthymics showed significantly *more* reminiscence than both hysterics and normals. On all other measures the reminiscence of the three groups was closely similar, a finding which is illustrated for the SAE experiment in Fig. 4.13. Also shown in this figure are the pre-rest SAE data for the three groups and it may be noted in passing that these support the main findings for this test described earlier. There was a clear separation between dysthymics and hysterics over the twelve trials of the experiment and a significant overall difference between the groups (F-ratio: $4 \cdot 769$, df 2/59, $p < 0 \cdot 05$).

The correlations between sedation threshold and the various reminiscence measures are shown, for neurotics and normals

TABLE 17. SCORES FOR THREE GROUPS ON SEVEN REMINISCENCE MEASURES

		Dysthymics	Normals	Hysterics	
Serial reaction time (unpaced)	N Mean SD	17 14·4 9·01	33 13·8 7·91	19 12·2 9·93	F-ratio: 2·831, N.S.
Serial reaction time (paced)	N Mean SD	24 89·2 70·20	15 158·2 100·73	17 78·1 32·41	F-ratio: 1·989, N.S.
Stroop test (colour condition)	N Mean SD	14 0·3 14·75	16 6·1 13·08	8 −0·2 9·04	F-ratio: 1·081, N.S.
Stroop test (word condition)	N Mean SD	14 12·9 10·25	16 4·2 6·68	8 0·8 6·55	F-ratio: 6·375, $p < 0.01$ Dysthymics vs. Hysterics: 3·232, $p < 0.01$ Dysthymics vs. Normals: 2·809, $p < 0.01$ Hysterics vs. Normals: 0·928, N.S.
Tsai–Partington test	N Mean SD	11 0·77 2·05	12 0·29 2·53	11 0·77 1·72	F-ratio: 0·177, N.S.
Symbol substitution test	N Mean SD	8 1·50 1·98	10 2·45 1·66	10 1·65 1·79	F-ratio: 0·674, N.S.
Spiral after-effect	N Mean SD	29 1·21 4·07	16 1·19 2·94	17 0·88 2·19	F-ratio: 0·053, N.S.

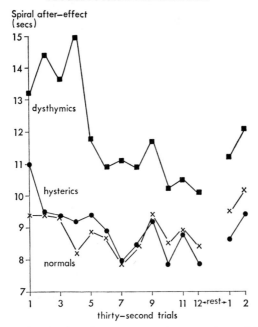

FIG. 4.13. Spiral after-effect curves under massed conditions in dysthymics, hysterics, and normal subjects.

separately, in Table 18. In no case was there a significant relationship between reminiscence and threshold, the correlations in both groups being apparently randomly distributed, from small negative to small positive values. The only possibly consistent finding occurred in the case of the paced serial reaction time and symbol substitution tests, where small positive correlations between threshold and reminiscence were found for both normal and neurotic subjects. This would imply rather greater reminiscence in subjects with high arousal.

Finally, Table 19 shows the intercorrelations between the seven measures of reminiscence. The correlations here are based on combined samples of neurotics and normals, since on one or two measures there were too few subjects to consider these groups separately. Perusal of the correlations for each of the groups taken separately indicated, in any case, that these were of a similar order. As can be seen in Table 19, the majority of the correlations were non-significant and in some cases negative. There were three exceptions to this finding. The reminiscence measure from the unpaced serial reaction time task correlated significantly and positively with

TABLE 18. CORRELATIONS IN NEUROTICS AND NORMALS
BETWEEN SEDATION THRESHOLD AND SEVEN MEASURES OF REMINISCENCE

	Neurotics		Normals	
	r	N	r	N
Serial reaction time (unpaced)	0·02	36	0·10	33
Serial reaction time (paced)	0·27	41	0·31	15
Stroop test (colour condition)	−0·14	22	0·12	16
Stroop test (word condition)	−0·19	22	0·01	16
Tsai–Partington test	0·15	22	0·10	12
Symbol substitution test	0·34	18	0·30	10
Spiral after-effect	−0·13	46	−0·13	16

those from both the Tsai–Partington test and the word condition half of the Stroop test. Not unexpectedly, the reminiscence scores from the two halves of the Stroop test also correlated significantly together.

In conclusion, there would seem to be little evidence to support the view that measures of reminiscence will differentiate dysthymics and hysterics, or that such measures will show any association with an index of arousability. Furthermore, there is little association between reminiscence scores obtained from different tests, the phenomenon being very task-specific. These findings do not, of course, invalidate the hypothesis that reminiscence reflects the influence of inhibition on performance. They do suggest, however, that it may be the result of a complex interaction between arousal and other factors associated with performance during the pre-rest period before reminiscence is measured.

DISCUSSION AND CONCLUSIONS

Extension of the research on dysthymia–hysteria to the study of psychological performance provided convincing evidence to support the arousability hypothesis developed in previous chapters. Significant correlations between sedation threshold and performance,

TABLE 19. Correlations between Seven Reminiscence Measures

		Tsai–Partington	Symbol substitution	SRT (unpaced)	SRT (paced)	Stroop (colour condition)	Stroop (word condition)	Spiral after-effect
Tsai–Partington	r	—	−0·04	0·59*	0·16	−0·39	−0·20	0·23
	N		38	12	32	17	17	30
Symbol substitution	r	—	—	0	0·12	−0·18	−0·37	−0·07
	N			10	27	15	15	25
SRT (unpaced)	r	—	—	—	−0·28	0·35	0·59*	0·16
	N				15	15	15	16
SRT (paced)	r	—	—	—	—	−0·14	−0·34	0·15
	N					23	23	50
Stroop (colour condition)	r	—	—	—	—	—	0·51†	0·07
	N						38	31
Stroop (word condition)	r	—	—	—	—	—	—	0·14
	N							31

* $p < 0.05$.
† $p < 0.01$.

and group differences on such simple tasks as vigilance and unpaced serial reaction time, were consistent in pointing to measures of *level* as the main variables differentiating dysthymics and hysterics. These findings accord with the drive interpretation of arousal and with the view that drive will be reflected in the speed or quality of performance. While not statistically significant, results for other simple tasks, such as the Tsai–Partington and symbol substitution tests, revealed similar trends, despite relatively small samples.

The operation of the Yerkes–Dodson law on certain complex tasks was also predictable from the arousal hypothesis, the high drive of dysthymics leading to a deterioration in performance under the stressful conditions imposed on paced serial reaction time and on the version of the Stroop test used here. It is perhaps surprising that the apparently curvilinear relationship between arousal and performance on these tests was revealed only with respect to group differences. The result suggests the need for further research on the association, in neurotic patients, between simultaneously recorded autonomic indices and performance on complex tasks. Such research may help to throw further light on the relative importance of the cue utilization and Yerkes–Dodson principles, particularly as explanations of Stroop performance. The cue utilization hypothesis found little support here, when drive was manipulated via individual differences, although this may have been due to the stressful nature of the colour-word task used.

Although variations in arousal could account for many of the individual differences, behaviour on some measures appeared, as anticipated, to implicate an inhibitory process. As a discriminating variable, however, inhibition seemed to be of secondary importance. Reminiscence measures, for example, clearly fail to differentiate dysthymics and hysterics, although the remarkably consistent negative results found here are of interest in themselves, since they may provide some clue to the role of inhibition in performance. This can be best illustrated with respect to unpaced serial reaction time. It has been argued elsewhere (Claridge and Herrington, 1960) that the similar reminiscence scores of dysthymics and hysterics on this task are due to the modulating or equilibrating effect that inhibition has on performance. High drive leads to a high initial rate of serial reaction time response. It also results in a more rapid decline in performance, rate of fall-off on the test being almost entirely a function of initial level. Claridge and Herrington suggested that, in the early phases of the test, high drive subjects will accumulate a greater amount of inhibition than low drive subjects, because they are making more responses. This inhibition will have the effect of gradually reducing the number of responses made, until performance reaches a level where the amount of inhibition being accumulated is tolerable for the individual. Subjects starting the task at low response rates will need to decline less to reach the same point of equilibrium; hence the high negative correlation between level and fall-off measures on serial reaction time. The implication of this modulation hypothesis of inhibition is that, if allowed to reach their respective points of equilibrium in performance, all subjects will end the task with a similar residual amount of inhibition. Reminiscence will then be similar in both high and low drive subjects.

Looked at in this way, the effect of inhibition on performance would be a secondary consequence of the primary influence of arousal, which will directly determine the degree of effort or number of responses made, and hence the absolute amount of inhibition induced. It is possible, of course, that individuals vary independently on some parameter of inhibition other than the absolute amount accumulated during performance. Eysenck (1962c), in fact, argued in just this way when presenting his revised hypothesis linking personality and reminiscence. He proposed that the crucial variables differentiating extraverts and introverts are the rates of accumulation and dissipation of inhibition, rather than its absolute amount, even though reminiscence is a measure of the latter. This hypothesis might be supported by the present data, in so far as the *relative* increment after rest shown by hysterics was clearly somewhat greater than that found in dysthymics, since on most tasks the two groups were still well separated at the end of the pre-rest period. It is also true that on unpaced serial reaction time, for example, subjects with low sedation thresholds committed significantly more errors, which might indicate that in these individuals inhibition was accumulating more rapidly; hence the greater need to take frequent rest pauses.

Unfortunately, in order to isolate the various factors influencing reminiscence it is necessary to control very carefully the conditions of practice during the pre-rest period; for example, by matching subjects for variations in drive. This is difficult in experiments where subjects differ widely in chronic drive and it was deliberately not attempted here, since the main aim of the study was to investigate natural variations in performance. Under these conditions, marked differences in arousal appeared to mask the influence of other variables, such as reactive inhibition. Thus, although internal inhibitory processes certainly appear to play a part in psychological performance, most of the differences between dysthymics and hysterics could be ascribed to primary variations in their respective levels of arousal.

Perhaps the most interesting results are those reported for the spiral after-effect. The full theoretical implication of these findings will become apparent in later chapters, but in the meantime a number of points are worth noting. The curvilinear relationship between sedation threshold and spiral after-effect finds an exact parallel in the similar departure from linearity demonstrated when sedation threshold and alpha index were compared in Chapter 3. This is of special interest because of the finding that the SAE is itself significantly correlated with both alpha index and alpha blocking time (Claridge and Herrington, 1963a). Thus, at high levels of cortical activation and where very long visual after-effects are reported, there is evidence that arousal as measured by the sedation threshold is low; the optimum SAE before threshold begins to decline being about 30 seconds. These results suggested that the concept of arousability as a simple unitary nervous process may have certain limitations and that the behavioural continuum of dysthymia–hysteria may be multiply determined. With these considerations in mind, a further analysis of dysthymia–hysteria was undertaken. This will be discussed in the next chapter, where Eysenck's hierarchical theory of personality will be examined in more detail.

SUMMARY

The performance of neurotic and normal subjects on eight perceptual and psychomotor tasks was examined, the results being looked at from two points of view: (a) group differences between dysthymics, hysterics, and normals and (b) the relationship of performance to psychophysiological variables, mainly the sedation threshold. The main predictions were derived from the hypothesis that dysthymics and hysterics differ in arousal or drive level.

Comparing the groups, dysthymics showed significantly longer spiral after-effects, better auditory vigilance, and faster unpaced serial reaction time than hysterics. Non-significant differences in the same direction were found on a symbol substitution task and on the Tsai–Partington number tracing test. Results for a time judgement test failed to conform with expectation, neurotics as a whole showing greater error in time perception than normals. On paced serial reaction time and on a complex version of the Stroop colour-word test both dysthymics and hysterics performed poorly relative to normal subjects, a finding which was in accordance with the inverted-U function relating drive to performance on complex tasks.

Variations in the susceptibility to internal inhibition were assumed to account for such performance parameters as rate of decline in psychomotor speed and reminiscence. Rate of decline was, however, largely a function of initial level and showed little relationship with personality factors; while seven reminiscence measures from various tests failed to discriminate dysthymics and hysterics. A homeostatic theory of reactive inhibition and reminiscence was proposed to explain these findings and the conclusion reached that drive was the primary variable accounting for individual differences in performance, the effects of inhibition being secondary to this influence.

As predicted, significant correlations were found between sedation threshold and the level of performance on some of the tasks, including vigilance. There was a weak relationship between vigilance and two autonomic functions monitored during performance of the task, while no association was found between vigilance decrement and rate of decline in autonomic arousal.

Although, as predicted, there was a significant positive correlation in neurotics between sedation threshold and spiral after-effect the relationship between the two tests showed a significant departure from linearity of regression. Both very high and very low spiral after-effects were associated with a low sedation threshold in the neurotic sample. In normal subjects the correlation between the two tests was zero. The significance of all of the results was discussed in relation to the arousal hypothesis proposed earlier.

CHAPTER 5

CAUSAL AND DESCRIPTIVE ANALYSIS OF DYSTHYMIA–HYSTERIA

INTRODUCTION

The hierarchical view of behaviour adopted here has made it possible to explore the causal links between different levels of psychophysiological and psychological function. Little account has been taken so far, however, of the descriptive phenomena forming the next stratum in the hierarchy of personality structure. Attention has been confined to the rather broad concept of dysthymia–hysteria, which has been used as a descriptive "anchor" for the causal analysis, allowing us to define some of the underlying correlates of a personality continuum that accounts for the major neurotic disorders recognized by clinical psychiatry.

Adoption of dysthymia–hysteria as a working descriptive model was, of course, based largely on Eysenck's theory, which attempts to explain the neuroses in terms of two personality dimensions of extraversion and neuroticism. Dysthymics and hysterics are assumed to differ in extraversion, while both of these neurotic groups differ from normal subjects in neuroticism. Thus, dysthymia–hysteria theoretically is compounded of both descriptive dimensions, though Eysenck himself has concentrated mainly on extraversion. In fact, as discussed in Chapter 1, introversion–extraversion and dysthymia–hysteria have often been regarded as synonymous.

Because the causal and descriptive status of extraversion and neuroticism was so uncertain, no assumptions were made at the beginning of the present research about their relative contribution to dysthymia–hysteria. It will be recalled from Chapter 1 that, at the causal level, both extraversion and neuroticism were considered to have some features in common with the arousal concept; while, at the descriptive level, the two dimensions appeared to be interrelated in a complex fashion, both in normal and neurotic individuals.

It is now necessary to examine Eysenck's theory in more detail, first in order to extend the descriptive analysis of personality and, secondly, in order to throw further light on the causal determinants of dysthymia–hysteria. The discussion may be usefully divided on the basis of some of the criticisms made of Eysenck's theory in recent years. These have been of two main types, aimed at different applications of his theory and at different hierarchical levels of personality.

The first criticism, made often by clinical psychologists, has been of Eysenck's contention that introverted and extraverted behaviour patterns are characteristic, respectively, of his neurotic criterion groups of dysthymics and hysterics. This kind of argument has been carried on mainly at the descriptive, trait, level of the theory. The second criticism has been of Eysenck's postulate that variations in extraversion, and hence cortical inhibition, are sufficient to account for individual differences in performance. This is a more fundamental criticism of the essential link joining the genotypic and phenotypic levels of the theory (see Fig. 1.1, p. 3). Each of these issues will be considered in turn and, following a review of previous evidence, the appropriate results from the present research will be described.

INTROVERSION–EXTRAVERSION AND DYSTHYMIA–HYSTERIA

It is now nearly twenty years since Eysenck (1947) described two factors of neuroticism and introversion–extraversion to account for hysterical disorders, on the one hand, and what at that time he named "dysthymic" disorders, on the other. The factor analysis in that study was based on psychiatric symptoms and other descriptive items, though similar conclusions about the position of hysterics and dysthymics in this two-dimensional framework were later reached by one of Eysenck's students, Hildebrand (1953), who used more objective personality tests, including questionnaires. Hildebrand's data were subsequently subjected to a good deal of re-analysis, first by Storms (1958) and then by Slater (1960). Storms criticized Hildebrand on two counts. In the first place, he maintained that it was unjustifiable to subsume the various diagnostic categories under the two broad headings of introverted and extraverted neurosis. This was particularly so in the case of hysterics and psychopaths, who could be shown to differ considerably from each other. Secondly, he demonstrated that discriminant function analysis differentiated the main groups of anxiety states and hysterics better than the factor analytic method used by Hildebrand. Furthermore, he claimed that the dimensions doing so bore little resemblance to introversion–extraversion. Slater accepted Storms' first criticism of Hildebrand and Eysenck, though he maintained that the second point was not a crucial attack on the extraversion hypothesis, since there were no *a priori* reasons for expecting the results of factor analysis to coincide with those of canonical variate analysis. He stated further that, although Hildebrand's solution for his data may not have been the optimum one, it had certain theoretical advantages. Essentially the same comment was made by Eysenck (1959c) who maintained that, while perhaps statistically more efficient, Storms' solution was of little theoretical value, since at no point was there any contact with current psychological or psychiatric thinking. On the whole, Hildebrand's results appear to have withstood their major criticism, though in experimental studies of neurosis at the descriptive level, at least, there may be some risks entailed in pooling patients with different diagnoses to form two broad categories of dysthymia and hysteria. The results reported here suggest that the risks may be less where causal measures, such as sedation threshold, are involved.

More recent criticisms of Eysenck's explanation of dysthymia–hysteria have centred upon results obtained with the Maudsley Personality Inventory (MPI) (Eysenck, 1956b). This two-part questionnaire was devised as a means of measuring an individual's position on the two dimensions of extraversion and neuroticism. It would follow from the theory that the extraversion or E-scale would differentiate the two major categories of dysthymia and hysteria. The neuroticism or N-scale would be expected to differentiate all neurotics from normal subjects.

The first study throwing some doubt on these assumptions was reported by Sigal *et al.* (1958a). They found that dysthymics and a mixed group of hysterico-psychopaths did not differ significantly in extraversion, though psychopaths alone were more extraverted than dysthymics. In line with Eysenck's prediction, dysthymics were significantly more introverted than normal subjects. Some of the more marked group differences appeared on the N-scale. Although dysthymics and psychopaths were, as expected, significantly more neurotic than normals, hysterics did not differ from the latter group and had significantly lower N-scores than the other neurotic patients.

McGuire *et al.* (1963) reported even lower E-scores in hysterics, a fact they explained by their restricted usage of the term "hysteria", which excluded personality disorders and psychopaths. The latter were included under the heading of "character neuroses" and patients carrying this diagnosis were slightly more extraverted than other neurotics. None of the group comparisons for neurotics on the E-scale was significant. On the N-scale patients with both character neuroses and hysteria were less neurotic than dysthymics, the difference being greater in the case of hysterics.

Ingham and Robinson (1964) reviewed the MPI performance of neurotics, with special reference to the problem of hysteria. They divided their own group into conversion hysterics and hysterical personalities. Conversion hysterics were found to be similar to normal subjects on extraversion and to be only slightly more neurotic. In this respect they resembled the hysterics studied by McGuire *et al.* (*op. cit.*), though the latter authors did not state whether their hysterics were restricted to patients with conversion symptoms. Ingham and Robinson found hysterical personalities to have much higher neuroticism scores than other hysterics and to be rather more extraverted. This group was similar, therefore, to the character neuroses described by McGuire *et al.* and the psychopaths described by Sigal *et al.* The authors concluded that there was no evidence relating classical conversion symptoms to extraversion, but that high E-scores on the MPI were associated with an hysterical personality and hysterical attitude. They further suggested that a possible reason for the low N-score of conversion hysterics is that they have successfully "converted" their anxiety or neuroticism into physical symptoms.

In the manual to the MPI Eysenck (1959a) summarized the results for various standardization groups gathered up to the time of its publication. There he accepted that hysterics were very similar to normal subjects in extraversion, as well as being less neurotic than dysthymics. The position of psychopaths—high scores on both scales—was seen to be more in line with that previously assigned to hysterics. Nevertheless, despite their unexpectedly low E-scores, hysterics were stated to be significantly more extraverted than dysthymics.

Eysenck's standardization sample for the MPI included a small group of hysterics and dysthymics tested by the present author (Claridge, 1960). The scores for this group, together with those of all subjects tested subsequently, are shown in Table 1. It can be seen from this table that results for both scales were generally very much in line with previous findings. Dysthymics were the most introverted

TABLE 1. MPI SCORES FOR DYSTHYMICS, HYSTERICS, AND NORMAL SUBJECTS

	Dysthymics	Normals	Hysterics
N	93	64	86
E-scale			
Mean	16·63	27·36	23·03
SD	9·13	8·99	8·64

F-ratio: 28·45, $p < 0·001$

t-tests {
Dysthymics vs. Hysterics: 4·77, $p < 0·001$
Dysthymics vs. Normals: 7·41, $p < 0·001$
Hysterics vs. Normals: 2·92, $p < 0·01$

	Dysthymics	Normals	Hysterics
N-scale			
Mean	34·38	21·23	31·83
SD	10·45	11·31	11·53

F-ratio: 27·84, $p < 0·001$

t-tests {
Dysthymics vs. Hysterics: 1·52, N.S.
Dysthymics vs. Normals: 7·24, $p < 0·001$
Hysterics vs. Normals: 5·76, $p < 0·001$

and neurotic while both neurotic groups had significantly higher N-scores than normal subjects. Hysterics were significantly more extraverted than dysthymics, but they were also significantly less extraverted than the normal sample tested here, a finding that requires further comment.

In the Introduction it was noted that the control group was almost certainly not a representative sample of "normal" subjects, since they were drawn, with the exception of two individuals, from a population known to be high on both neuroticism and extraversion. The evidence for this is shown in Table 2, where the E- and N-scores of a large group of military personnel are shown, together with Eysenck's English quota sample of normal subjects. It will be seen

TABLE 2. MAUDSLEY PERSONALITY INVENTORY
Comparison of military personnel with other English norms

	Military group	Eysenck English sample
N	628	1800
	E-scale	
Mean	28·07	24·91
SD	7·98	9·71

$t = 7·33, p < 0·001.$

	N-scale	
Mean	23·88	19·89
SD	9·91	11·02

$t = 8·03, p < 0·001.$

that the military sample had significantly higher scores on both scales. Comparison between Tables 1 and 2 will show that, with respect to extraversion at least, the small experimental group of normal subjects resembled the RAMC population from which they were drawn more closely than Eysenck's sample. Compared with the latter, hysterics were, therefore, only slightly less extraverted. This bias in the MPI scores of the "normal" subjects used in the present research is in some ways unfortunate. It does, however, help to account for the close resemblance between hysterics and control subjects on some of the causal measures described in the previous chapters.

In the present data, a further finding that should be mentioned was a significant negative correlation in neurotics between the E- and N-scales. The value for r in 179 neurotic patients was $-0·40$, ($p < 0·001$) falling to $-0·20$ (N.S.) in sixty-four normal subjects. The result is in accordance with most other investigations of the MPI using neurotic populations (Bartholomew, 1959; Jensen, 1958; Brengelmann, 1959, 1960; McGuire et al., op. cit.). It has been explained by Eysenck (1959a) as being due to non-linearity of regression between E and N at high introversion scores. This in turn is said to be the result of a positive feedback effect between the processes underlying neuroticism and extraversion. At a descriptive level this presumably means that high neuroticism will have an introverting effect on behaviour. The association between the two scales is said to have been removed in the latest version of the questionnaire, namely the Eysenck Personality Inventory (EPI). In the manual to that test zero correlations are reported between E and N in all groups (Eysenck and Eysenck, 1964). Group differences on both scales are very similar to those found on the MPI, hysterics again emerging as rather more introverted than normal subjects.

It seems fairly well-established, therefore, that hysterics as a group, while certainly more extraverted than dysthymics, do not score as high on the E-scale as originally anticipated by Eysenck. In his defence against the criticism by Sigal *et al.* (1958a), Eysenck (1958) did not regard this as being important, since he maintained that the relative extraversion of dysthymics and hysterics was a more crucial test of his theory. This argument was rejected by Sigal *et al.* (1958b) in their rejoinder to Eysenck, on the grounds that, in order to demonstrate that hysterics are extraverted, it is necessary to show that they are towards the extraverted end of the scale and not just "less introverted introverts".

The controversy has continued unabated, almost to the point of futility. Foulds (1961) has tried to argue the logical impossibility of using dysthymics and hysterics at all as criterion groups for studying introversion–extraversion. He has, therefore, been led to reject the validity of any results obtained with the MPI. Foulds' paper resulted in a series of exchanges between himself, Eysenck, and Ingham (Eysenck, 1962b), Eysenck stressing the heuristic convenience of using dysthymics and hysterics to study variables that appear, on theoretical grounds, to be associated with both introversion–extraversion and dysthymia–hysteria. He reasserted his view, however, that these two concepts were not meant to be equated, as Foulds had claimed, since the neurotic criterion groups differ from normal subjects on at least one other major dimension of personality, i.e. neuroticism.

To the present author it seems that the arguments on both sides have been vitiated by constant changes in the level of discourse. Foulds, on the one hand, has failed to distinguish between the descriptive and causal aspects of Eysenck's theory. Eysenck, on the other hand, has invited misunderstanding on the part of casual readers of his work by synonymous use of such terms as "excitation–inhibition", "introversion–extraversion", and "dysthymia–hysteria". Thus, objective measures of excitation–inhibition have often been named as tests of extraversion, even though, strictly speaking, the latter term refers to behaviour at a different level of personality. An example of this confusion in terminology is found in the argument between Foulds and Eysenck. In defending his position against Foulds, Eysenck quoted an experiment on the performance of dysthymics and hysterics, carried out by himself and the present author (Eysenck and Claridge, 1962). The results strongly supported those reported in earlier chapters of this book, namely significant discrimination between dysthymics and hysterics on tests like sedation threshold. A causal theory of dysthymia–hysteria was thus confirmed, but at the descriptive level introverted and extraverted behaviour patterns did not correspond closely with performance on objective tests. This led the authors to reach the following conclusion:

> Questionnaires such as the MPI are sensitive measures of *behavioural* extraversion; objective tests such as those used in this experiment are probably sensitive measures of *constitutional* extraversion. Factorial studies such as those of Claridge (1960), and the one reported here, show that constitutional and behavioural measures are not unrelated, but it would be a mistake not to distinguish between them. The interesting question arises therefore whether hysteria and dysthymia are more closely related to constitutional or behavioural extraversion; the present results suggest the former.

It is perhaps unfortunate that a factor derived from objective measures should have been given a label derived from descriptive terminology. At best, it would seem to lead to semantic confusion. At worst, it may result in faulty conclusions being drawn about the causal basis of dysthymia–hysteria, as distinct from introversion–extraversion. It is now becoming increasingly clear that the reason these two behavioural continua do not coincide is because dys-thymia–hysteria has several causal determinants, a fact which probably accounts for the lack of correspondence between measures of behavioural and constitutional "extraversion". The evidence to support this view will be considered in the following section.

THE CAUSAL INTERACTION OF EXTRAVERSION AND NEUROTICISM

One of the main points of controversy in Eysenck's theory has been his causal explanation of introversion–extraversion. The bulk of evidence adduced for his excitation–inhibition hypothesis has been gathered on normal introverts and extraverts, distinguished by their performance on the E-scale of the MPI. Its enormous volume precludes a detailed review of this evidence and the discussion will be confined to those studies that are relevant to the argument here. Some of the work has, in any case, been referred to earlier when discussing the particular tests used in the present research; while the general degree of support for this part of the theory can be assessed from the extensive writings of Eysenck himself and from that of some of his critics (e.g. Storms and Sigal, 1958; Hamilton, 1959b).

The experiments most crucial to the present discussion are not those that have looked for or demonstrated a simple relationship between extraversion and performance measures, but those that have shown an interacting influence of both extraversion and neuroticism on such measures. Following its demonstration in neurotics (Claridge, 1960), a number of more recent studies have confirmed, in normal subjects, an apparent influence of neuroticism on measures of "excitation–inhibition". Rodnight and Gooch (1963) reported a complex relationship between susceptibility to nitrous oxide anaesthesia and MPI scores. In their total group neither personality scale from that test correlated with gas susceptibility. Some interesting relationships emerged, however, when they broke their group down into four subtypes in terms of high and low scores on the E- and N-scales. Among members of the group having a low N-score, introverts tended to be significantly more susceptible to the gas than extraverts. Gas susceptibility was also higher in the "neurotic" members of the very extraverted subgroup, the greater the E-score the closer the relationship between neuroticism and gas susceptibility.

Comparable findings have been described by Knowles and Krasner (to appear) using the spiral after-effect in normal subjects. They reported a negative correlation between the spiral after-effect and E-score in subjects with high N-scores and a positive correlation between these two measures in those with low N-scores. In other words, in the "neurotic" half of the sample introverts had longer spiral after-effects than extraverts, while the opposite was true in the stable half of the sample. Similarly, in reporting a significant relationship between alpha amplitude and extraversion, Savage (1964) noted that, while neuroticism as such did not correlate with this EEG measure, at high levels of extraversion it did tend to reduce the amplitude of alpha rhythm.

Arguments about the relative influence of introversion and neuroticism have also formed the crux of the long-standing controversy over personality and conditioning. The Spence–Taylor hypothesis, for example, has attributed individual differences in conditionability to variations in manifest anxiety level (Taylor, 1951; Spence, 1956; Spence and Taylor, 1951). Here manifest anxiety is visualized as a drive that facilitates learned connections of the simple conditioning type. Implicit in this view is the identification of manifest anxiety with neuroticism, an assumption that is confirmed by the very high correlation (Eysenck, 1959a) between the N-scale of the MPI and the Manifest Anxiety Scale used by the Iowa group as their measure of anxiety (Taylor, 1953).

Eysenck (1957b), on the other hand, in attempting to account for similar conditioning data, argued originally that the crucial variable determining individual differences was not drive (manifest anxiety or neuroticism), but some aspect of the excitation–inhibition balance underlying extraversion. In a later publication (Eysenck, 1962a) he considered that habit growth may be affected either directly by variations in excitatory potential or indirectly by variations in inhibitory potential. Either way he claimed at that time that there was no support for the Spence–Taylor hypothesis, because results using the Manifest Anxiety Scale could be explained by its low negative correlation with the E-scale of the MPI.

In stating his case for introversion as the exclusive mediating variable, Eysenck relied heavily on the findings of Franks, who demonstrated more rapid eyeblink conditioning in normal introverts compared with normal extraverts (1957), and in dysthymic compared with hysterical neurotics (1956). Subsequently, however, Franks (1963b) failed to confirm his own original findings and, after reviewing other work on conditioning and personality, he concluded:

> . . . it is becoming increasingly apparent that attempts to account for individual differences in eyeblink conditioning in terms of *either* habit strength and its excitatory–inhibitory components (associated with introversion-extraversion) *or* drive strength and its autonomic and other components (associated with anxiety, neuroticism and emotionality) are incomplete and limited in their abilities to account for the facts. Both components of total response strength seem to be pertinent to the majority of conditioning situations, and their relative contributions and interactions to be operating in an as yet only partially understood manner.

Finally, quite recently Eysenck (1965) accepted that both anxiety/neuroticism and introversion may be important determinants of the rate of eyeblink and GSR conditioning. He suggested that which variable predominates would depend on the nature of the experimental procedure, i.e. whether the conditions of the experiment were such as to produce anxiety or reactive inhibition.

There is thus increasing evidence in the literature that at least two psychophysiological processes interact to produce variations not only in conditionability, but also on other objective measures of behaviour. Although there is some suggestion that these processes are roughly paralleled in such personality dimensions as extraversion and neuroticism, the study of individual correlations between, for example, E- and N-scores and single experimental measures is likely to prove an unsatisfactory method of investigating the link between these causal and descriptive phenomena. In the present research, for example, over forty correlations were calculated, for normals and neurotics separately, between the two MPI scales and various objective, including physiological, measures. In neurotics neither scale correlated significantly with any other measure, the only acceptably significant relationship being that referred to in the previous section, viz. a highly significant correlation between the two scales themselves. In normal subjects a similar picture emerged, with one exception. This was a significant negative correlation of -0.36 ($p < 0.05$, $N = 34$) between the N-scale and sedation threshold.

Rather more promising results were found, however, when a principal components analysis was carried out on some of the measures. Because of the large amount of missing data this analysis had to be severely restricted with respect both to sample size and number of variables. At least this was so if the theoretically more important variables were to be included. After careful inspection of the data twelve measures were chosen that yielded a sample of reasonable size. This was still relatively small, consisting of twenty-seven neurotic and ten normal subjects. A principal components analysis of the data was then carried out and the four components extracted subjected to a Varimax rotation to orthogonal simple structure. This was transformed to Promax oblique simple structure, according to the procedure described by Hendrickson and White (1964).

Rotated factor loadings for the first two components are shown in Table 3, together with a description of the measures subjected to analysis. Inspection of the loadings for the first factor suggests that it defines an arousal component associated, at the high end, with raised sedation threshold, long spiral after-effect, good auditory vigilance, and high autonomic activation. The factor has poor loadings on EEG measures and virtually zero loadings on the two MPI scales. These measures, on the other hand, appear to be mainly responsible for the second factor, which could also be interpreted as an arousal component in view of its loadings on indices of cortical activity. There high introversion—i.e. low E-score—and high neuroticism are associated with long alpha blocking time, low alpha index, and high alpha frequency. The moderate negative loading of alpha amplitude would also be consistent with the direction in which the other EEG measures are weighted, reduced amplitude of

TABLE 3. ROTATED LOADINGS FOR TWO FIRST-ORDER FACTORS

| | Factor | |
	I	II
Sedation threshold	0·74	0·04
Spiral after-effect	0·61	0·42
Alpha blocking time	0·31	0·51
Alpha frequency	−0·32	0·58
Alpha index	−0·11	−0·60
Alpha amplitude	0·10	−0·36
Vigilance—signals detected	0·68	−0·28
Vigilance—decline	−0·25	0·26
Vigilance—heart rate level	0·65	−0·19
Vigilance—heart rate decline	0·52	0·07
E-score	0·08	−0·68
N-score	0·00	0·69

alpha rhythm being associated with high cortical activation. Apart from the spiral after-effect no other test is well saturated with this second factor.

Further analysis of the first-order components was carried out following the method described by Hendrickson and White (1966) for rotating higher-order factors. The resulting second-order factor is shown in Table 4. As expected, at the causal level it seems to be determined by a combination of all of the "arousal" measures, and at the descriptive level by both MPI scales, operating in opposite directions, high neuroticism being associated with introversion and vice versa. If a descriptive label were to be attached to this second-order factor then that of "dysthymia–hysteria" seems most appropriate; more so than "introversion–extraversion" which is roughly equal, as a source of variation, to neuroticism.

The results of the first-order analysis are remarkably similar to those reported by Davies *et al.* (1963), who carried out a centroid factor analysis of six tests from the battery used in the present research. The factor loadings for the first two factors after rotation in that experiment are shown, for comparison, in Table 5. Comparing

TABLE 4. FACTOR LOADINGS FOR SECOND-ORDER FACTOR

Sedation threshold	0·58
Spiral after-effect	0·76
Alpha blocking time	0·61
Alpha frequency	0·19
Alpha index	−0·52
Alpha amplitude	−0·20
Vigilance—signals detected	0·30
Vigilance—decline	0·00
Vigilance—heart rate level	0·34
Vigilance—heart rate decline	0·43
E-score	−0·44
N-score	0·51

TABLE 5. ROTATED LOADINGS FOR TWO FACTORS
(FROM DAVIES *et al.*, 1963)

	Factor	
	I	II
Sedation threshold	0·05	0·68
Spiral after-effect	0·66	0·12
Rogitine test—Basal Systolic BP	0·49	0·38
Rogitine test—Maximum Systolic BP Change	0·24	0·68
E-score	−0·71	0·17
N-score	0·60	−0·36

Tables 3 and 5 it can be seen that, although the order of factors is reversed, the pattern of loadings for each is similar. Table 5 once more shows the separation of the MPI E-scale from the more important physiological measures, i.e. sedation threshold and blood pressure response to stress. Results for the spiral after-effect differ in the two analyses, any substantial loading being confined to only one of the factors in the Davies *et al.* experiment. There the factors were rotated to orthogonal simple structure and it is possible that closer agreement between the two analyses would have been achieved had an oblique rotational method been used. Even so, the results of the two investigations parallel each other to a very acceptable degree, considering the different methods of analysis used, the small samples and number of variables involved, and the fact that the two experiments were carried out on entirely independent groups of subjects.

DISCUSSION AND CONCLUSIONS

The results presented in this and previous chapters, and the findings of other related studies, suggest the need for an extension and modification of Eysenck's theory, if it is to account adequately for all of the available evidence. In some respects it finds ample support, in so far as profound individual differences in the psychophysiological status of neurotics can be demonstrated, exactly as predicted by Eysenck. At the descriptive level, however, and in attempting to link the two levels of personality, the theory runs into some difficulty. It is clearly not possible to accept the hypothesis that all of the differences between dysthymics and hysterics can be explained by a single psychophysiological process having introversion–extraversion as its sole behavioural counterpart. Instead, it seems necessary to propose two correlated nervous processes, both of which have arousal properties. Arousability, as defined in Chapter 1, and its behavioural counterpart, dysthymia–hysteria, appear to be the end-result of an interaction between autonomic factors and some other central nervous process, which on present evidence seems to be most highly weighted on measures of cortical activity. The nature of these two causal processes will be discussed in more detail in the final chapter after the results for psychotics, which are of considerable theoretical importance, have been presented.

Demonstration of a descriptive continuum of dysthymia–hysteria to account for neurosis accords well with the findings of other workers. Shagass and Jones (1958), for example, proposed a similar continuum ranging from obsessionality to hysteria in order to explain their sedation threshold findings. They noted its similarity to introversion–extraversion, but emphasized the additional influence of anxiety as one of its determinants. Similarly, Caine and Hope (1964) recently demonstrated that in neurotics the MPI E-scale appears to measure an obsessoid–hysteroid dimension; while Fahrenberg and Delius (1963), after factor analysing a large quantity of autonomic data, extracted a factor recognizable as dysthymia–hysteria, having loadings on both scales of the MPI.

E

Because of the high correlation between the two MPI scales, only tentative conclusions can be reached about their relative contribution to dysthymia–hysteria, or about the extent to which they can be identified with the two causal mechanisms isolated here. It seems probable, however, that the sedation threshold and its autonomic correlates are mainly associated with anxiety/neuroticism and the second component with extraversion. This view would coincide with other supporting evidence and with the earlier speculations of Claridge (1960) and Claridge and Herrington (1963b) that the "excitation–inhibition balance" is determined by the causal processes underlying *both* personality dimensions recognized by Eysenck.

There is one difficulty of equating neuroticism with an autonomic or similar component contributing to arousability. This concerns the apparent discrepancy between the psychophysiological status of the hysterical patient and his position on Eysenck's neuroticism dimension. On objective tests the hysteric gives evidence of being extremely underaroused. On the MPI N-scale, however, he emerges, while less neurotic than the dysthymic, significantly more neurotic than the normal subject. This, as we noted earlier, is even more true of the psychopath. There are at least two possible explanations for this discrepancy.

One possibility is that tests such as the N-scale may not accurately reflect causal variations in arousal. Certainly, in the two analyses reported above the scale had low or zero loadings on the main factor qualifying as an arousal component, namely that weighted highly on sedation threshold and various autonomic indices. Instead, it tended to be associated consistently with the E-scale, thus supporting the findings obtained from individual correlations between the two parts of the MPI. Of course, neuroticism has been visualized by Eysenck at the descriptive level as a dimension of behavioural maladjustment and it is feasible that this may have as its autonomic basis any kind of departure from normality, whether it be the result of increased or decreased sympathetic reactivity. The findings for the Mecholyl and phentolamine experiments may help to illustrate this. There the most "normal" response is a small fall in blood pressure and its rapid restoration to the pre-stress level. Large prolonged falls in blood pressure were interpreted as being the result of defective sympathetic reactivity, or poor arousability. Yet such responses clearly reflect a degree of autonomic instability equivalent to that of patients showing a marked sympathetic reaction to stress, resulting in an overshoot of the blood pressure beyond the baseline. This interpretation would be consistent with the demonstration by van der Merwe (1948) that, while dysthymics and hysterics differ on some aspects of autonomic activity, they are alike with respect to a factor he identified as "emotional lability". The hysteric might therefore emerge as "neurotic", or emotionally maladjusted, even though his autonomic responses are not in the direction normally associated with heightened arousal. The rather higher N-scores consistently found in dysthymics could also be explained, because the neuroticism scales of the MPI and EPI tend to be weighted on items that describe the "sympathetic" anxiety of the introverted neurotic. This partial, but not complete, identification of the neuroticism dimension with anxiety as normally defined is supported by the demonstration (Knowles and Kreitman, 1965) that the N-scale of the EPI correlated only to the extent of about $0 \cdot 4$, with the total score from the Hamilton Anxiety Rating Scale (Hamilton, 1959a). It showed an even lower correlation with the two constituent parts from the Hamilton scale, namely physical and psychological anxiety.

An alternative interpretation of the discrepant N-scale findings in hysterics is that a downward shift in arousal occurs in these patients when they become ill. This may not be completely reflected in the neuroticism score, though, as noted earlier, Ingham and Robinson (*op. cit.*) did suggest that the relatively low N-scores of conversion hysterics may be due to their denial of anxiety. Certainly, shifts in test performance do occur in neurosis, at both the causal and descriptive levels, though the evidence for this is confined to dysthymics and to changes occurring on recovery. Shagass *et al.* (1957), for example, demonstrated that the sedation threshold of some dysthymics decreases when their anxiety symptoms are relieved. This finding is paralleled by the fact that, compared with the E-scale, which is relatively stable over time (Bartholomew and Marley, 1959; Mezey *et al.*, 1963), the N-scores of neurotics are known to fluctuate (Knowles, 1960). In anxiety states, in particular, it has been shown that good clinical remission is accompanied by a small but significant fall in the N-score on the EPI (Knowles and Kreitman, *op. cit.*). Changes in the reverse direction in hysteria do not appear to have been reported, at either the causal or descriptive levels. The hypothesis proposed by Ingham and Robinson to account for conversion hysteria therefore still remains to be tested. In any case, a major difficulty with this explanation of the behaviour of hysterics in general is that the greatest discrepancy between causal and descriptive measures is found in those patients in whom the conversion mechanism is presumably not operating, namely hysterical personalities and psychopaths. Both of these groups tend to show high N-scores, yet both resemble conversion hysterics in being poorly arousable on tests such as the spiral after-effect and sedation threshold. This suggests that the first explanation considered is more acceptable, namely that the N-scale is more a measure of "maladjustment" than of sympathetic or introverted anxiety. It indicates too that this scale of the MPI and EPI may not be a particularly suitable instrument for identifying the behavioural counterpart of autonomic arousal.

In conclusion, it may be said that an arousal interpretation of Eysenck's theory has been amply justified, in so far as it has led to a number of testable hypotheses, the investigation of which has made it possible to demonstrate some of the strengths and weaknesses of his hierarchical system of personality. The extraversion hypothesis as an explanation of dysthymia–hysteria finds only partial support at the descriptive level. At the causal level its continued use may be misleading and result in a failure to take account of the several sources of individual variation contributing to neurosis. It is at this level of analysis that most progress is likely to be made in understanding neurotic disorder, a fact that few of Eysenck's critics, armed with MPI results, seem to have realized. Indeed, it may scarcely matter whether dysthymics and hysterics are behaviourally introverted or extraverted. The descriptive theory will have served its main purpose by providing a working framework for research at the causal level of personality. Here the evidence certainly supports the view that dysthymics and hysterics can be used successfully as criterion groups to study some of the psychophysiological correlates of personality; even though the processes involved are more complex than originally anticipated by Eysenck.

In future research on the causal aspects of neurosis it may be less ambiguous to maintain the link with the descriptive level by means of the concept of dysthymia–hysteria, rather than by reference to such personality parameters as introversion–extraversion. Further breakdown of dysthymia–hysteria could then be undertaken by defining more precisely the causal links with less crude psychiatric criteria, such as those obtained from well-validated symptom rating scales. In this way it should be possible to establish in abnormal groups some of the causal processes responsible for normal personality variation. Such a procedure would give personality theory a psychiatric bias, but this would not be outwith the long tradition in this field of seeking to describe normal personality in terms of its abnormal manifestations. Once the causal processes and their interaction had been established in psychiatric populations, their relationship with such characteristics as extraversion could then be re-examined.

SUMMARY

Eysenck's descriptive theory of personality was discussed, particularly in relation to the controversy concerning the position of his neurotic criterion groups in the two-dimensional framework of introversion–extraversion and neuroticism. The Maudsley Personality Inventory scores of three groups of dysthymics, hysterics, and normal subjects were presented. These were found to be exactly in line with those reported previously on smaller samples and with the findings of other workers. While, as predicted, dysthymics were significantly more introverted and more neurotic than normal subjects, hysterics were less extraverted and less neurotic than would be expected from Eysenck's theory. MPI scores did not, therefore, exactly parallel results obtained with causal measures, where dysthymics and hysterics occupied opposite ends of a continuum.

A principal components analysis of some of the objective measures described in previous chapters was reported. Two correlated factors were found, both of which could qualify for interpretation as factors of arousal. It was concluded that dysthymia–hysteria was the result of an interaction between two causal processes and that a simple identification of introversion–extraversion with dysthymia–hysteria was untenable. It was suggested that dysthymics and hysterics could be used as criterion groups for studying the causal processes underlying personality but not for studying the descriptive dimension of introversion–extraversion.

CHAPTER 6

STUDIES IN PSYCHOSIS
I. INTER-GROUP COMPARISONS

INTRODUCTION

No other group of psychiatric syndromes has inspired a greater volume of research or more diverse theoretical viewpoints than those clinical conditions subsumed under the general heading of the "functional psychoses".[1] Social, psychological, neurophysiological, and biochemical explanations abound, as witnessed by such compendious reviews of schizophrenia as those of Bellak (1958) and Jackson (1960).

Even within those studies that can be broadly considered to be of an experimental psychological nature, a wide spectrum of research interests has been represented. Furthermore, different, and some-sometimes contradictory, hypotheses have been proposed to account for similar behavioural phenomena. For example, the impairment of psychomotor performance in psychosis is well documented (Hunt and Cofer, 1944). It has, however, been variously ascribed to disturbances in "set" (Rodnick and Shakow, 1940; Shakow, 1962) and to abnormalities of internal inhibitory processes, either in terms of the growth rate (Venables and Tizard, 1956) or dissipation rate (Eysenck, 1961) of reactive inhibition. Similarly, studies of thought disorder have led some workers to argue that the schizophrenic is abnormally concrete in his thinking and unable to make

---

[1] The generic term "psychosis" is used here to cover both schizophrenic and manic-depressive reactions. At the outset there were no theoretical or empirical grounds for thinking that the experimental measures used would differentiate these two conditions; while there is considerable difficulty in distinguishing clinically between them in young adult patients of the kind taking part in the present study. Reference will be made later, however, to conventional diagnostic categories and the distinction between psychotic depression and schizophrenia will be retained when reviewing other work reported in the literature.

abstract generalizations (Goldstein and Scheerer, 1941; Kasanin and Hanfmann, 1938). Others have claimed that the schizophrenic is unable to maintain normal conceptual boundaries, so that his thinking becomes over-generalized or "overinclusive" (Cameron, 1938, 1944). Overinclusion itself and related aspects of schizophrenic behaviour have been explained from various theoretical viewpoints. Payne et al. (1959) have regarded overinclusive thinking as a breakdown of filtering mechanisms in the CNS that normally screen out irrelevant stimuli; while Mednick (1955, 1958) proposed a stimulus generalization explanation of similar disorders of response in the schizophrenic patient.

On the whole there have been relatively few large-scale attempts to interrelate measures from different levels of function in psychosis, though the mammoth interdisciplinary study by Greenblatt and Solomon (1953) is a notable exception. There are increasing signs in the very recent literature, however, that a more unified theoretical view of psychosis is developing, with greater integration of previously disparate approaches to the problem. This is undoubtedly due partly to the influence on psychology of advances in neurophysiology. As a result, a theoretical viewpoint is beginning to emerge which, however ill-defined at present, holds some promise of being able to handle such different phenomena as the disorders of perception, emotion, thinking, attention, and drive so characteristic of psychosis.

Evidence for this new approach to psychosis is seen in the recent review by Venables (1964) of what he calls "input dysfunction" in schizophrenia. Within the broad conceptual framework of arousal theory Venables discusses a wide variety of investigations, ranging from those of a purely experimental kind to more clinical observational studies such as that of McGhie and Chapman (1961). While pointing towards a more unified view of psychosis, Venables' paper at the same time underlines the confusion that still exists in this field. Comparisons between even similar experiments may be difficult because of variations in the patient populations studied. Chronic and acute patients cannot be considered similar; while, as Venables' own work has shown, there may be differences between various subgroups within the general category of schizophrenia (Venables and Wing, 1962).

The same point has been lucidly stated by Kety (1960), whose comments on the sources of error likely to be encountered in biochemical research apply equally well to other experimental studies of psychosis. He says:

> Despite the phenomenological similarities which permitted the concept of schizophrenia to emerge as a fairly well-defined symptom-complex, there is little evidence that all of its forms have a common aetiology or pathogenesis. The likelihood that one is dealing with a number of different disorders with a common symptomatology must be recognized and included in one's experimental design. Errors involved in sampling from heterogeneous populations may help to explain the high frequency with which findings of one group fail to be confirmed by another. Recognition of the probability that any sample of schizophrenics is a heterogeneous one should seem to emphasize the importance of analyzing data not only for mean values but also for significant deviations of individual values from the group.

It is unlikely, therefore, that any general statement can be made, or any basis for prediction provided, about the behaviour of psychotics as a group. Despite this, there have been numerous attempts to theorize about the neurophysiological changes that occur during the course of a psychotic illness. Quite recently, for example, Fish (1961) suggested that the acute phase of psychosis is characterized by a high state of arousal, which subsides as the illness becomes more chronic. By contrast, other authors (e.g. Weckowicz, 1958) have proposed that early in the psychotic breakdown there is a shift towards parasympathetic predominance, due to a low level of activity in the diencephalon. According to this theory the progression into chronicity is accompanied by a shift in the opposite direction towards increased sympathetic activity. The apparent contradiction between these two explanations is a sign of the theoretical immaturity that still exists in this field.

It was against this complex and rapidly changing theoretical background that the studies reported here were undertaken. At the outset the orientation adopted was unashamedly empirical, since when the investigation was started nearly eight years ago it was not possible to take advantage of the developments that have occurred in the field even since that time. The study of neurosis to which previous reference has been made (Claridge, 1960) included a group of acute psychotic patients to whom the same battery of tests was administered. The results of that experiment need not be considered in detail here, though some of the conclusions drawn from it are perhaps worth mentioning, despite their apparent naivety on re-reading some six years later.

A general similarity was noted between the performance of psychotics as a group and hysterics, though the variability among psychotics was greater than among other subjects, markedly so on some of the measures used. Certain features of the psychomotor performance of psychotic patients led to the tentative conclusion that there may be some disturbance of inhibitory processes in schizophrenia. No firmer link with general personality theory could be discerned at that time and the investigation remained largely an exploratory one. Adoption of an arousal orientation towards neurosis subsequently led to a further series of experiments in psychotic patients, carried out from a similar viewpoint. The sedation threshold again played a prominent part in these experiments and their course was greatly influenced by parallel results being obtained with this technique in neurotics. Eventually, as will be shown later, both sets of data became theoretically supportive of each other. As with neurotics, the main aim of this part of the research was to try and account, not for psychosis as a homogeneous entity, but for variations within what was clearly a very hetereogeneous group of conditions.

In presenting the results for psychotic patients here and in the next chapter the procedure followed will be basically similar to that adopted earlier for neurotics. That is to say, an attempt will be made to study psychosis at various hierarchical levels of function on a variety of tests of psychomotor performance, attention, and conceptual thinking, as well as on autonomic and other putative measures of arousal. The presentation differs, however, in two respects. First, the amount of data available on some of the tests used with psychotics was relatively small and to this extent the investigation can only be regarded as a preliminary one. Secondly, the theoretical framework guiding the investigation was less firm than in the case of neurosis, where Eysenck's theory had provided a closely interlocked network of testable postulates at both the causal and descriptive levels of personality. It should also be noted that any conclusions to be drawn from the results are limited to the early phases of psychosis. All of the patients studied were acutely rather than chronically ill, using the term "chronic" in its generally accepted sense as an illness marked by two or more years continuous stay in hospital (Brown, 1960).

In this chapter the results for psychotics as a group on the major tests studied will be presented, while in the following chapter the interrelationships between various measures will be discussed. From what has been said already, the latter aspect of the data is clearly more important theoretically, though the average trends in behaviour are of some interest too. This chapter will in any case allow some of the data to be presented upon which the subsequent intra-group analysis is based. The comparison here will be mainly with normal subjects, though similarities, where they exist, with the two neurotic groups will also be noted. All of the experimental procedures discussed below have been described in previous chapters and, since these did not differ in the case of psychotic patients, the reader is referred for further details to the appropriate parts of Chapters 2, 3, and 4.

DESCRIPTION OF SUBJECTS

The total sample of psychotics available for study consisted of sixty-seven male patients, all but five of whom had been given the diagnosis of schizophrenia by the psychiatrist in charge of the case. Of these sixty-two schizophrenics, seven were classified as paranoid, eleven as simple, and thirty-four as hebephrenic; while ten were not assigned to any subtype of schizophrenia. Three of the five exceptions were diagnosed as psychotic depressives, one as a hypomanic, and one as a schizo-affective state.

As noted above, all were early acute patients, only one having previously been admitted to hospital for a psychotic illness. This patient had had only a very short stay in hospital and minimal treatment with tranquillizers. One other patient had also received a short course of tranquillizers a few weeks before testing. Otherwise, apart from temporary sedation, all patients were untreated and five were thought to be remitting spontaneously at the time of testing. No patient was receiving medication when tested.

The normal and neurotic groups with whom comparisons will be made consisted of the military subjects used in the main part of the research described in previous chapters. Full details of these subjects have already been given and comparisons with respect to age and weight indicated that psychotics were closely similar to other groups on both of these variables. The mean age of the psychotic group was $23 \cdot 6$ yr SD $5 \cdot 59$, which did not differ significantly from that of normal subjects ($t = 0 \cdot 34$), dysthymics ($t = 1 \cdot 91$) or hysterics ($t = 0 \cdot 53$). The mean weight of psychotics was $148 \cdot 5$ lb SD $15 \cdot 90$, which again did not differ significantly from that of other groups, the values for t in comparison with normals, dysthymics, and hysterics being, respectively, $1 \cdot 20$, $0 \cdot 28$, and $0 \cdot 89$.

An adequate assessment of intelligence was not obtained on all of the psychotic patients, though Matrices IQ's were available on thirteen subjects. The mean IQ of this subgroup was $101 \cdot 5$ SD $15 \cdot 51$. This value was significantly lower than the mean IQ's of dysthymics ($t = 2 \cdot 47$, $p < 0 \cdot 02$), hysterics ($t = 2 \cdot 41$, $p < 0 \cdot 02$), and normal subjects ($t = 2 \cdot 53$, $p < 0 \cdot 02$). The finding is consistent with other studies of intelligence in psychiatric groups (Payne, 1960) and could be explained by the known effect of an ongoing psychosis on Matrices performance (Foulds and Dixon, 1962a). A similar result was found by Herrington and Claridge (1965) on thirty patients forming part of the present sample. They based their comparison on the Summed Selection Group ratings (Claridge, 1960), obtained on entry to the Services and therefore providing an estimate of intelligence prior to breakdown. The relative intellectual dullness of their subgroup was thought to be due to the inclusion of a high proportion of hebephrenic patients, who probably have a low premorbid intelligence (Mason, 1956; Foulds et al., 1962; Foulds and Dixon, 1962b). Since roughly the same proportion of hebephrenics was contained in the larger sample reported on here, it seems reasonable to assume that the overall intelligence level of the group was lower than that of neurotic and normal subjects at least on performance tests of intelligence. This in turn was presumably a composite effect of innate dullness and an active psychotic process.

EXPERIMENTAL FINDINGS

Sedation Threshold

Previous work on the sedation threshold and allied procedures in psychosis is fairly clearly divided into studies of schizophrenia, on the one hand, and studies comparing neurotic and psychotic depressives, on the other. Considering the latter group of experiments first, one of the major claims made for the technique as a diagnostic tool was that it would successfully differentiate these two kinds of depression (Shagass et al., 1956). Despite the technical difficulties met by other workers trying to replicate Shagass' original sedation threshold procedure, there is a remarkable consistency with which this particular claim for the method has been supported. Although some authors have reported equivocal findings (Ackner and Pampiglione, 1959; Martin and Davies, 1962), most agree that there is increased barbiturate sensitivity in psychotic depression. Using an EEG criterion, Boudreau (1958), Nymgaard (1959), Seager (1960a), and Perris and Brattemo (1963) all reported significantly lower sedation thresholds in psychotic compared with neurotic depressives. This result was replicated for the sleep threshold by Shagass and Kerenyi (1959) and Perez-Reyes and Cochrane (1964) and for the GSR-inhibition threshold by Perez-Reyes et al. (1962). Findings for depressant drug thresholds have also been supported using a stimulant drug to measure the "stimulation threshold", Giberti and Rossi (1962) reporting significantly higher tolerance of methamphetamine in psychotic compared with neurotic depression. There have been few studies of drug tolerance in mania and hypomania, though Shagass and Jones (1958) reported the mean sedation threshold of a small group of such patients to be higher than normal, but showing marked individual variability. Of two hypomanic patients tested by Claridge et al. (1964) one had a high, and one a low, sedation threshold.

A complex picture emerges with respect to the sedation threshold in schizophrenia, since the heterogeneity of this condition is reflected in experimental findings with the test. Shagass (1957b) and Shagass and Jones (op. cit.) reported that in acute patients, i.e. those in whom the illness was of less than six months duration, thresholds were consistently low. Chronic patients were shown to have higher than average thresholds, though simple schizophrenics were an exception to this. A group of "borderline" or pseudoneurotic schizophrenics had an average threshold higher than that of chronic patients and falling near that of dysthymic neurotics. High sedation thresholds were also reported in chronic schizophrenia by Boudreau (op. cit.) and by Krishnamoorti and Shagass (1964). The latter authors confirmed the significantly lower thresholds of acute patients, though this group contained cases of both affective psychosis and schizophrenia.

In considering further the relationship between chronicity and barbiturate tolerance, Shagass (1957b) demonstrated that the sedation threshold increased as a function of duration of psychotic symptoms, levelling off at about two years. The data on which this conclusion was based did not, however, include three types of patient: borderline, acute or chronic, and acute recurrent schizophrenics. The last two groups, although having had their first episode at least a year before testing, had low sedation thresholds, resembling those of acute patients.

From the foregoing discussion it would be expected that the population from which our own sample was drawn would tend, on average, to have low sedation thresholds. This was shown to be true by Herrington and Claridge (1965). The result for the larger sample studied here is shown in Table 1, together with that for the normal group. It can be seen that the means for the two groups are similar, though in assessing this result account must be taken of the bias towards low thresholds in the normal sample used here. That

TABLE 1. SEDATION THRESHOLD (MG/KG) IN PSYCHOTICS
AND NORMAL SUBJECTS

	Psychotics	Normals
N	67	34
Mean	7·12	7·36
SD	2·13	2·32

$t = 0·50$, N.S.

the psychotics tended to fall near the end of increased, rather than decreased, barbiturate sensitivity is indicated by the fact that there was a highly significant difference between their mean sedation threshold and that of dysthymic neurotics ($t = 6·546$, df 131, $p < 0·001$). Psychotics did not, on the other hand, differ significantly from hysterics, t being 1·344 (df 122). It is possible to conclude from these results, therefore, that early acute psychotics as a group tend to have relatively low sedation thresholds.

Archimedes Spiral After-effect

Although some authors (Price and Deabler, 1955; Krishnamoorti and Shagass, *op. cit.*) have noted no marked variation from normal in the performance of psychotics on this test, Claridge (1960) reported a significantly longer mean spiral after-effect in acute schizophrenics compared with his normal group. He emphasized, however, the somewhat greater standard deviation among psychotic patients. This result was closely replicated by Herrington and

Claridge (*op. cit.*) on a further sample of patients from the same population. In the expanded sample now available the result shown in Table 2 was found. As can be seen there, the trend for acute psychotics as a group to report significantly longer after-effects than normals was continued. As would be expected their mean SAE was also significantly greater than that of hysterics, *t* being 4·198 (df 122, *p* < 0·001). It was also significantly smaller, however, than that of dysthymic neurotics, *t* being 2·671 (df 131, *p* < 0·01). The mean SAE of acute psychotics would seem to fall, therefore, somewhere midway between that of normal subjects and dysthymics, though the bias towards low values in the present normal group should again be recalled. The only other comment necessary at this

TABLE 2. SPIRAL AFTER-EFFECT (SEC) IN PSYCHOTICS AND NORMAL SUBJECTS

	Psychotics	Normals
N	67	34
Mean	15·95	12·71
SD	6·75	5·48

$t = 2·59, p < 0·01.$

point is to draw attention to the difference between this test and the sedation threshold, where psychotics tended to resemble hysterics rather than dysthymics. The significance of this finding will be taken up in more detail in the following chapter.

Auditory Vigilance

Mainly on the basis of clinical observation and the well-known inferiority in the performance of psychotics, it was predicted and demonstrated by Claridge (1960) that acute schizophrenics would perform badly on the auditory vigilance task described earlier (p. 64 ff.). Subsequent results with the sedation threshold, in both neurotics and psychotics, provided some *post hoc* explanation of the finding, since the generally low sedation thresholds of acute psychotics had suggested a poor level of arousal in these patients, similar to that demonstrated in hysterics. Further experiments were carried out, with continuous recording, in a few cases, of the autonomic functions measured in the other groups, viz. heart rate and skin conductance. The total number of patients on whom performance scores were available was thirty-one. Heart rate was recorded in fourteen of these patients and both heart rate and skin conductance in thirteen cases.

Considering the performance data first, it can be seen from Table 3 and Fig. 6.1 that, confirming the earlier findings, psychotics were significantly inferior to normal subjects. In this respect they resembled

TABLE 3. VIGILANCE SCORE (TOTAL SIGNALS DETECTED) IN PSYCHOTICS AND NORMAL SUBJECTS

	Psychotics	Normals
N	31	55
Mean	13·3	21·0
SD	10·62	5·31

$$t = 3 \cdot 78, p < 0 \cdot 001$$

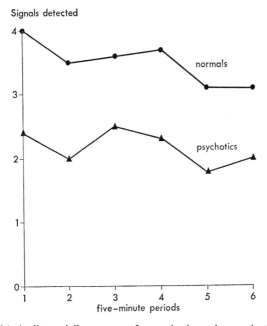

FIG. 6.1. Auditory vigilance curves for psychotics and normal subjects.

hysterics, from whom they did not differ significantly ($t = 0 \cdot 759$, df 77). As expected, dysthymics performed significantly better than psychotics, t being $4 \cdot 747$ (df 86, $p < 0 \cdot 001$). Perhaps the most marked feature of the performance of psychotics, however, was the very wide variability in their vigilance performance. As can be seen in Table 3 the standard deviation for psychotics was exactly twice that of normal subjects, a difference that was statistically significant ($F = 4 \cdot 00$, df 30/54, $p < 0 \cdot 01$).

Turning to the autonomic measures taken during vigilance, the means for the slope and level scores of heart rate and skin conductance are shown, respectively, in Tables 4 and 5. Figures 6.2 and 6.3 illustrate the trends in these two functions over the course of the vigilance task. It can be seen that there was no marked difference between psychotic and normal subjects on either autonomic measure. Psychotics tended to show a slightly lower heart rate during most of the test (Fig. 6.2), but normals declined more. The opposite trend occurred in the case of skin conductance (Fig. 6.3). Only one of the group comparisons on the various measures reached significance: psychotics tended to show a significantly lower heart rate level than dysthymic neurotics, t being $3 \cdot 879$ (df 37, $p < 0 \cdot 001$).

An unusual feature of the heart rate level findings was the much *smaller* standard deviation shown by psychotics compared with

TABLE 4. VIGILANCE—HEART RATE

Level and rate of decline (beats per min) in psychotics and normal subjects

	Psychotics	Normals
N	14	24
(a) *Level*		
Mean	74·6	79·3
SD	7·96	16·43
$t = 1 \cdot 18$, N.S.		
(b) *Rate of decline*		
Mean	−0·79	−1·68
SD	1·59	0·99
$t = 1 \cdot 86$, N.S.		

TABLE 5. VIGILANCE—SKIN CONDUCTANCE

Level and rate of decline (micromhos) in psychotics and normal subjects

	Psychotics	Normals
N	13	14
	(a) Level	
Mean	151·7	158·7
SD	152·47	193·16
	$t = 0·32$, N.S.	
	(b) Rate of decline	
Mean	−3·60	−10·04
SD	14·63	16·48
	$t = 1·03$, N.S.	

normal subjects (Table 4). This difference was found to be significant at the 0·05 level, F being 4·26 (df 23/13). The result is, of course, contrary to the normally greater variability to be expected in samples of psychotic patients.

In general, the results for the vigilance test supported earlier findings in so far as there was an average tendency for psychotics to perform poorly, though with much greater variability than normal

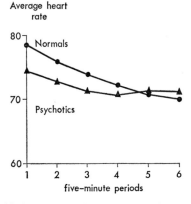

FIG. 6.2. Trend in heart rate during vigilance performance in psychotics and normal subjects.

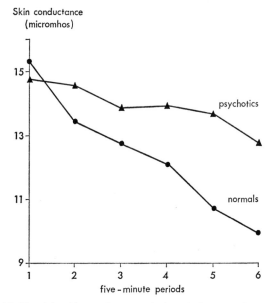

Fig. 6.3. Trend in skin conductance during vigilance performance in psychotics and normal subjects.

subjects. This overall trend is in keeping with the rather low sedation thresholds found in acute psychotics and the somewhat greater tendency towards low, rather than high, levels of autonomic arousal, at least in the particular sample on whom these measures were taken.

Serial Reaction Time (unpaced)

In a previous study of serial reaction time, using the same apparatus as that employed here, Venables (1959) demonstrated the very marked inferiority in the performance of both psychotic depressive and schizophrenic patients compared with a control group of normal subjects. Within the schizophrenic group active patients performed better than withdrawn patients, while no differences were found in the reminiscence scores of psychotic and normal subjects.

In a more recent study Bills (1964) compared serial reaction time performance in brain-damage, functional psychosis, and personality disorder, paying particular attention to the problem of involuntary rest pauses, or "blocks". Both blocks and errors were shown to occur far more often in schizophrenics than in personality disorders, though paranoid patients were an exception to this. Paranoid and other schizophrenics were alike, however, in performing at a significantly slower rate than patients with personality disorder.

Both of these experiments were carried out on chronic psychotics and the task does not appear to have been used previously with acute patients. On the pursuit-rotor, however, Claridge (1960) demonstrated that there were no marked differences from normals in the level at which acute psychotics performed, but the nature of their learning curve was rather unusual. A conspicuous feature was the marked lack of reminiscence in psychotics, a result replicated with chronic patients by Broadhurst and Broadhurst (1964). This failure of reminiscence to appear in psychotics after the normal short rest interposed in massed practice led Eysenck (1961) to postulate that psychotics dissipate reactive inhibition extremely slowly. He claimed there was no evidence for an abnormal lack of drive in psychotics, quoting studies by Ley (unpublished) and Rachman (1963) to support this view.

In the present experiment, using the apparatus described on p. 72, serial reaction time under unpaced conditions was studied in thirteen patients from the total sample of psychotics. As with the other groups, performance scores for the first 5 minutes of practice were analyzed by means of regression lines. The mean level and slope measures for psychotics and normal subjects are shown in Table 6, while performance curves for these two groups are

TABLE 6. SERIAL REACTION TIME (UNPACED)
Level and rate of decline (responses per min) in psychotics and normal subjects

	Psychotics	Normals
N	13	33
	(a) *Level*	
Mean	90·3	88·6
SD	11·11	13·35
	$t = 0·44$, N.S.	
	(b) *Rate of decline*	
Mean	−1·34	−0·66
SD	1·08	1·49
	$t = 1·72$, N.S.	

illustrated in Fig. 6.4. It can be seen that there was no difference between the groups either in level or slope of performance, psychotics and normal subjects overlapping considerably throughout the task. Comparison with the performance of neurotic patients revealed only one significant finding, viz. that psychotics responded at a markedly faster rate than hysterics, t for the mean level scores of these groups being $3 \cdot 125$ (df 30, $p < 0 \cdot 01$).

It is evident from Fig. 6.4 and Table 7 that there was little difference in the reminiscence scores of normal and psychotic subjects, though there was a significant tendency for the latter to make more errors

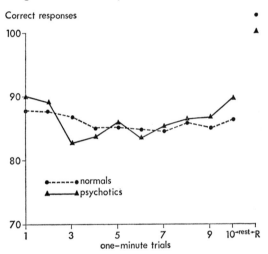

FIG. 6.4. Serial reaction time performance and reminiscence in psychotics and normal subjects.

during the course of the task (Table 8). Psychotics also made significantly more errors than dysthymics, t being $2 \cdot 07$ (df 28, $p < 0 \cdot 05$). No other comparison with neurotics was significant, either for errors or reminiscence.

In summary, apart from a significant tendency to make more frequent errors, acute psychotic patients do not seem to differ noticeably from normal subjects on the serial reaction time task. In fact, their performance appears to be less impaired than that of hysterics, who have consistently shown low response rates. In this respect the findings parallel those reported earlier for the pursuit-rotor, though a conspicuous difference is the failure here to confirm that psychotics will not show a reminiscence effect.

TABLE 7. SERIAL REACTION TIME (UNPACED)

Reminiscence scores in psychotics and normal subjects

	Psychotics	Normals
N	13	33
Mean	13·0	13·8
SD	7·53	7·91

$t = 0·30$, N.S.

TABLE 8. SERIAL REACTION TIME (UNPACED)

Error score in psychotics and normal subjects

	Psychotics	Normals
N	13	33
Mean	19·6	11·5
SD	11·48	11·18

$t = 2·15, p < 0·05$

Colour-word (Stroop) Test

In Chapter 4 we discussed in some detail the rationale for using this test to investigate the narrowed attention hypothesis of arousal. It will be recalled that the hypothesis found little support using individual differences within a neurotic population to manipulate arousal level. Both dysthymics and hysterics performed poorly compared with normal subjects and it was concluded that the result could be most easily explained by invoking the Yerkes–Dodson Law applied to complex tasks. Further investigation of the Stroop test in psychotic patients was of some interest because of the possibility that the attentional defects present in psychosis might be reflected in performance on the task and these in turn linked with disturbances in arousal level.

When the experiment was carried out there was little firm ground for forming a precise hypothesis about the Stroop performance of acute psychotic patients as a group. In his recent discussion of input dysfunction in schizophrenia Venables (1964) considered the relevance of the narrowed attention hypothesis and once more emphasized the heterogeneity of psychosis, though he did conclude from the evidence reviewed that chronic patients appear to behave as though their attention were narrowed.

In the present study the low sedation thresholds that were being found might have suggested that the opposite would be the case in acute patients who would, because of low arousal, perform poorly on the Stroop test. On the other hand, some authors, such as Fish (*op. cit.*), have argued for high arousal in early psychosis, an hypothesis that would lead one to predict improved Stroop performance in the acute schizophrenic. Looked at from yet a different viewpoint, it would have been possible to predict impaired performance on this rather complex task simply on the basis of the "illness" factor, i.e. because of his disturbed behaviour generally the acute psychotic should have difficulty coping with the Stroop test, at least as administered here. It was, in fact, on the basis of this entirely empirical observation that we anticipated poor Stroop performance in psychotics as a group, although it was hoped that subsequent intra-group analysis might throw some light on the relationship between attention and arousal in early psychosis. Apart from the performance measures, the two indices of reminiscence derived from the test were also of interest because they provided a further opportunity to test Eysenck's reactive inhibition explanation of psychosis.

A group of thirteen psychotics was examined on the test following the procedure described in Chapter 4 (p. 83 ff.). The mean correct and incorrect scores under the colour and word conditions are shown, respectively, in Tables 9 and 10, together with the comparable

TABLE 9. STROOP TEST (COLOUR CONDITION)

Mean correct and incorrect responses in psychotics and normal subjects

	Psychotics	Normals
N	13	16
(a) *Total correct score*		
Mean	169·9	211·8
SD	46·32	50·35

$t = 2·22, p < 0·05$

(b) *Total incorrect score*		
Mean	62·6	64·7
SD	26·06	23·71

$t = 0·22$, N.S.

TABLE 10. STROOP TEST (WORD CONDITION)

Mean correct and incorrect responses in psychotics and normal subjects

	Psychotics	Normals
N	13	16
	(a) *Total correct score*	
Mean	182·6	230·6
SD	56·47	58·16
	$t = 2·15, p < 0·05$	
	(b) *Total incorrect score*	
Mean	50·0	48·6
SD	18·23	32·31
	$t = 0·13$, N.S.	

values for the normal group. Performance curves for the two halves
of the test in each group are shown in Fig. 6.5. As anticipated, under
both colour and word conditions, psychotics made significantly
fewer correct responses than normal subjects, though the groups
did not differ significantly in error score. Confirming the findings for
serial reaction time, no difference was found in reminiscence under
either condition, as can be seen in Table 11. There were no significant differences between psychotics and either neurotic group on
any of the measures derived from the Stroop test.

TABLE 11. STROOP TEST

Reminiscence scores in psychotics and normal subjects

	Psychotics	Normals
N	13	16
	(a) *Colour condition*	
Mean	10·1	6·1
SD	10·45	13·08
	$t = 0·86$, N.S.	
	(b) *Word condition*	
Mean	6·6	4·2
SD	12·21	6·68
	$t = 0·64$, N.S.	

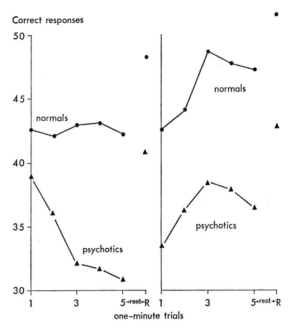

FIG. 6.5. Performance of psychotics and normal subjects on Stroop
test under colour condition and word condition.

The Stroop performance of acute psychotics as a group thus
conformed very much to expectation. It is significant, perhaps, that
all three psychiatric groups performed poorly relative to normal
subjects and it is possible that the average trend found in psychotics
as a whole is explicable, as in neurotics, in terms of the Yerkes–
Dodson principle. Again there was no evidence that a lack of
reminiscence effect is particularly characteristic of psychosis.

Maudsley Personality Inventory

Although falling into a somewhat different category from the
other tests described so far, it is convenient to consider here the
group findings for the Maudsley Personality Inventory, which was
administered to a proportion of the psychotic sample. As with the
other measures, the main purpose of gathering this data was to
examine intra-group variability, particularly in this case to investigate

how far the superficial traits tapped by the MPI were related, within a group of psychotics, to more objective behavioural indices. However, it was also of interest to determine the overall status of psychotics on the two scales of the MPI, since Eysenck (1960a) has argued that psychoticism is a personality dimension orthogonal to extraversion and neuroticism. Theoretically, therefore, psychotics should not differ, as a group, from normal subjects on either of the MPI scales.

In the manual to the test no norms are given for psychotic patients (Eysenck, 1959a), though McGuire et al. (1963) reported on a small group of acute schizophrenics. These patients tended to resemble neurotics on both scales, being more introverted and more neurotic than normal subjects. The same authors also tested a group of depressed patients, but did not specify the type of depression predominating in the sample. This presumably mixed group were also found to resemble neurotics but to be significantly more extraverted than schizophrenics.

Coppen and Metcalfe (1965) studied changes in the MPI scales after treatment in depressed patients and, though finding a dysthymic-like pattern of low E- and high N-score before treatment, demonstrated significant increases in extraversion and significant decreases in neuroticism with recovery. This was most marked in endogenous cases but the pre-treatment scores did not differentiate the two types of depression.

The manual for the more recent Eysenck Personality Inventory does include standardization samples of psychotic patients (Eysenck and Eysenck, 1964). According to these norms both psychotic depressives and schizophrenics are more introverted than normal. This is particularly true of schizophrenics. On the N-scale both psychotic groups fall between normals and neurotics, with depressives nearer the neurotic mean and schizophrenics nearer the normal mean. It is not specified in the manual whether the schizophrenic sample consisted of chronic or acute patients, though Al-Issa (1964), also using the EPI, reported the mean N-score of a group of chronic schizophrenics to be below the published mean for normal subjects. The mean E-score for that group was similar to the figure reported by Eysenck and Eysenck (op. cit.) in schizophrenics.

In the present study the MPI was administered to thirty-two acute psychotics with the results shown in Table 12. Also included in the table are the mean scores for the experimental sample of normal subjects used here and, because of the bias towards extraversion in that group, the data for Eysenck's quota sample of English normals. It can be seen that on extraversion psychotics did not differ significantly from either normal sample though they had a significantly higher N-score than both of these groups. Comparison with the MPI results for neurotic patients discussed in Chapter 5 indicated

TABLE 12. MPI SCORES FOR PSYCHOTICS, NORMAL SUBJECTS, AND EYSENCK'S ENGLISH SAMPLE

	Psychotics	Normals	Eysenck's English sample
N	32	64	1800
		E-scale	
Mean	23·65	27·36	24·91
SD	9·03	8·99	9·71

t-tests { Psychotics vs. Normals: 1·91, N.S.
Psychotics vs. Eysenck's English sample: 0·78, N.S.

		N-scale	
Mean	29·91	21·23	19·89
SD	11·47	11·31	11·02

t-tests { Psychotics vs. Normals: 3·51, $p < 0·001$
Psychotics vs. Eysenck's English sample: 4·92, $p < 0·001$

that psychotics were, if anything, closer to hysterics than dysthymics. They were significantly more extraverted than dysthymics ($t = 3·799$, df 123, $p < 0·001$), but did not differ significantly from hysterics on the E-scale or from either neurotic group on the N-scale.

These findings suggest that acute psychotics, even when ill, do not as a group deviate markedly towards either extraversion or introversion, though they do rate themselves as significantly more neurotic. It is possible that this conclusion applies only to the acute phase of psychosis, since Al-Issa's results suggest that there may be a decrease in N-score with chronicity.

The high N-score of the present group of patients is consistent with earlier findings that psychotics score highly on tests of neuroticism (S. B. G. Eysenck, 1956; Trouton and Maxwell, 1956).

Eysenck (1960a) has suggested that the effect is due to the stress imposed by a developing psychotic illness. This explanation seems acceptable in view of the frequency with which neurotic symptoms appear in the early stages of psychosis and the difficulty often encountered in making the differential diagnosis between neurosis and psychosis on the basis of symptomatology alone.

CONCLUSIONS

One of the main conclusions to be drawn from the group data presented here is the lack of consistency in the performance of psychotics relative to that of the neurotic and normal subjects described in previous chapters. Although on a number of tests, such as sedation threshold and vigilance, acute psychotics as a group appear to resemble hysterics, this is not true for other measures. Serial reaction time, and more particularly the spiral after-effect, place the psychotic nearer, if anything, to the dysthymic patient. Furthermore, the within group variability on some measures suggests considerable heterogeneity even in a sample of patients that was very carefully selected with respect to such important variables as age, chronicity of illness, and treatment history.

One consistent finding was the failure to confirm that psychotics do not show reminiscence. On the particular tasks used here there was no evidence that such patients differ from other individuals in this respect. Since previous work demonstrating the effect has been done with the pursuit-rotor, it is possible that the result is specific to that particular task. The pursuit-rotor does, of course, differ considerably from the serial reaction time and Stroop procedures used in the present research. Serial reaction time, for example, was self-paced and the argument used earlier with respect to the behaviour of neurotics on the test might apply equally to psychotics, namely that performance level is self-modulated in order to maintain inhibition within critical limits. The relatively normal pre-rest performance of the small group of psychotics studied here would tend to argue against this, but a more thorough investigation comparing different types of psychomotor task might help to settle the issue.

Nevertheless, to the present author it seems unlikely that a limited hypothesis based on one aspect of reactive inhibition will prove capable of accounting for the very varied dysfunction found in psychosis. The emerging view of psychosis as a disturbance of the arousal mechanisms would seem to provide a more promising approach, some of the findings described here, particularly those for sedation threshold, tending to support this conclusion. Thus, despite the apparent differences between neurotics and psychotics, the results using the same experimental measures in both of these groups indicate that it may be possible to provide an explanation of psychosis within the same theoretical framework as that applied to neurosis. Because of its complex nature it would not be expected, of course, that psychotic illness would be accompanied by a simple upward or downward change in arousal of the kind visualized in the neuroses. Even in the case of the latter, doubt has already been thrown on the tenability of such a unitary view of arousal. How the mechanisms contributing to arousal are disturbed in psychosis can be best examined by considering how various measures relate to each other within a group of psychotic patients. This problem is taken up in the following chapter.

SUMMARY

Some of the theoretical problems entailed in studying psychosis were discussed, its heterogeneity stressed, and the limitations of studying average trends in psychotic groups particularly underlined. A sample of sixty-seven acute psychotics was then described, followed by results for a number of measures obtained in all or part of this sample. As expected, the performance of psychotics was impaired on such tests as vigilance and colour-word naming (Stroop test), but a very large variance in vigilance score was noted. On the Maudsley Personality Inventory psychotics were not significantly different from normals in extraversion, but were significantly more neurotic. The main findings presented, those for sedation threshold and spiral after-effect, indicated that on the former measure psychotics as a group resembled hysterics, having generally low thresholds. The spiral after-effect, on the other hand, tended to approach that of dysthymics. It was concluded that the variability of psychotic behaviour can only be properly understood by comparing the interrelationship between various measures, a problem considered in the next chapter.

CHAPTER 7

STUDIES IN PSYCHOSIS
II. INTRA-GROUP ANALYSIS

INTRODUCTION

From what has been said already it is clear that progress in understanding the nature of psychosis can only be made if some account can be given of its heterogeneity. It is also clear that this can only be partly achieved by the method of analysis used in the previous chapter, viz. the investigation of overall trends in groups of psychotics, even where the patient material is carefully selected with respect to the more important clinical variables. An alternative procedure is that discussed by Stern and McDonald (1965) who, after reviewing some of the current work in this field, concluded that a more fruitful approach may be to define subgroups of psychosis in terms of physiological and psychophysiological parameters and then to examine the clinical and other behavioural correlates of these parameters. The choice of relevant parameters itself poses a major problem, particularly in view of the unsatisfactory nature of most theories in this area, none of which provides a sound basis for selection. In planning the present study it was necessary, therefore, to be guided by what appeared to be empirically the most important, if theoretically the least understood, of our own findings.

This was a discovery first referred to briefly by Claridge (1961b) and later described in more detail by Herrington and Claridge (1965). They demonstrated that in early psychosis there is a significant *negative* correlation between the sedation threshold and the spiral after-effect. This, of course, contrasts markedly with the positive relationship found between these two measures in neurosis, the correlations for the two populations being, in fact, significantly different in sign. The result indicated that, although opposite in direction to that found in neurosis, there was nevertheless a significant co-variation between the tests in psychosis, from High ST/Low SAE to Low ST/High SAE.

While no explanation could be given for this rather curious finding, it did seem to provide a possible definitive framework within which to study psychosis. It suggested, for example, that the differences between psychotics and neurotics may lie, not so much in their performance on single tests, but rather in the relationship between the same pairs of measures. If this were true, then there were several important consequences. First, the heterogeneity of psychosis might be more clearly understood in terms of variations along continua defined by such pairs of measures. Secondly, useful comparisons could be made with neurotics on whom similar measures had been taken. Thirdly, in view of the detailed relationships established in neurotics, considerable light might be thrown on the disturbances in arousal perhaps underlying psychosis.

The decision to use the ST/SAE performance of psychotics as a starting-point for the intra-group analysis was subsequently strengthened by the results of two other studies carried out independently. The first was an experiment by Krishnamoorti and Shagass (1964) who also investigated the spiral after-effect and sedation threshold in neurotic and psychotic patients. They reported results identical with those of Herrington and Claridge (*op. cit.*), though the negative correlation between the two measures in psychotics was somewhat lower than that found by the latter authors. As will become clear later, the most likely explanation of this is that the group of psychotics studied by Krishnamoorti and Shagass was very heterogeneous, containing acute and chronic schizophrenics, as well as patients diagnosed as suffering from affective illnesses. Their replication of the original finding is, therefore, all the more convincing.

The second study to be mentioned is that reported by Venables (1963b) who compared normal subjects and chronic schizophrenics on two quite different arousal indices. These were skin potential and the two-flash threshold, the latter being a measure of the threshold for fusion of brief paired flashes of light. Venables demonstrated that in schizophrenics the sign of the correlation between these measures is opposite to that found in normal subjects. In detail Venables' finding differs somewhat from those obtained with sedation threshold and spiral after-effect, a discrepancy that will demand further consideration later. In the meantime, however, it is sufficient to note his confirmation of the sign-reversal effect in psychosis.

Because of the apparent importance of this group of results, the discussion below will begin with a comparison of neurotic, psychotic, and normal subjects on the sedation threshold and spiral after-effect, giving data for the larger samples that have subsequently become available. The autonomic correlates of ST/SAE performance will then be examined in order to determine how far the relationships found in neurotics also hold in psychotic patients. The data will next be discussed with reference to the clinical features of psychosis. Finally, we shall consider relationships with the performance measures described in the previous chapter.

SEDATION THRESHOLD AND SPIRAL AFTER-EFFECT
IN PSYCHOSIS

In their original study Herrington and Claridge (*op. cit.*) demonstrated that in thirty acute, previously untreated psychotics the correlation between sedation threshold and spiral after-effect was -0.44 ($p < 0.02$). When this sample was divided into two subgroups of fifteen patients who recovered and fifteen who did not recover with treatment, the correlations in each differed somewhat. In those who did not recover the value for r was -0.55 ($p < 0.02$), compared with a lower and non-significant, though still negative, correlation of -0.23 in those who subsequently responded to treatment.

In the larger group of sixty-seven patients described here the negative correlation between threshold and spiral after-effect was maintained, r being -0.29 ($p < 0.02$). The fact that the correlation is lower than that in Herrington and Claridge's original group may be due to the eventual inclusion of a number of patients who were thought to be remitting and of two who had had some previous treatment. As further subjects were added, the group certainly became rather less homogeneous, unavoidably so, because of a subsequent difficulty experienced in obtaining suitable patients. It is interesting to note, therefore, that the correlation of -0.24 reported by Krishnamoorti and Shagass (*op. cit.*) in their mixed group of psychotics was very similar to that given here for the larger group.

The possible effects of remission and/or treatment on the ST/SAE performance of psychotics were very clearly demonstrated by Herrington and Claridge (*op. cit.*) who reported that on recovery, the correlation between these two measures reverted to the positive one usually found in neurotics. The correlation between sedation threshold and spiral after-effect after treatment in their recovered subgroup of fifteen patients was positive and significant, r being $+0 \cdot 74 \, (p < 0 \cdot 01)$. This result is illustrated in Fig. 7.1, where the post-treatment scores of these fifteen patients are plotted,

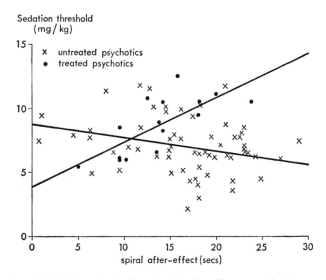

FIG. 7.1. Sedation threshold and spiral after-effect scores in sixty-seven psychotic patients before treatment and in fifteen patients following treatment.

together with the pre-treatment scores of the total sample of sixty-seven psychotics. The negative relationship in untreated patients is shown, though the fairly wide scatter of scores should be noted. It can also be seen that there is a relative preponderance of patients with high spiral after-effects and low sedation thresholds, a fact that accounts for the group findings on these two tests taken individually.

Herrington and Claridge reported a complex relationship between pre- and post-treatment scores on the threshold and spiral after-effect and the shifts in each of these measures with recovery. Interpreting the post-treatment measures as representing "premorbid" values, they concluded that there was a significant tendency for patients with high sedation thresholds to show a fall and those with low thresholds to show a rise in threshold on entering psychosis. The other two findings of interest in this part of the data are illustrated in Fig. 7.2 where the pre- and post-treatment scores of the fifteen re-tested patients are shown. First, there was a significant average rise in sedation threshold after treatment, though, as can be seen in Fig. 7.2, three patients showed a small fall in threshold. Secondly, on recovery there was a significant decrease in the variance of the SAE scores, patients with long after-effects showing a fall and those with short after-effects an increase in SAE.

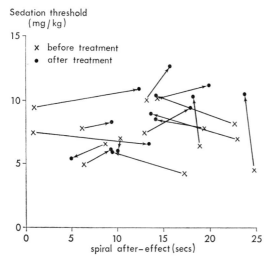

FIG. 7.2. Pre-treatment and post-treatment scores in fifteen psychotics, showing individual shifts in sedation threshold and spiral after-effect with treatment.

In making their comparison with non-psychotic individuals Herrington and Claridge assumed a linear relationship between sedation threshold and spiral after-effect in neurotic and normal subjects. However, as seen in Chapter 4 the addition of further data to the neurotic sample suggested a more complex picture. It will be recalled that in neurotics there was a significant tendency towards curvilinearity, while in normal subjects the correlation between threshold and spiral after-effect was zero. The comparison based on these larger samples is illustrated in Fig. 7.3. There the regression line for all sixty-seven untreated psychotics is shown, together with the best-fit curve for the 168 neurotic patients, whose scores were plotted individually in Fig. 4.2 of Chapter 4 (p. 61).

Also shown in Fig. 7.3 are the scores for the thirty-four normal subjects tested.

A number of points should be noted. First, the range of scores—approximately represented in the respective lengths of the regression line and parabola—is considerably less in psychotics than in neurotics. Secondly, the tendency towards decreasing threshold with increasing SAE in neurotics begins to appear beyond about 30

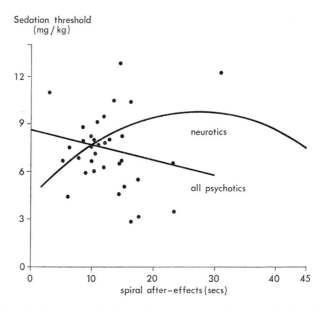

FIG. 7.3. Summary of relationship between sedation threshold and spiral after-effect in neurotics and psychotics. The individual scores for thirty-four normal subjects are also shown.

seconds, that is near the end of the range for the spiral after-effect in psychotics. Within the range 0–30 seconds the relationship between the two tests in neurotics is reasonably linear, the product moment correlation in fact being significantly positive, as will be recalled from Chapter 4. Thirdly, the status of normal subjects within the framework illustrated in Fig. 7.3 is unpredictable. As can be seen there, they appear to be scattered over the whole range of scores found in neurotic and psychotic patients. The possible significance of this group of findings will be considered later.

Further analysis of the ST/SAE performance of psychotics was possible using several scores extracted from the data. The most obvious were the absolute values for the sedation threshold and spiral after-effect themselves. A measure of each individual's departure from "normality" could also be obtained, following the procedure described by Herrington and Claridge (*op. cit.*). They entered the SAE value for each psychotic in one of the regression equations for their combined neurotic–normal group. The difference between the sedation threshold value estimated from this equation and the patient's actual threshold thus provided a measure of that individual's departure from "normality". This measure could, of course, be used ignoring or taking account of the sign of the deviation.

In the present analysis, because of the subsequent findings for the non-patient group, the performance of neurotics only was considered to provide a more logical criterion of "normality". It was also decided to use the appropriate regression equation for linear, rather than parabolic, regression. There were two reasons for this decision. First, as noted earlier, the ST/SAE relationship in neurotics was, in any case, linear over most of the range covered by psychotics. Secondly, inspection of the plotted scores for neurotics indicated that, up to an SAE value of about 30 seconds, a linear regression line provided a better fit to the data than the rising part of the parabola which was somewhat "flattened" by a preponderance of subjects in the middle range.

The regression equation for predicting sedation threshold (y) from spiral after-effect (x) in the sample of 168 neurotic patients was $y = 6 \cdot 619 + 0 \cdot 116x$. The convention followed in calculating each psychotic patient's deviation from the line described by this equation was to subtract his estimated threshold from its actual value. Where the sign was taken account of, a positive value thus indicated a higher actual threshold than would be predicted from the patient's SAE, and vice versa. Where the sign was ignored the size of the deviation simply indicated, of course, the patient's degree of departure from "normality", irrespective of its direction.

Where previously published results involving this deviation measure are referred to below they will, of course, be based on the regression equation given in the paper cited. However, although the deviation value for any particular individual may be changed a little, the trends over groups are unlikely to be altered to any significant degree by the use of slightly different regression coefficients.

AUTONOMIC CORRELATES

The autonomic dysfunction found in the psychoses is, of course, well-known (Shattock, 1950) and this fact has led some authors to postulate in these illnesses a primary disturbance of the central mechanisms regulating autonomic activity (Gellhorn, 1953). The implications of this interpretation for an arousal theory of the functional disorders, including schizophrenia, have been discussed by Duffy (1962), who has reviewed a variety of studies on the autonomic physiology of the psychotic patient. Duffy suggests that results in this area are sufficiently consistent to make them capable of being handled eventually within a theory of the arousal type. In common with other reviewers, however, she reaches the now familiar conclusion that psychotics are very heterogeneous on autonomic measures, a heterogeneity that has been recently demonstrated by Rubin (1960, 1962) in a series of studies of the pupillary response in schizophrenic patients.

It is logical to enquire whether there is any parallel variation in the sedation threshold and autonomic response of psychotics. It will be recalled that this was so in neurotics, where raised barbiturate tolerance was consistently correlated with increased sympathetic reactivity. If a similar relationship could be demonstrated in psychotics then this would provide further support for the arousal hypothesis. It might also help to account for some of the variable findings from previous studies of psychosis.

In addition to the skin conductance and heart rate measures monitored during the vigilance experiment, data for this part of the research was obtained from an investigation of the Mecholyl and cold pressor tests in some patients from the psychotic sample. Of these two procedures most previous work in psychotic patients has been done on the Mecholyl test, principally with the aim of predicting the response to ECT in depressive states. Attempts to differentiate various clinical groups by means of the test have produced conflicting results, Funkenstein and his colleagues noting that the variety of blood pressure responses to Mecholyl cuts across diagnostic categories (Funkenstein *et al.*, 1948, 1949). In these studies there was, however, a greater tendency for psychotic depressives to show a hypotensive reaction, that is a prolonged BP fall in response to the drug. Schizophrenics showed a variety of responses, a result also reported by Alexander (1955) and Jones

(1956). Both of these authors agreed with Funkenstein in finding a greater tendency towards hyporeaction in depressives. In a study preceding all of these Altman *et al.* (1943) showed that hebephrenic patients were characterized by even greater hypotensive responses than depressives of the manic-depressive type.

Sloane *et al.* (1957) reported, however, that acute schizophrenics differed from depressives in responding to Mecholyl with a small initial fall and a pronounced secondary rise in blood pressure following injection. They interpreted this result as evidence against the view that schizophrenics show a sluggish response to stress. Gellhorn and Loofbourrow (1963), on the other hand, summarizing their own extensive work with the Mecholyl test, claimed that first-admission schizophrenics did not differ from chronic patients. While reiterating their view that response to the drug measures central sympathetic reactivity, they reached the now somewhat obvious conclusion that both hypo- and hyper-reactors were more frequent among psychotics than in control groups.

Systematic study of the cold pressor test in psychosis appears to have been confined to schizophrenic patients, who on average have been found to show a diminished blood pressure rise, or even a paradoxical fall, in response to this stress (Igersheimer, 1953; Earle and Earle, 1955). The latter authors, and also Glaser (1952), demonstrated that this sympathetic hyporeactivity tended, however, to be most marked in hebephrenic schizophrenics, paranoid patients showing a more normal cold pressor response.

Since it has been suggested that rise in blood pressure on the cold pressor test is proportional to the degree of pain experienced (Wolff, 1951), studies of pain responsiveness as such are perhaps relevant here. In his survey of experiments in this area Hall (1953) concluded that they were few in number, though he and his colleagues demonstrated that endogenous depressives appeared to be very insensitive to pain (Hemphill *et al.*, 1952). This perhaps suggests a low degree of autonomic arousability in these patients. In early schizophrenics Malmo and Shagass (1949a), measuring a number of physiological variables, including GSR and EKG, demonstrated a high degree of autonomic response to pain. These patients resembled anxiety neurotics in this respect. In another study the same authors (Malmo and Shagass, 1952) measured only blood pressure and again found a similarity between acute psychotics and neurotics, confined however to measures of pre-stress level. Chronic schizophrenics differed most significantly from other subjects in showing a high resting diastolic blood pressure.

The variability of these and other findings reported in the vast literature on the subject made it difficult to formulate precise hypotheses about the outcome of the present study. Theoretical considerations provided some general guidance in so far as, on the basis of the earlier work with neurotics, it was expected that sympathetic reactivity might be greater in psychotic patients with high sedation thresholds and low spiral after-effects. The apparent dissociation between the sedation threshold and spiral after-effect, however, suggested a complex disturbance of arousal in psychosis. The investigations reported below were therefore largely exploratory. As anticipated, an intricate picture emerged, particularly with respect to the Mecholyl test, where a large number of measures were intercorrelated, both before and after treatment. Many of the correlations did not permit a simple interpretation and, in the case of the post-treatment measures, involved very small samples. In this, and later sections where the autonomic data are referred to again, the discussion will be confined, therefore, to results that bear directly on the findings of previous workers and are relevant to the theoretical model under review.

Mecholyl Test[1]

The Mecholyl test was administered to twenty-one psychotics, following the procedure described by Wawman *et al.* (1963). The four measures derived from the data for each subject were Basal Systolic BP, Basal Diastolic BP, Mean Systolic BP Change, and Mean Diastolic BP Change. A full description of the criteria used for obtaining these measures has already been given in Chapter 3 (p. 32).

Table 1 shows the correlations between each of the four measures and the sedation threshold and spiral after-effect. Considering the sedation threshold first, it can be seen from Table 1 that there was no correlation between this measure and the change in systolic blood pressure, though the correlation with the change in diastolic pressure was positive and marginally significant at the 10 per cent level of confidence. Both measures of basal blood pressure also correlated positively with sedation threshold, but only in the case of the

[1] The author is grateful to Dr. R. N. Herrington for making these data available for analysis.

TABLE 1. CORRELATIONS OF SEDATION THRESHOLD AND SPIRAL AFTER-EFFECT
WITH FOUR MEASURES FROM MECHOLYL TEST (N = 21)

	Basal Systolic BP	Basal Diastolic BP	Mean Systolic BP Change	Mean Diastolic BP Change
Sedation threshold	+0·32 N.S.	+0·39 $p < 0·1$	−0·13 N.S.	+0·38 $p < 0·1$
Spiral after-effect	+0·05 N.S.	+0·23 N.S.	−0·13 N.S.	−0·28 N.S.

diastolic pressure did the correlation reach significance. Results for the spiral after-effect were even less clear-cut, none of the correlations being significant. There was, however, a slight tendency for diastolic blood pressure change to be greater in those with low SAE's.

Further examination of the data revealed two other findings of interest, though neither added much further information to that already described. First, there was a positive correlation of +0·37 (N = 21, $p < 0·1$) between diastolic change and the deviation measure ignoring the sign. This result simply confirmed the correlation of the same order between diastolic change and the threshold itself. Secondly, there was a significant negative correlation of −0·46 ($p < 0·05$) between sedation threshold and pulse pressure change following injection. That is, patients with high thresholds tended to show a greater reduction in pulse pressure in response to Mecholyl. This latter finding again probably reflects the relatively greater rise in diastolic pressure and therefore the presumably greater increase in peripheral resistance in high threshold psychotics.

One final aspect of the data should be mentioned. Rather unexpectedly, as will be discussed fully later, a significant positive association was found between age and sedation threshold in psychotics. Since it has been shown that response to Mecholyl varies with age (Nelson and Gellhorn, 1957, 1958), it seemed possible that the age variable might contaminate the relationship between sedation threshold and blood pressure change. However, within the narrow range covered by the present sample, age did not appear to be a significant variable affecting the results and it was given no further consideration.

In conclusion it can perhaps be said that there was a slight tendency for sympathetic reactivity on the Mecholyl test to be greater in psychotics with high sedation thresholds and low spiral after-effects. The general pattern of the results is clearly very different, however, from that found in neurotics. There it was systolic rather than diastolic change that showed the closest association with sedation threshold, while the basal blood pressure measures did not correlate highly at all with barbiturate tolerance.

Cold Pressor Test

The cold pressor response was measured in twelve psychotics according to the procedure described by Claridge *et al.* (1963). The four measures taken from the test were those given in Chapter 3 viz. Basal Systolic BP, Basal Diastolic BP, Systolic BP Change, and Diastolic BP Change. Correlations between these measures and the sedation threshold and spiral after-effect are shown in Table 2. It can be seen that in neither case was there a significant correlation

TABLE 2. CORRELATIONS OF SEDATION THRESHOLD AND SPIRAL AFTER-EFFECT WITH FOUR MEASURES FROM THE COLD PRESSOR TEST (N = 12)

	Basal Systolic BP	Basal Diastolic BP	Systolic BP Change	Diastolic BP Change
Sedation threshold	+0·14 N.S.	+0·36 N.S.	+0·17 N.S.	−0·03 N.S.
Spiral after-effect	−0·03 N.S.	−0·39 N.S.	−0·48 N.S.	−0·46 N.S.

with the autonomic indices, though the trend of results followed that found on the Mecholyl test. There was a moderate positive correlation between basal diastolic pressure and sedation threshold, while all four cold pressor measures correlated negatively with the spiral after-effect. There was again a slight tendency, therefore, for sympathetic reactivity to be greater in High ST/Low SAE psychotics.

Other Measures

It will be recalled from the previous chapter that measures of level and rate of change in skin conductance and heart rate were collected on thirteen psychotic patients during performance of the auditory vigilance task. In no case, however, was there a significant correlation between any of these autonomic measures and either the sedation threshold or the spiral after-effect. In the case of the threshold, values for r were all near-zero. This was also true with respect to the spiral after-effect and the measures of rate of change, though SAE did show small negative correlations with levels of both heart rate and skin conductance. The values for r here were respectively $-0 \cdot 25$ and $-0 \cdot 39$. Neither of these correlations was significant, but they did follow the trends found in the Mecholyl and cold pressor tests.

In view of the obvious autonomic instability of the psychotic patient, particularly the diurnal variability of his responses, it is of interest to consider briefly here the extent of intercorrelation between some of the autonomic measures themselves. In the case of the only two functions monitored simultaneously, heart rate and skin conductance, the correlation was surprisingly high, the value for r between the level measures of these two variables being $+0 \cdot 74$ ($N = 13$, $p < 0 \cdot 02$). The blood pressure measures from the cold pressor test correlated less well with skin conductance and heart rate, though both showed a consistent positive association with basal systolic blood pressure. Values for r here were $+0 \cdot 45$ ($N = 10$, N.S.) in the case of skin conductance and $+0 \cdot 41$ ($N = 11$, N.S.) in the case of heart rate. The latter also correlated $+0 \cdot 40$ (N.S.) with basal diastolic blood pressure. The order of these correlations was not markedly different, therefore, from that found in neurotic and normal subjects.

Despite these trends, the known fluctuations in the physiology of the psychotic patient must undoubtedly be regarded as a major factor contributing to the findings in this part of the research. In this respect the behaviour of one patient from the sample is worth recalling. It was intended that this patient should be a subject for the vigilance experiment, but attempts to record his skin resistance level on two consecutive days were unsuccessful. On the first day his resistance level proved to be so low that it was unrecordable, his hands being found to be literally dripping perspiration in pools on to the floor. The next day his hands appeared to be excessively dry and, in fact, his resistance level was too high to be recorded.

This, admittedly extreme, case illustrates the importance of taking serial measures of autonomic response in psychotic patients. The failure to do so was clearly a weakness of the present research. The conclusions to be drawn from it can therefore only be tentative, and based on the additive effect of a number of similar but marginally significant findings, rather than on any single result. Looked at in this way, it can perhaps be concluded that there is some, obviously complex, relationship between peripheral indices of arousal level and ST/SAE performance. This is shown rather more in the negative correlations between autonomic measures and spiral after-effect than in any direct positive association with the sedation threshold itself.

CLINICAL CORRELATES

Type of Illness

The most convenient way of considering the data in relation to the subtype of psychosis was in terms of the ST/SAE deviation measures described earlier. The distribution of diagnoses according to the degree of departure from the neurotic regression line was therefore considered, both taking account of and ignoring the sign of the deviation. For this purpose the total sample of sixty-seven patients was divided each time into two groups. Because of the odd number of subjects one patient was assigned at random in each case.

Where the sign of the deviation was taken account of, this procedure gave thirty-three subjects showing moderate to high negative deviation (Low ST/High SAE) and thirty-four subjects, twenty of whom showed positive deviation (High ST/Low SAE) and fourteen low negative deviation. The distribution of diagnoses over these two groups is shown in Table 3, where it should be noted that the patient assigned randomly fell into the hebephrenic, or most frequently diagnosed, subtype of schizophrenia. The most obvious finding in Table 3 is the consistent behaviour of paranoid patients, all seven of whom fell into the positive/low negative group. Six of these paranoids, in fact, showed positive deviation, i.e. had high sedation thresholds relative to their spiral after-effects. Hebephrenics were almost exactly evenly divided between the two groups, while there was a slight preponderance of simple schizophrenics in the high negative group. Little can be concluded from the remaining results because of the small number of subjects, but it is perhaps interesting to note that the only hypomanic patient tested resembled the paranoid schizophrenics.

Results disregarding the sign of deviation are shown in Table 4. As before, the one patient assigned at random was diagnosed as

TABLE 3. DISTRIBUTION OF TYPE OF PSYCHOSIS ACCORDING TO DEGREE OF DEVIATION FROM NEUROTIC REGRESSION LINE, TAKING ACCOUNT OF SIGN

	Paranoid	Hebephrenic	Simple	Unclassified	Hypomanic	Depressive	Schizo-affective
Positive or low negative deviation (High ST/Low SAE)	7	16	4	5	1	1	0
High negative deviation (Low ST/High SAE)	0	18	7	5	0	2	1

TABLE 4. DISTRIBUTION OF TYPE OF PSYCHOSIS ACCORDING TO DEGREE OF DEVIATION FROM NEUROTIC REGRESSION LINE, IGNORING THE SIGN

	Paranoid	Hebephrenic	Simple	Unclassified	Hypomanic	Depressive	Schizo-affective
High deviation	1	16	7	6	0	2	1
Low deviation	6	18	4	4	1	1	0

hebephrenic. The distribution of diagnoses shown in Table 4 resembles that of Table 3 in many respects. Paranoid patients again stand out from other psychotics. Six out of seven tended to deviate little from "normality", in the sense that they were most similar to neurotics. Hebephrenics were evenly scattered into those showing high and those showing low absolute departure from the neurotic regression line.

Taking the results for both tables together, it can be concluded that paranoid patients seem to be most "normal" of all psychotics and show high sedation thresholds relative to other psychotic patients. Simple schizophrenics show a slight tendency towards lower thresholds and greater absolute deviation from "normality" than other patients. Equivocal findings emerge for hebephrenic patients who may show both high and low absolute and relative deviations from the neurotic regression line. Some caution is necessary in interpreting these results because of the known unreliability of psychiatric diagnosis, particularly with respect to the subtyping of psychosis. Nevertheless, there does seem to be some systematic relationship between the psychophysiological status of the psychotic patient and the subcategory to which he is assigned. This is most marked in the case of paranoids, a finding which supports the increasing evidence that paranoid patients stand out as a distinctly different group from other schizophrenics (see Venables, 1964).

Age and Duration of Illness

An accurate assessment of the duration of illness was not made in all patients seen and the most reliable information concerning this variable comes from the original sample reported on by Herrington and Claridge (1965). Using the deviation measure and disregarding its sign, they demonstrated a significant tendency for greater deviation from "normality" to be associated with longer duration of illness. Only limited conclusions can, of course, be drawn from this finding, since all of the patients were acutely ill, the length of illness being assessed as greater or less than 6 months. The result may partly reflect variations in the severity of illness, which while presumably correlated with duration is not identical with it. In this respect we should recall that, as noted earlier, patients who recovered, and were perhaps therefore less ill, also tended to deviate less from "normality" than those who did not respond to treatment.

In the Herrington and Claridge study neither the sedation threshold nor the spiral after-effect themselves correlated with duration of illness, though in the larger group described here there was a significant positive correlation between age and threshold, the value for r being $+0\cdot40$ (N $= 67$, $p < 0\cdot001$). This was rather unexpected in view of the fact that in neither neurotics nor normals was any significant relationship between age and threshold found, the respective correlations in these two groups being $+0\cdot18$ and $+0\cdot07$.

The explanation of the apparently discrepant result in psychotics probably lies in the covariation between age and type of illness, viz. the later presentation of paranoid psychoses in which, as noted above, high thresholds tended to predominate. This explanation is confirmed by the fact that there was also a significant positive correlation between age and deviation taking account of the sign, the value for r here being $+0 \cdot 40$ (N $= 67$, $p < 0 \cdot 001$). Thus the older individuals tended to be those with high thresholds and low spiral after-effects, a pattern most typical of paranoids. One might have supposed that the age finding was due to a relationship between sedation threshold and chronicity or severity of illness. That the result was not due to this would tend to be supported by the low and non-significant correlation of $-0 \cdot 16$ between age and deviation disregarding the sign, a measure shown above to be related to both duration and severity of psychosis.

Process–Reactive Classification

An approach to the problem of heterogeneity in the psychoses that has been favoured by some workers, particularly in the United States, is their subdivision in terms of process–reactive factors. This classification is based on the assumption that the schizophrenias fall on a continuum the end-points of which are labelled "process" and "reactive", respectively. The process schizophrenic is said to be typically characterized by a slow insidious onset of illness, an inadequate premorbid personality, and a poor prognosis. By contrast, the illness of the reactive schizophrenic is said to occur in the setting of a reasonably normal premorbid personality, to be significantly related to external stress, and to carry a good prognosis.

Considerable experimental work has been carried out at various levels of function in order to determine the psychological and physiological correlates of the process–reactive continuum. Some of the more recent and important studies in this area, as well as the process–reactive concept itself, have been critically appraised by Higgins (1964). There appear to have been no previous studies of the sedation threshold in this context, though a number of workers have tried to discriminate process and reactive schizophrenics in terms of the Mecholyl test. Results here have been contradictory, some experiments demonstrating that the reactive schizophrenic is autonomically hyperresponsive (King, 1958) and others that the opposite is true (Zuckerman and Grosz, 1959). In a study of critical flicker fusion and the spiral after-effect McDonough (1960), using an all-or-none criterion for perception of the latter, demonstrated that it did not differentiate process and reactive patients.

In two unpublished studies three colleagues of the present writer have attempted to link the process–reactive classification of psychosis with variations in ST/SAE performance. In both cases only part of the total sample was available for what were retrospective studies of the patients' histories and eventual disposal. The first investigation was carried out by Hume and Treacher who examined the case-notes of forty-seven of the patients studied here and rated each according to the Premorbid History (PMH) section of the Phillips Prognostic Scale for assessing process–reactive factors in schizophrenia (Phillips, 1953). In its complete form the latter consists of three parts, though it is claimed that the PMH correlates very highly with the full scale (Seidel, 1960).

Hume and Treacher found zero or near-zero correlations between PMH score and sedation threshold, spiral after-effect, and the deviation measure disregarding the sign. Using a cut-off score of three points on the PMH scale they classified sixteen cases as reactive and thirty-one as process patients. The mean scores of these two groups were almost identical on both the sedation threshold and spiral after-effect.

In an extension to this study the same workers considered only prognosis on discharge, using as their criterion the nature of each patient's disposal. Here thirty-nine patients were assigned to one of the following three categories:

> Good—discharged to next of kin without maintenance therapy.
> Fair—discharged to next of kin with maintenance therapy.
> Poor—discharged to a civilian mental hospital.

The mean sedation threshold and spiral after-effect for these three categories are shown in Table 5, where it can be seen that in

TABLE 5. SEDATION THRESHOLD AND SPIRAL AFTER-EFFECT
IN RELATION TO PROGNOSIS ON DISCHARGE (HUME AND TREACHER)

		Good	Fair	Poor
Sedation threshold	N	5	24	10
	Mean	7·95	7·41	8·01
	SD	2·27	1·81	2·02
Spiral after-effect	Mean	13·55	15·41	18·35
	SD	4·31	7·37	4·81

no case was there a significant relationship with prognosis, at least as assessed in this way. A finding of interest, however, in view of results to be reported below was the orderly, but non-significant, increase in spiral after-effect with worsening prognosis.

In a later investigation Wawman estimated the process–reactive status of forty-four patients from the present sample, using the criteria shown in Table 6. Of this group of patients sixteen were regarded as process and ten as reactive cases, while eighteen were assigned to an indeterminate category. Before discussing Wawman's findings we should perhaps comment briefly on the extent of agreement between his categorization of patients and that of Hume and

TABLE 6. CRITERIA USED BY WAWMAN TO ASSESS
PROCESS–REACTIVE STATUS

1. Duration of hospitalization.
2. Estimated duration of illness prior to admission.
3. Premorbid personality (good, fair, poor, bad).
4. Estimated extent of recovery (complete, much improved, improved, unchanged, worse).
5. Disposal (civilian mental hospital, next of kin, own care with psychiatric after-care, return to duty).
6. Extent of treatment, e.g. whether spontaneous remission.
7. Whether on treatment when discharged.
8. Relevance of environmental stress (important, possible, irrelevant).

Treacher using the PMH score. Because there was not complete overlap in the samples of patients studied this could only be done for a proportion of the cases. However, of nine cases assigned by Wawman to the process category eight were also considered to be process patients by Hume and Treacher. Agreement was rather poorer in the reactive group, three out of seven of Wawman's reactive patients being classified as process cases by Hume and Treacher. The latter regarded ten out of fourteen patients in Wawman's indeterminate group as falling into the process category.

The discussion here will be confined to Wawman's two extreme groups, ST/SAE performance data of which are shown in Table 7. It can be seen that process patients had significantly lower sedation thresholds and longer spiral after-effects than reactive patients. The results for the spiral, though not for the threshold, thus paralleled the trend reported by Hume and Treacher, using prognosis alone as a criterion. This is perhaps not too surprising in view of Wawman's heavy reliance on prognostic signs in his assessment of process–reactive status.

As also shown in Table 7, there were significant differences between the groups on the deviation measure, both ignoring and regarding sign. Process patients showed a significantly greater absolute deviation from the neurotic regression line and also deviated in a negative direction—i.e. towards low threshold and high spiral after-effect—to a significantly greater degree than reactive patients. The latter finding, of course, reflects the lower absolute sedation thresholds in

TABLE 7. SEDATION THRESHOLD AND SPIRAL AFTER-EFFECT IN RELATION TO PROCESS–REACTIVE STATUS (WAWMAN)

		Process patients	Reactive patients	t	p
Sedation threshold	N	16	10		
	Mean	6·13	7·70	4·13	0·001
	SD	1·28	0·97		
Spiral after-effect	Mean	19·62	12·00	2·97	0·01
	SD	5·37	6·92		
ST/SAE deviation (regarding sign)	Mean	−2·53	−0·07	4·71	0·001
	SD	1·15	1·36		
ST/SAE deviation (ignoring sign)	Mean	2·53	1·14	3·66	0·002
	SD	1·15	0·80		

process schizophrenics; while the former result is consistent with Herrington and Claridge's demonstration that before treatment unrecovered patients depart more from "normality" than recovered patients. These authors did not, however, find any difference in the absolute pre-treatment values for threshold and spiral in their two subgroups.

The trend of Wawman's results suggests that there may be some relationship between the process–reactive classification and the breakdown of the sample in terms of type of illness, reported in a previous section. Examination of the data revealed that Wawman's group of ten reactive patients contained four of the seven paranoid psychotics tested during the research programme. The remainder of his reactive group was made up of three hebephrenic, one simple, and two unclassified schizophrenics. His process group consisted almost entirely of hebephrenic patients, twelve out of sixteen falling into this category. The remaining four cases were either unclassified (one patient) or diagnosed as simple schizophrenics.

The main conclusion to be drawn from these findings is that there does seem to be some general relationship between prognosis, assessed in various ways, and ST/SAE performance as reflected either in the absolute values of the measures themselves or in their relative departure from "normality", or in both. The evidence does not permit any more precise statement than this, especially as differences in the criteria of prognosis make comparisons between the various results difficult. The studies both by Hume and Treacher and by Wawman suffer from the hazards of retrospective enquiries, but they do perhaps provide some guidance for undertaking more systematic investigations.

Support for the process–reactive classification of psychosis remains uncertain. Although in assessing a patient's position on the process–reactive continuum reliance is placed on prognostic signs, the concept, almost by definition, also emphasizes the importance of premorbid personality and of precipitating factors in psychosis. When these were assessed by Hume and Treacher using a standard rating scale the findings were inconclusive, though this may have been due again to the retrospective nature of the study and the unreliability of hospital case-histories as a source of evidence. In the Wawman enquiry the patients' histories were only superficially examined and so its results throw little light on this aspect of the process–reactive concept.

The concept seems in any case to be somewhat unsatisfactory since it appears to overlap with and be compounded of other features of psychosis such as type of illness and chronicity. The evidence cited here, for example, suggests that some paranoid schizophrenics have characteristics typical of reactive psychosis, even though the two methods of classification may not coincide. Similarly, many acutely ill patients will be classified as process schizophrenics. So, however, will almost all chronic schizophrenics who, by virtue of the nature of their illness, inevitably fall into that category. Yet one of the most marked features of the psychoses are the psychological and physiological differences between the acute and chronic phases of the illnesses.

Those workers favouring the process–reactive classification of schizophrenia have, on the other hand, focused attention on qualities of the psychotic patient and his illness that may prove, as descriptive items, to have correlates with the underlying psychophysiological disturbance. In future investigations, however, it may be better to avoid the crude categorization of patients into "reactive" or "process". A more profitable approach would be to consider separately such factors as premorbid personality and environmental stress and to assess their influence as a source of individual variation, alongside the many other variables affecting the nature and course of the psychoses.

Activity Level and Thought Disorder

Recent experimental work has suggested that a promising approach to the problem of classifying the psychoses is to describe precisely or statistically isolate discrete and easily definable "dimensions" or areas of behaviour in the psychotic patient. One attempt to do this with respect to chronic schizophrenia has been made by Venables, who in a series of studies has related variations along behavioural continua of social activity–withdrawal and paranoid/non-paranoid psychosis to psychophysiological measures of arousal (Venables, 1960; Venables and Wing, 1962).

In a rather different group of experiments Payne and his co-workers have investigated the factors determining psychotic thought disorder (Payne et al., 1959; Payne and Hewlett, 1960). The latter authors demonstrated that performance on a large battery of tests was partly accounted for by two correlated factors which they identified as "overinclusion" and "retardation". They reported that overinclusive thinking was marked in some schizophrenics but was not present in all patients carrying this diagnosis. Some schizophrenics in their sample of acute patients showed little disturbance of thought content, but resembled endogenous depressives in being abnormally slow and retarded in their thought processes. Payne and Hewlett tentatively concluded that overinclusive thinking might be more characteristic of the paranoid and retarded thinking of the non-paranoid schizophrenic.

The behavioural continua described by both Payne and Venables to some extent cut across the traditional subclassification of the psychoses, though like the process–reactive dimension some overlap is clearly evident. Further, despite the different orientations from which they were carried out and the different kinds of patient studied, both groups of experiments appear to be tapping somewhat similar aspects of psychotic behaviour. There is, for example, at least some superficial resemblance between Payne's retardation and Venables' withdrawal dimensions; while, as noted above, Payne has linked overinclusion specifically with the paranoid reaction type. Both authors have suggested a relationship between psychotic behaviour and an underlying dysfunction of arousal and attention. Payne (1960), for example, has postulated a breakdown of filtering mechanisms in the CNS to account for overinclusion; while Venables (1963a) has demonstrated that selectivity or narrowing of attention— perhaps the reciprocal of overinclusion—varies with arousal level in chronic psychotics. Although Venables has laid more stress on psychophysiological parameters than Payne, the similarity between their two approaches led us to investigate the possible co-variation between ST/SAE performance and such behavioural features of psychosis as activity level, retardation, and thought disorder. For this reason, and because of the results that subsequently emerged, it is appropriate to consider all of these here under the same heading.

Using clinical ratings of mood disturbance and thought disorder, as well as the Venables Activity Rating Scale (Venables, 1957), Herrington and Claridge (1965) demonstrated systematic relationships with the continuous variation in performance from High ST/Low SAE to Low ST/High SAE. Psychotics with high thresholds and short spiral after-effects were found to show a significantly higher level of activity and a significantly greater degree of thought disorder and mood deviation than those with low thresholds and long after-effects to the spiral. There was also a non-significant tendency towards increased affective flattening in patients with long after-effects and low thresholds.

In a subsequent sample the possibility was investigated that the relationship between ST/SAE performance and activity level might also be revealed with respect to the MPI scores of psychotics. The correlations between SAE and both scales of this questionnaire were near-zero, however. There were, on the other hand, slight positive correlations between sedation threshold and both extraversion and neuroticism. The values for r were $+0.32$ and $+0.34$ respectively. Neither of these correlations was significant for the rather small sample of fifteen subjects. The tendency towards slightly increased extraversion in high threshold psychotics is, however, theoretically consistent with the other findings and is perhaps worth investigating further on a larger sample.

The finding that clinically rated thought disorder is greater in High ST/Low SAE patients was later confirmed by Claridge *et al.* (1966) using a more objective measure of conceptual thinking, the Payne Object Classification Test (Payne, 1962). Here the subject is required to sort twelve objects into groups according to their various characteristics, such as shape, colour, size and so on. Payne (*op. cit.*) has claimed that the Non-A score on the test—the number of incorrect sortings—is a measure of overinclusive thinking.

Claridge *et al.* (1966) demonstrated that psychotics with high sedation thresholds produced a significantly greater number of Non-A sortings than those with low thresholds, though no relationship with the spiral after-effect was found. The latter result led them to analyse the sorting test responses in more detail. It was argued that the sorting methods produced by psychotics on the Payne test are so heterogeneous that it is doubtful whether they should be considered under one general heading such as "overinclusion". The Non-A responses of each patient were therefore assigned to one of three categories: overinclusive, abstract–bizarre, and concrete–bizarre. Overinclusive responses were strictly defined as those where the patient attempted to sort the objects as instructed, but was unable to confine himself to one concept, such as shape. The other two categories referred to sorting methods in which the patient made no use at all of the required concepts, but formed patterns with the test pieces and gave explanations in terms either of abstract ideas or concrete objects.

Breakdown of the responses in this way revealed that overinclusive sortings were significantly more common in patients with short spiral after-effects and in those who deviated from the neurotic regression line in the direction of High ST/Low SAE. Abstract–bizarre sortings were also slightly more frequent in the latter group and it was suggested that such responses may reflect, in a more extreme form, the loosening of conceptual boundaries assumed to underlie overinclusive thinking. Concrete–bizarre sortings were common to all psychotics, though they formed a rather higher proportion of the responses produced by patients with low thresholds and long spiral after-effects. Thus, while such patients produced few responses anyway on the test, if they did so these tended to be of a concrete–bizarre type. It was concluded that the latter kind of response, far from reflecting overinclusive thinking, probably arose as a result of constriction or poverty of thought.

An interesting feature of this experiment was that some of the relationships between sorting test and ST/SAE performance were not confined to psychotic patients, but appeared in neurotic and normal subjects as well. There was, for example, a significant positive correlation between sedation threshold and the total output of responses on the Payne test, i.e. the sum of the correct and incorrect sortings. In psychotics this was not unexpected because of the significant correlation, already mentioned, between threshold and Non-A responses considered alone. However, similar correlations were found in the neurotic and normal groups, the only difference between neurotics and psychotics being that in the former the correlation was largely due to a positive association between sedation threshold and the number of *correct* sortings produced. It was demonstrated that this relationship was not due to a co-variation with intelligence and suggested that it may reflect a greater "drive" level in high threshold patients, whatever their diagnosis. This interpretation would be consistent with the tendency for psychotics with high thresholds to show greater activity as rated on the Venables scale.

The other finding that should be mentioned concerns the behaviour of the normal group used in the experiment. Rather unexpectedly four control subjects showed extreme deviation in ST/SAE performance. Three had long spiral after-effects and very low sedation thresholds; the fourth a very high threshold and an abnormally short after-effect. The extent of their deviation in ST/SAE performance can be judged from Fig. 7.3 on page 144, where their scores were included with those of other control subjects for comparison with psychotic and neurotic patients.

Three of these control subjects showed a highly abnormal performance on the Payne test, characterized by patterning responses. The High ST/Low SAE subject was most disturbed in this respect and, despite his superior intelligence level, had considerable difficulty in understanding the instructions for the test. After making only one correct response he continued to produce four Non-A sortings of a very bizarre kind. One of these deviant "normals" was subsequently found to be a florid homosexual, although a 2-year follow-up of the other three subjects revealed no overt evidence of psychiatric abnormality.

Returning to the psychotic sample, subsequent analysis has uncovered further, previously unpublished evidence, supporting the results already described here. This evidence mainly concerns the relationship between sorting test performance and the autonomic measures described earlier. The correlations between these two sets of data are brought together in Table 8. The sorting test measures considered there are the three sub-categories of the Non-A score discussed above. The Non-A score itself was not included since in no case did it correlate consistently or significantly with any autonomic measure, a finding which itself provides some validity for the breakdown of this category made by Claridge et al. (1966). Because of the apparent similarity between the overinclusive and abstract–bizarre responses a measure of the sum of these two scores was included in the analysis. The correlations for this measure are also shown in Table 8.

Inspection of this table reveals an internally consistent pattern of correlations, despite the small samples involved. Considering skin conductance and heart rate first, it can be seen that both over-inclusive and abstract–bizarre responses were significantly more frequent in patients with high initial levels of arousal. This was true whether these two sorting test scores were considered separately or in combination. The same relationship also held for basal systolic blood pressure on the cold pressor test, at a very high level of significance in the case of abstract–bizarre responses, which were much more common in patients with a high resting blood pressure. The remaining cold pressor indices showed poor correlations with sorting test performance, with the exception of a significant association between diastolic BP change and the concrete–bizarre measure. Apart from this latter correlation, concrete–bizarre responses were uniformly unrelated to autonomic activity, a fact which supports the earlier conclusion that sortings of this type differ from those classified as overinclusive or abstract–bizarre.

Two further findings should be mentioned here. The E-scale of the MPI was found to correlate positively and significantly with both the overinclusive and abstract–bizarre scores on the Object Classification Test, the values for r being, respectively, $+0 \cdot 57$ and $+0 \cdot 55$ ($N = 15$, $p < 0 \cdot 05$). When these two sorting test scores were combined they correlated $+0 \cdot 73$ ($p < 0 \cdot 01$) with the E-scale. This tendency for more extraverted psychotics to show greater thought content disorder is, therefore, consistent with the evidence described earlier relating the Payne test and the E-scale to ST/SAE performance.

TABLE 8. CORRELATIONS BETWEEN AUTONOMIC MEASURES AND VARIOUS CATEGORIES OF INCORRECT SORTING TEST RESPONSE

		Overinclusive	Abstract–bizarre	Overinclusive + abstract–bizarre	Concrete–bizarre
Cold pressor test measures (N = 12)	Basal Systolic BP	+0·51 $p < 0·1$	+0·86 $p < 0·001$	+0·72 $p < 0·01$	+0·30 N.S.
	Basal Diastolic BP	−0·11 N.S.	+0·39 N.S.	+0·09 N.S.	−0·12 N.S.
	Systolic BP Change	+0·24 N.S.	+0·15 N.S.	+0·23 N.S.	+0·44 N.S.
	Diastolic BP Change	+0·23 N.S.	+0·29 N.S.	+0·29 N.S.	+0·69 $p < 0·05$
Vigilance measures (N = 14)	Heart rate level	+0·36 N.S.	+0·52 $p < 0·1$	+0·46 $p < 0·1$	−0·12 N.S.
	Skin conductance level	+0·67 $p < 0·02$	+0·61 $p < 0·05$	+0·71 $p < 0·01$	−0·26 N.S.

Finally, the three Non-A score subcategories were found to be differentially related to intelligence, though the Non-A score itself was not correlated with this variable ($r = +0.17$, N = 13, N.S.) Matrices performance was significantly better in patients producing a greater number of abstract–bizarre sortings, r being $+0.5$ (N = 13, $p < 0.05$). Complementing this, tested intelligence was slightly, but not significantly, lower in those producing a greater number of concrete–bizarre sortings. The value for r here was -0.40 (N = 13, N.S.). Overinclusive responses were not significantly correlated with intelligence, r being $+0.20$.

These results clearly suggest a parallel variation in the psychophysiological status of acute psychotics and such clinical–behavioural features as thought disorder and social activity level. The kind of relationship found between these two strata of behaviour is also in keeping with the distribution of diagnoses along the ST/SAD continuum which, as we saw in a previous section, appears to approximate roughly to the paranoid/non-paranoid division of psychosis.

The sorting test findings are somewhat reminiscent of those reported by Meadow and his colleagues, who examined the relationship between response to the Mecholyl test and various tests of conceptual thinking. Meadow and Funkenstein (1952) demonstrated that the greatest impairment of abstract thinking occurred in those schizophrenics who showed a marked sympathetic overshoot in response to Mecholyl. Schizophrenics having a large and extended fall in BP had retained an intact capacity for abstract thinking. In a further paper Meadow et al. (1953) confirmed that in both acute and chronic schizophrenics there were significant correlations between impairment of abstraction capacity on a proverbs test and three measures from the Mecholyl test. Sympathetically more aroused patients were again found to be more impaired than those with hypotensive responses.

It should be noted that these results cannot be compared directly with our own, since, in carrying out his experiments, Meadow followed Goldstein's view of schizophrenic thought disorder as a shift towards more concrete thinking (Goldstein and Scheerer 1941). Here, of course, we have been more concerned with Cameron's overinclusion explanation (Cameron, 1938) and its subsequent modification by Payne and his colleagues. Payne and Hewlett (1960) claimed, in fact, that there was no evidence for greater concreteness of thinking in schizophrenics and that any thought impairment demonstrated was largely explicable in terms either of overinclusion or retardation, or both. Elsewhere Payne (1962) did suggest that concrete thinking might be measured by the number of correct responses (A-score) made on his test, though he maintained that, because of the correlation between the A-score and intelligence, it was impossible to distinguish operationally between lack of intelligence and concrete thinking.

From the present evidence there would appear to be some grounds for regarding psychotic thought disorder as a continuum running from the loosening of associations characteristic of overinclusion at one end to what we described earlier as the constriction or poverty of thought at the other. At the latter end there may be some overlap with Payne's retardation factor, on the one hand, and with features associated with concrete thinking and poor intelligence test performance, on the other. This hypothesis would find some support from the finding here that the affectively flattened, withdrawn, Low ST/High SAE psychotic shows a poor output of sortings on the Payne test and a high relative proportion of concrete–bizarre responses.

PERFORMANCE CORRELATES

On the basis of what had been found in neurotic patients it was expected that variations in sedation threshold and spiral after-effect might help to account for the variability of performance found in psychotics on such tests as vigilance and serial reaction time. On the whole the findings in this part of the research were suggestive rather than definitive and, because of the small samples, the conclusions to be drawn from them can only be regarded as tentative.

It will be recalled that in neurotics there was a significant association between sedation threshold and auditory vigilance performance. In psychotics this finding was replicated only to the extent that the correlation between threshold and total signals detected was positive, r being $+0 \cdot 39$. In the sample of only fourteen subjects this correlation was not significant. There was no discernible consistent pattern of correlations between vigilance and other measures derived either from the ST/SAE data or from the autonomic measures monitored during vigilance performance.

The most promising result that emerged with respect to vigilance concerned its possible relationship with some of the clinical features, in particular the process–reactive classification. Process–reactive ratings were available on fourteen subjects, seven of whom were classified as process and seven as reactive schizophrenics. The ratings used here were those made by Hume and Treacher in their study of the PMH to which we have already referred. Dividing the patients in this way, it was found that reactive psychotics showed far superior vigilance to process psychotics, the mean number of signals detected by these two subgroups being 22·1 and 7·7 respectively. The respective ranges were 15–27 and 0–20. Only one process patient in fact detected more than a third of the total signals presented on the test, while no reactive patient detected fewer than half this number.

The sample involved here was too small to make a detailed examination of performance in relation to illness type, though it is perhaps of interest that two of the seven reactive patients were diagnosed as paranoid schizophrenics, while no patient in the process group carried this diagnosis. Five of the process patients were diagnosed as either simple or hebephrenic schizophrenics. That the gross clinical features of psychosis were probably important determinants of vigilance efficiency was supported by the finding that at least one measure from the Object Classification Test showed a positive association with performance on the vigilance task. Total vigilance score correlated $+0·46$ ($N = 14$, $p < 0·1$) with the number of abstract–bizarre sortings, a type of response most commonly found in the more active High ST/Low SAE psychotic. It is apparent that no single characteristic of psychosis was an accurate predictor of vigilance performance; rather, it was the presence of a cluster of factors—associated with high sedation threshold—that seemed to favour relatively efficient auditory vigilance.

A similar conclusion could be reached about serial reaction time, where the only relationship with the ST/SAE scores was a significant correlation of $+0·64$ ($N = 13$, $p < 0·02$) between sedation threshold and rate of decline in serial reaction time. That is to say, high threshold psychotics tended to show a slower decrement in performance over time than low threshold psychotics. This result would be in keeping with the greater retardation thought to characterize the low threshold patient, a conclusion which finds further support in two correlations between serial reaction time and Object

Classification Test performance. There were correlations of -0.52 (N $= 13$, $p < 0.1$) and -0.65 ($p < 0.02$), respectively, between the concrete–bizarre response score and the level and slope measures from the reaction time task. In other words, psychotics performing in a concrete fashion on the sorting test were slower in psychomotor response and showed a steeper decline over time.

Although on this task the speed of performance tended to be more impaired in the retarded, low threshold patient, the opposite tended to be true of the error score. There was some evidence that errors in serial reaction time were more frequent in patients showing a high frequency of abstract–bizarre and overinclusive responses on the sorting test, the correlation between the error score and each of these OCT scores being, respectively, $+0.55$ (N $= 13$, $p < 0.1$) and $+0.66$ ($p < 0.02$). A possible explanation of this finding is that the five-choice reaction time situation acts as a distraction for the overinclusive patient.

It might have been supposed that the results from the Stroop test would have thrown some light on this hypothesis, since it will be recalled from earlier discussions of this task that greater distraction in colour- and word-naming would be expected in overinclusive psychotics, that is in patients assumed to show poor narrowing of attention. However, no relationship was found between any of the sorting test scores and Stroop performance. On the other hand, there was a significant negative correlation between total errors committed on both halves of the Stroop test and the spiral after-effect, the value for r being -0.72 (N $= 13$, $p < 0.01$). Thus, patients with low spiral after-effects tended to suffer more distraction when naming both words and colours. Since overinclusive responses were more frequent in patients with low SAE's, there was at least some indirect evidence that the process common to both of these measures also determined some aspects of Stroop performance. On theoretical grounds it might be supposed that this process was concerned with the mechanisms determining directed attention. As will be discussed in more detail in the following chapter, an attention dysfunction could account for the psychotic's performance on all three measures.

Results for the performance measures as a whole were clearly too complex to make any simple explanation of them possible, though they did reveal a number of trends that are worth investigating further using larger samples. One conclusion that can be reached with certainty is that performance on tasks of the kind described here is complicated by the more obvious clinical features of psychotic illness. This is especially true if we include among these the abnormalities found on tests of thought disorder. Clinical characteristics such as thinking difficulty, co-operativeness, and degree of contact with reality may obscure relationships between performance and simple psychophysiological variables. These latter relationships can often only be inferred from the independently demonstrable association between psychophysiological status and the behavioural symptoms of psychosis. Thus, on performance parameters such as speed of response, the High ST/Low SAE psychotic may be superior to his more retarded Low ST/High SAE counterpart; but this superiority will only be relative to the generally chaotic effect that any psychotic illness will have on psychological performance. On certain tasks an attention dysfunction such as overinclusion may slow down the performance of a psychotic who, in other respects, is potentially capable of relatively normal response. The end-result of both retardation and overinclusion may, therefore, be similar. The same conclusion has been reached by Payne and Hewlett (1960) who demonstrated a correlation between their two factors of overinclusion and retardation. They suggested that the overinclusive patient is handicapped by his tendency to consider too many alternative possibilities before he responds, an abnormality that will secondarily retard his performance.

Partialling out the multitude of factors affecting the psychotic's performance poses a major research problem that was by no means solved in the present study, though the positive results that did emerge were theoretically consistent with the findings from other parts of the research. The main value of the investigation was in focusing attention on what may be profitable areas for further study. By correct choice of parameters it may be possible to use performance tests to throw further light on the basic dysfunction underlying such clinical features of psychosis as thought content disorder. Of the experimental techniques described the colour-word (Stroop) test is perhaps the most promising and is certainly the most interesting. Observation of the patients' behaviour suggested that in the form used here the presentation of stimuli was probably too rapid. Performance seemed to represent a complex interaction between anxiety, psychomotor slowness, and perceptual difficulty. In a modified form, however, it may be possible to isolate the separate effects of these variables. Such an investigation would be well worth doing since the colour-word technique promises to be a particularly suitable method of investigating what is clearly a fundamental disorder in psychosis: a disturbance of the relationship between arousal level and the processing of sensory input into the nervous system.

DISCUSSION

In this chapter an attempt has been made to link together the various functional levels of psychotic behaviour, running from the descriptive clinical characteristics of psychosis, through performance measures, to psychophysiological variables. The value of this hierarchical approach has been well-established with respect to neurosis and its application to psychosis is equally promising. Compared with neurosis, of course, the problems encountered are conceptually more difficult, the links established more tenuous, and the theoretical framework guiding the research much less adequate. Nevertheless, there does seem to be a consistent theme running through the results which we shall try to summarize here.

Perhaps the most important single finding was the behaviour of psychotic patients on the spiral after-effect and sedation threshold. The theoretical implications of this result will be discussed in detail in the next chapter. In providing an empirical framework within which to investigate other aspects of psychosis it proved extremely valuable and justified our selection of it as an "anchor" for the subsequent research. For this reason the continuum of behaviour described by these two measures will be used as the basis for the present discussion.

In Table 9 the results from the various sections of the research are brought together making a comparison between High ST/Low SAE patients, on one hand, and Low ST/High SAE patients, on the other. It goes without saying that in evaluating the data in this table a number of points should be borne in mind. First, conclusions drawn from the results are valid only for psychotics—mainly schizophrenics—of the early, acute type used in the present research. Secondly, the division into two extreme types is made only to bring out the main features of the results. It scarcely needs emphasizing that there is continuous variation from one extreme to the other, possibly with a number of subgroups that were not isolated here.

TABLE 9. SUMMARY OF CHARACTERISTICS THOUGHT TO BE ASSOCIATED
WITH VARIATIONS IN SEDATION THRESHOLD AND SPIRAL AFTER-EFFECT

	High sedation threshold/ Low spiral after-effect	Low sedation threshold/High spiral after-effect
Type of illness	Paranoid if older/hebephrenic	Non-paranoid
Age	Older if paranoid	Younger
Process–reactive status	Reactive	Process
Activity level	Active	Withdrawn
Prognosis	Good	Poor
Personality	Extraverted	Introverted
Mood	More fluctuant	Less fluctuant
Affective flattening	Less	More
Thought disorder	More	Less
Conceptual thinking	Abstract–bizarre if more intelligent/overinclusive	Concrete–bizarre if less intelligent/ retarded
Sympathetic reactivity	High	Low
Psychomotor speed	Quick with many errors	Slow with few errors
Effect of treatment	Rise in SAE	Fall in SAE

Thirdly, this continuous variation is itself presumably the result of a
complex interaction between a number of underlying "dimensions"
so that, while the parameters described in Table 9 overlap, they
almost certainly do not coincide exactly. Finally, and perhaps most
important of all, some of the links suggested are regarded not as
factual statements but rather as hypotheses requiring further investigation. The extent to which this is true can be judged by the
reader himself from the detailed results already presented.

Bearing these cautionary remarks in mind, the picture that
emerges from Table 9 is of two broad clusters of psychotic behaviour,
corresponding roughly with variations in ST/SAE performance. At
the High ST/Low SAE end the tendency is towards greater behavioural and social activity, overinclusive thinking, more responsive and labile mood, and greater disorder of thought content.
The suggestion is that patients here, in keeping with their clinical
features, show relatively less impaired psychomotor performance
and are sympathetically more reactive than psychotics at the
Low ST/High SAE end. The latter are characteristically less responsive in all respects. They are more introverted and socially
withdrawn, their thought processes are more retarded, and their
mood is flatter and less fluctuant.

Paranoid psychoses seem to be confined to the High ST/Low SAE group, age being the main variable differentiating them from other patients showing similar ST/SAE performance. In younger patients hebephrenic reactions are also very common at this end of the continuum, though they occur with equal frequency in the Low ST/High SAE group. It may be that the distribution of hebephrenic illnesses is to some extent related to intelligence, a suggestion that would be supported by the sorting test results.

One possibility is that the more intelligent individual will develop a hebephrenic psychosis characterized by a high sedation threshold and bizarre responses of an abstract kind on the sorting test. In the less intelligent the illness may be revealed in a low threshold and an increased tendency towards concrete–bizarre thinking. An alternative interpretation, of course, is that both the intelligence test performance and the concrete responses of some hebephrenics are themselves the result of a common underlying impairment associated with that particular kind of psychotic reaction, or with some other feature of psychosis such as severity or duration of illness, or with some quite different variable, like premorbid personality. Unfortunately, in the present study it was impossible to disentangle the separate effects, on the one hand, of basic intelligence on the course of psychosis and, on the other, of the impact of the illness itself on intelligence test performance. Further studies clearly need to be carried out to determine how far premorbid intelligence influences the presentation of psychotic symptoms.

The picture of psychosis presented here partly cuts across traditional diagnostic categories, although it roughly coincides with that described by a number of authors in the experimental literature. We have, for example, already noted the suggestion by Payne and Hewlett (1960) that there may be a relationship between their factors of overinclusion and retardation and the paranoid/non-paranoid dichotomy of schizophrenia. Similar dichotomies have appeared in a number of other contexts, but particularly in studies of the autonomic system.

Meadow *et al.* (1953), on the basis of their work relating the Mecholyl test to thought disorder, distinguished two polar types of psychosis not unlike those referred to here. Similarly, Monroe *et al.* (1961) compared hypertensive and hypotensive schizophrenics. They concluded that hypertensive patients were emotionally responsive, oriented, aware of subtle changes in their environment, showed press of speech, flight of ideas, and obvious evidence of thought disorder. By contrast, hypotensive patients were lethargic, retarded, emotionally flat, and showed sparse verbal productions. We have already noted too that the cold pressor response in paranoid patients differs from that in other schizophrenics (Earle and Earle, *op. cit.*).

Paralleling these findings on the cardiovascular system have been some results obtained with electrodermal measures in schizophrenia. In a very early investigation of skin resistance Richter (1928) demonstrated higher than normal resistance in schizophrenics with passivity feelings and lower than normal resistance in paranoid patients. At about the same time Syz (1926) and Syz and Kinder (1928) also reported that normal subjects fell midway between paranoids and catatonics, both in skin resistance level and GSR responsiveness. Paranoids, in particular, were found to show a high frequency of spontaneous GSR's, suggesting a higher level of sympathetic reactivity in these patients.

In a more recent series of studies, to which brief reference has already been made, Venables and his co-workers investigated the relationship between skin potential and two aspects of schizophrenic behaviour, viz. the activity/withdrawal continuum and the paranoid/non-paranoid dichotomy. In one of the earliest papers in this series Venables (1960) reported that active schizophrenics showed a significantly higher frequency of skin potential responses than withdrawn schizophrenics. He also found that active patients responded more when background stimulation was reduced and withdrawn patients when it was increased. Venables interpreted this finding in terms of an inverted-U relationship, suggesting that altering the level of background stimulation shifted the state of arousal towards the optimum. Thus, active schizophrenics were considered to be overaroused and to benefit, therefore, from a reduction in stimulus input, while the opposite was assumed to be true for withdrawn schizophrenics.

Apparently contradicting these findings, Venables and Wing (1962) reported a relationship between activity/withdrawal and skin potential, such that greater behavioural withdrawal was associated with a higher arousal level. In summarizing his work Venables (1964) restated this conclusion and also reported that coherent paranoid schizophrenics differed from other patients in showing the opposite relationship between skin potential and activity/withdrawal. In this group high physiological arousal was associated with greater behavioural activity. Venables also emphasized the distinction between level and reactivity measures as indices of arousal, a difference that might account for the discrepancy between his earlier and later experiments.

One of the most interesting results reported by Venables is that referred to at the beginning of this chapter, namely his demonstration that in non-paranoid schizophrenics the correlation between the two-flash threshold and skin potential was opposite in sign to that found in normal subjects (Venables, 1963b). The sign-reversal effect thus confirms the present results for sedation threshold and spiral after-effect although in other respects the two findings do not coincide. In Venables' experiment it was normal subjects who showed a dissociation between his two arousal measures, non-paranoid schizophrenics showing a *positive* association between skin potential and two-flash threshold.[1] A small group of coherently deluded patients resembled normal subjects rather than other schizophrenics.

On available evidence it is difficult to reconcile our own findings with those of Venables. This is particularly so with respect to the behaviour of his normal group where, on *a priori* grounds, a positive or at the very least a zero relationship, rather than a dissociation, between his two arousal measures might have been expected. In fact, in a replication of Venables' experiment with normal subjects Hume and Claridge (1965) found little evidence of any relationship between skin potential and two-flash threshold. Two-flash threshold was estimated for six flash durations and only in one case was there a significant correlation with the autonomic variable. There the correlation was opposite in sign to that reported by Venables, indicating a slight tendency in normal subjects for high arousal on one measure to be associated with high arousal on the other. A similar result was obtained in neurotic patients by Rose (personal communication) correlating two-flash threshold with skin resistance

[1] It is necessary to point out here that the signs of the actual correlations reported by Venables were positive for normals and negative for schizophrenics. However, this was due to the statistical convention he adopted when analysing his results. Thus, higher arousal is reflected in a *lower* value for the two-flash threshold and a greater negativity of skin potential. By ignoring the negative sign of his skin potential values, Venables obtained, in normals for example, a correlation positive in sign but indicating negative co-variation between the two variables. To make comparison with our own results easier and in order to avoid confusing the reader, Venables' data will be looked at here from the standpoint of their arousal interpretation.

Hume and Claridge (*op. cit.*) concluded that the discrepancy between Venables' and their own virtually identical experiment with normals was probably due to sampling differences. Certainly, in the case of the sedation threshold and spiral after-effect the continued addition of further subjects to the normal group resulted eventually, as we have seen, in a zero correlation between these measures, even though in various sub-samples the correlations fluctuated between positive and negative values. For example, in one experiment (Claridge *et al.*, 1966) the correlation was significantly negative, due to the inclusion of the four deviant control subjects described earlier. It is possible that the normal group used by Venables was unusual in some way.

It is still difficult, however, to account for his results in non-paranoid schizophrenics. The explanation may lie partly in the difference between the two patient populations studied, Venables using chronic compared with our own acute psychotic material. The shift back to "normality" reported here in treated acute patients might imply that a similar natural change in psychophysiological status could occur with chronicity, but this remains to be demonstrated. The only evidence bearing on this point is the finding that sedation threshold, at least, appears to rise progressively with increasing length of illness (Shagass, 1957).

It is fairly clear that only further research can disentangle some of these apparently conflicting findings. Little is known, for example, about the relationship between the measures used by Venables and those used in the present studies. In one preliminary unpublished experiment Hume did demonstrate a significant correlation between two-flash threshold and spiral after-effect, the value for r in twenty acute psychotics being $+0\cdot66$ ($p < 0\cdot01$). In this group of patients, therefore, the two-flash threshold resembled the sedation threshold, high spiral after-effect being associated with poor perceptual discrimination and vice versa. However, the two measures were only significantly dissociated at one flash duration, the correlations at other durations being low and non-significant. No firm conclusions can be reached about the interrelationship of these various arousal indices until they have been thoroughly investigated in sufficiently large samples of normal subjects as well as in neurotic and both chronic and acute psychotic patients.

Nevertheless, it does seem possible to conclude that many of the measures used in this and other research cannot be regarded as interchangeable indices of a single arousal process. This became evident, of course, as a result of the research on neurotic patients reported in earlier chapters. It is considerably strengthened by the findings in psychosis, where a systematic dissociation between at least two psychophysiological measures appears to occur in the early phases of the illness. Furthermore, there seems to be acceptable evidence that the kind of dissociation occurring is related to other aspects of psychotic behaviour at various functional levels.

From the theoretical point of view the results are of interest for two reasons. First, they suggest a possible way of accounting for the heterogeneity of psychosis. Secondly, they provide a means whereby both neurosis and psychosis can be brought within the same theoretical framework, since a major difference between these two psychiatric conditions would seem to be not a qualitative one, but rather to lie in the functional organization within the CNS of similar psychophysiological processes. The implications of this conclusion will be discussed in the following chapters, where a theoretical appraisal of all of the results will be attempted.

SUMMARY

An attempt was made to interrelate data from various functional levels of psychotic behaviour, ranging from the psychophysiological to the clinical. The starting-point for the investigation was the classification of a group of psychotics according to their performance on the sedation threshold and spiral after-effect. It had previously been shown that, in contrast to neurotics, these two tests are negatively correlated in psychotics and define a broad continuum of psychosis running from High sedation threshold/Low spiral after-effect at one end to Low sedation threshold/High spiral after-effect at the other. Variations along this continuum showed some rather complex relationships with autonomic function.

A variety of clinical features was associated with threshold/spiral performance. Patients at the high threshold end of the continuum were more often diagnosed as paranoid, had a better prognosis, were more active, and showed greater mood deviation and thought disorder than patients at the low threshold end. The relationship between thought disorder and threshold/spiral performance was confirmed using a sorting test of conceptual thinking. Incorrect sortings as a whole on the test were more frequent in patients with high sedation thresholds, while overinclusive responses were more frequent in patients with short spiral after-effects.

Relationships with perceptual-motor performance were complex and thought to be contaminated by the gross effects of psychotic illness on such tests as vigilance and serial reaction time. However, there was some evidence that the more active, thought-disordered psychotic was relatively quicker on these tasks, though more prone to make errors, possibly because of the intrusion of overinclusive thinking. A significant tendency for patients with low spiral after-effects to make more errors in word- and colour-naming on the Stroop test was thought to be due to the basic attentional dysfunction characteristic of these individuals.

A tentative classification of psychosis was suggested and the results discussed in relation to other supportive evidence. It was concluded that there is substantial support for the view developed in previous chapters that several mechanisms contribute to arousal and that neurosis and psychosis may differ mainly in the functional organization of these mechanisms within the central nervous system.

CHAPTER 8

THEORETICAL INTEGRATION
I. A THEORY OF NEUROSIS AND PSYCHOSIS

Any attempt at a theoretical integration of the varied experiments reported in this book must inevitably be found wanting in many respects. Numerous questions remain unanswered and many inconsistencies in the data are unresolved. That the attempt is made at all is partly justified on the grounds that it may help the reader himself to integrate all of the results described and perhaps stimulate him to suggest some alternative explanation. It is hoped that the particular interpretation given here will be benevolently regarded as a series of speculative guesses, some of which find more empirical support than others, many of which will undoubtedly be wrong, but most of which can be subjected to further experimental tests. The theoretical evaluation will be undertaken in two halves, in this and the following chapter. In this chapter a theory of psychiatric disorder will be proposed to take account of the findings described in the earlier chapters of the book. In the next chapter we shall consider some of the implications of this theory for the study of problems in the field of personality that were not directly touched upon in the present research. An attempt will also be made there to integrate the theory with other empirical data and theoretical viewpoints.

Since Eysenck's theory of personality occupied a place of central importance, particularly in the early phases of the research, it is appropriate to begin by briefly reappraising its status in the light of the results described here. It should be noted at the outset that attention will be confined to Eysenck's theory of neurosis, for two reasons. First, his explanation of psychosis is too ill-defined and limited in scope to give a sufficiently comprehensive account of the anomalies of behaviour found in this diagnostic category. Secondly,

179

and perhaps somewhat paradoxically, the results for psychotics can probably be more easily contained, as will be seen later, within a theoretical framework developed out of Eysenck's attempts to explain neurosis.

Considering, to begin with, the results described in the earlier chapters of the book, it is clear that in its most generally stated form Eysenck's theory finds very considerable support. As predicted, experimental techniques such as sedation threshold, spiral after-effect, vigilance, and other similar procedures significantly differentiate the two major types of neurosis, dysthymia and hysteria. In other respects, however, the theory has several fairly obvious weaknesses. Although the objective test performance of the neurotic criterion groups does appear to define a distinct behavioural continuum, the causal determinants of this continuum and its correlates with other descriptive personality phenomena are not exactly those proposed by Eysenck. The continuum does not, for example, coincide either with a single behavioural dimension of introversion–extraversion or with a single underlying causal process. Instead, at the causal level it appears to be compounded of at least two correlated nervous processes, both of which operate, in neurosis at least, in the same direction.

Three findings support these conclusions. First, factor analyses of the experimental measures in neurotics reveal two components both of which could qualify as causal processes of the kind proposed by Eysenck. Secondly, the psychophysiological status of normal subjects is indeterminate from the dysthymia–hysteria and intro-version–extraversion postulates, suggesting that the neurotic criterion groups are widely separated because they occupy extreme and opposite positions not on one, but on two, causal dimensions. Thirdly, two important measures, both of which were previously assumed to reflect a single process, become completely dissociated in psychotic patients.

Although these findings suggest that, as it stands, Eysenck's excitation–inhibition hypothesis is inadequate, they nevertheless indicate that, with suitable modification and extension, it may be able to provide a common theoretical framework for both neurosis and psychosis. The lines along which such modification might be most usefully attempted has, of course, provided the theoretical orientation of this book, namely a reinterpretation of Eysenck's 1955 postulates in terms of current notions about arousal. The common features of these two approaches to behaviour were noted in Chapter 1 and confirmed by the results reported in subsequent chapters. As anticipated, both of Eysenck's dimensions—extraversion and neuroticism—appear to qualify as dimensions of arousal. In fact, such important putative measures of "introversion-extraversion" as the sedation threshold are strongly correlated with autonomic variables assumed by Eysenck to underly neuroticism.

Any attempt to provide an alternative explanation to that offered by Eysenck faces two major problems. The first is to identify the two psychophysiological components of arousal that have consistently appeared throughout the research. The second is to define the descriptive personality characteristics that are determined by the two components and by the interaction between them. An adequate theoretical model must therefore be able to give an account of personality at both the genotypic or aetiological and at the phenotypic or descriptive levels of personality. Before presenting such a model some of the relevant neurophysiological evidence will be reviewed.

NEUROPHYSIOLOGICAL EVIDENCE

It has become traditional in books of this kind to precede the psychological theorizing by reviewing supportive evidence from neurophysiology; presumably in order to give a simulated air of respectability to what is often mistakenly thought to be less authentic psychological data. We shall not depart from this practice here, though we do apologize to those readers who face yet another psychologist's account of what are now well-known experiments on the reticular mechanisms of arousal. Brief reference to these and other studies here can perhaps be justified on three counts. First, it can be fairly safely assumed at the most general level that variations in behaviour of the kind investigated almost certainly imply particular involvement of the reticular formation. Secondly, it will provide a framework within which the reader can more readily assess the specific neurophysiological evidence concerning barbiturate tolerance, reviewed by Dr. Herrington in the Appendix to this book. Thirdly, it may draw attention to some of the possible lines along which a neurophysiological explanation of the behavioural data might eventually be sought. It must be stated at the outset, however, that the account given here is selective and to some extent interpretative. This is inevitable because contemporary neurophysiology is developing so rapidly that the functional significance of different areas in the nervous system and their interaction changes constantly as new facts emerge. As a result, the field presents a bewildering complex of hypotheses and experimental data, often with little discernible boundary between them. In this respect, of course, it resembles psychology.

Nevertheless, as most readers will be aware, the reticular formation has a well-established place in neurophysiology as a system intimately concerned with the maintenance of consciousness. To the psychologist the most well-known and most often-quoted function of the reticular formation is the role played by its more caudal, mesencephalic portion. This "ascending reticular activating system", particularly associated, of course, with the work of Moruzzi and Magoun (1949), is known to exert a generalized tonic arousal influence on the cortex which is relatively long-lasting and non-specific in its effect. This arousal depends upon afferent input from peripheral receptors, though the contribution of the *intérieur milieu* has also been emphasized, particularly by Dell (1958). He has suggested that the primary nervous activation arising from exteroceptive sources is intensified and maintained by a secondary sympathetic arousal involving the secretion and circulation of adrenaline (Dell, 1957b). In this respect it should be noted that the midbrain component has been said to be adrenaline-sensitive (Bonvallet *et al.*, 1954; Rothballer, 1956), a humoral aspect of its function which Jasper (1960) has suggested might account for the tonic nature of its arousing influence on the cortex.[1]

The hypothalamus undoubtedly plays a major role, of course, in the effect described by Dell (Ingram, 1960). This important structure has anatomical connections with the midbrain (Nauta and Kuypers, 1957) and can probably be considered functionally part of the

---

[1] At this point it is necessary to sound a cautionary note, warning against the simple identification of arousal or excitation with increased adrenergic activity within the central nervous system. Sympathin (adrenaline and noradrenaline) is, in fact, among the candidates for the role of a neurohumoral transmitter for synaptic inhibition (see McLennan 1961); while the depressant effect on behaviour of intraventricular administration of adrenaline has also been described (Feldberg, 1964). Further consideration of these studies is beyond the scope of this review, but they do serve to emphasize that the neurophysiological processes being discussed are more complex than the account given here might suggest.

reticular formation. The interplay between reticular and hypo-thalamic influences on the cortex has been extensively discussed by Gellhorn and Loofbourrow (1963), who point out that excitation of the reticular formation in the intact organism will certainly be followed by excitation of the posterior hypothalamus, leading to an increase in sympathetic discharge. This will result in additional activation of the cortex, contributing, they suggest, an emotional component to the arousal derived directly from afferent input into the nervous system. It was on the basis of this analysis that Gellhorn and Loofbourrow were led to predict the positive relationship demonstrated here between sympathetic reactivity and the sedation threshold. As noted above, the detailed neurophysiological evidence relating to the sedation threshold is reviewed later by Dr. Herrington. In brief, however, it may be stated that an important locus of action of the barbiturates is the midbrain level of the reticular formation (Killam, 1962).

In addition to those portions of the reticular formation lying within the brainstem, a more discretely organized component in the diencephalon has also been recognized, the diffuse thalamic projection system (Jasper, 1949). The activating function of this system requires the energizing influences of the more caudal segments (French, 1960) and, compared with the brainstem component, its effects on the cortex are of a shorter-lasting and more phasic character (Jasper, 1957). This thalamic system is topographically more organized (Jasper et al., 1955) and can probably therefore regulate the activity of limited areas of the cortex without affecting the cortex as a whole (Jasper, 1960).

In comparing the brainstem and thalamic portions of the reticular formation Lindsley (1960) suggests that the ascending reticular activating system perhaps serves preliminary arousal through its influence on the cortex via an extrathalamic route. The phasic diencephalic system, on the other hand, contributes to a scanning or screening mechanism which controls the distribution and integration of impulses arriving at the cortex. It appears, therefore, to play a crucial role in the focusing and shifting of attention and, according to Jasper (1954), may be an important underlying regulator of alpha rhythm. The latter, of course, is particularly sensitive to momentary variations in awareness and has itself been considered by Walter (1953) to be a correlate of a scanning device in the nervous system.

The integrated activity of the reticular formation may be said to depend upon both excitatory and inhibitory mechanisms. With respect to tonic arousal, the caudally projecting, bulbar inhibitory centre of Magoun and Rhines (1946) is known to modify spinal motor discharge and may contribute to a feedback mechanism controlling the activating effects of proprioceptive impulses due to changes in muscle tone. As Moruzzi (1960) has suggested, this centre may form part of a more general cephalically directed system in the brainstem, having both activating and inhibitory effects on the cortex. Variations along the sleep–wake continuum are, probably, therefore, the end-result of a complex interaction between reciprocally acting facilitatory and suppressor mechanisms, some of which may involve not only the brainstem, but also the diencephalon (Hess, 1954).

The thalamic reticular formation also contains functionally antagonistic components (Tissot and Mounier, 1959), an arrangement that would be well suited to its role as a system for mediating the regional activation or inhibition of the cortex during attention. The more caudal portion of the reticular formation may contribute to this process by differentially affecting the specific thalamocortical projection system at a subcortical level (Jasper, 1957). The latter author concludes that attention probably depends on an interaction between ascending and descending influences of the reticular formation.

The ability of the reticular formation to filter incoming information almost certainly extends beyond its own anatomical boundaries, allowing some direct central control over afferent activity (Livingston, 1957). There is well-documented evidence that reticular stimulation can modify potentials at various stages along the sensory pathways themselves (Galambos, 1956; Hernández-Péon et al., 1956; Granit, 1955). Thus the screening of sensory input into the nervous system may occur at an early stage in its route from the peripheral receptors.

In spite of the crucial role they play in regulating consciousness, the functions of the reticular formation and hypothalamus can only be properly assessed within the context of their interaction with more recently developed parts of the central nervous system. It is probable, for example, that the cortex can modulate its own arousal level and, as Dell (1957a) has commented, it is not at all certain that finally it is not the cortex that has the last word in deciding the stimuli to which it will respond and the intensity with which it will react. There is well-established evidence concerning the cortical control of autonomic mechanisms (Fulton, 1949), while the existence of corticofugal projections to the reticular formation (French *et al.*, 1955) indicates that activity generated within the brainstem can itself be modified by stimulation of appropriate cortical areas (Segundo *et al.*, 1955; Adey *et al.*, 1957). These effects may be excitatory or inhibitory. With respect to the latter it is possible that the cerebral cortex exerts a tonic inhibitory control over sub-cortical centres (Hugelin and Bonvallet, 1958), the reticular–cortical relationship forming a negative feedback loop (Dell *et al.*, 1961).

Finally, interspersed between the neocortex and the brainstem, and forming part of the limbic system, is the rhinencephalon. The functional relationship of this area with the reticular formation is not entirely certain (Green, 1957). However, it was recognized early on as forming, with parts of the thalamus and the hypothalamus, a circuit intimately associated with emotional expression (Papez, 1937). Because of its many anatomical connections with both older and newer parts of the brain, the limbic system probably forms a vital link in the functional chain which, in the intact organism, issues in an integrated arousal response (Gellhorn and Loofbourrow, 1963). It therefore almost certainly plays an important aetiological role in psychiatric disorder (see Smythies, 1966).

It is clear, even from this brief account of the evidence, that the current view of the nervous system emphasizes its dynamic, functional character more than was true of classical neurophysiology. This view is summarized by Hernández-Péon (1961) who, after an excellent survey of the contemporary scene, points out how nervous regulation and integration of sensory information from the external and internal environment involve a delicate interplay between functional excitatory and inhibitory circuits at all levels of the nervous system. These circuits, he says, maintain a dynamic equilibrium by processing and filtering sensory input and by protecting the brain from excessive stimulation. Such a concept of nervous activity has two contrary implications for psychology. On the one hand, it now becomes easier to visualize possible neural substrates for some overt behavioural phenomena. On the other hand, the functional connections between various parts of the nervous system offer so many alternative possibilities that, whatever theoretical model he erects, the behavioural scientist can scarcely be entirely wrong! This is not meant to imply that such models are valueless, but only to suggest that their main purpose is to provide a working framework for guiding further experimental research.

A CAUSAL AND DESCRIPTIVE MODEL OF PSYCHIATRIC DISORDER

Before turning to the problem of individual differences it is necessary to provide a general psychophysiological model of arousal which is compatible with the neurophysiological and psychological evidence. It will be recalled that the two causal components revealed in the present data were associated, on the one hand, with the sedation threshold and its autonomic correlates and, on the other hand, with the spiral after-effect, the EEG correlates of which seem to be at least partly established. It is tempting, therefore, to identify the processes underlying these measures with subcortical and cortical arousal respectively. This interpretation would coincide with the views of some other workers; for example, Venables (1963b) has used this terminology to account for his skin potential and two-flash threshold findings.

It is obvious, however, from the studies reviewed in the previous section that usage of such terms as "cortical" and "subcortical" implies a localization of function that is unreal in the context of what are essentially psychophysiological, rather than neurophysiological, theories of behaviour. It can almost certainly be assumed with confidence that all of the behavioural phenomena studied by the psychophysiologist are determined by an interplay between both cortical and subcortical mechanisms; while functional concepts such as "arousal" cannot be visualized in neuroanatomical terms. It cannot be emphasized too strongly, therefore, that the theoretical model to be proposed here is regarded as a purely molar one, even though the theory is inevitably framed in such a way as to provide some link with the physiological evidence.

The theoretical account given here arises out of less formally stated attempts to explain previously published data from the research (Claridge and Herrington, 1963b; Davies *et al.*, 1963). Essentially it proposes the existence of two functionally related arousal mechanisms, approximately corresponding at the behavioural level to the two components defined by the sedation threshold and spiral after-effect. The first, identified as a *tonic arousal system,* is considered responsible for maintaining the individual's gross level of arousal, derived from exteroceptive and interoceptive sources. The second, named here the *arousal modulating system,* serves two main regulating functions. These are (a) to control directly, through suppressor influences, the level of activity in the tonic arousal system; and (b) to integrate the stimulus input into both systems, by appropriate facilitation and suppression of incoming information. These two arousal mechanisms and their functional properties are illustrated schematically in Fig. 8.1.

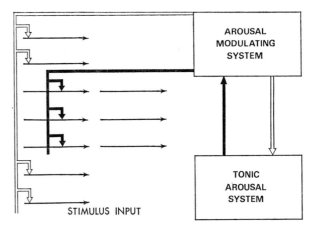

FIG. 8.1. Schematic diagram illustrating causal model of arousal. Thick black arrows represent activating or facilitating influences and white arrows inhibitory influences. The arousal modulating system is assumed to exert an inhibitory control over the tonic arousal system as well as to filter, by inhibition and facilitation, the sensory input into both systems (see text for full explanation).

It is assumed that under normal circumstances a balance is maintained between these two systems, the arrangement forming an efficient negative feedback loop. It is important to note, therefore, that a high level of activity in the arousal modulating system implies a high level of inhibition as well as excitation. As far as its direct control over tonic arousal is concerned, this implies that the strength of inhibition from the arousal modulating system will normally be matched in intensity to the level of tonic activation.

Thus, if for any reason the level of tonic arousal increases excessively, the modulating system will damp down the tonic system, protecting the CNS from over-stimulation. At the same time, because of its additional filtering control over sensory input, the modulating system will be actively facilitating the reception of relevant information and suppressing irrelevant information.[1] This part of its function is assumed to be responsible for the directional and attentional aspects of arousal, and to be involved in the narrowing and widening of attention under different conditions of arousal.

It is proposed that at this causal level there are two main sources of individual variation. The first is the overall level of excitability at which the total system operates. The second is the degree of equilibrium or homeostasis that is maintained between the two arousal mechanisms. It is assumed that the behavioural continuum from dysthymia to hysteria represents a state of affairs in which the tonic arousal and arousal modulating systems operate in equilibrium, but at varying levels of excitability. In the dysthymic high tonic arousal is matched by an efficient modulating inhibitory system. In the hysteric the reverse is true, both tonic arousal and arousal modulation being at a low level.

In psychosis it is postulated that the two systems become functionally dissociated, due to a failure at some point in the negative feedback loop illustrated in Fig. 8.1. The dissociation may occur in either of two directions, issuing in the varied behavioural reactions found in psychotic patients. Thus, in some psychotics weakening of the arousal modulating system would have two consequences. First, it would release the tonic system from its normal inhibitory control, leading to an increase in general arousal. Secondly, because of inadequate filtering (poor inhibition and facilitation) of sensory input it would result in a failure of directed attention. In other psychotics an increase in the excitability of the arousal modulating system would lead to strong inhibitory control over tonic arousal and a severe narrowing of attention.

---

[1] It may seem more parsimonious to assign a purely inhibitory role to the arousal modulating system. However, the evidence from neurophysiology would tend to argue against this, since the regulation of CNS arousal seems to involve both active facilitation and suppression of stimuli. Under certain extreme circumstances, such as sensory deprivation, one of the main functions of such a system may be to facilitate sensory input in order to try and maintain an adequate level and variety of stimulation. This also presumably underlies the phenomenon of stimulus hunger or "arousal jag" (Berlyne, 1960).

The descriptive and causal levels of this theory are brought together in Fig. 8.2, which shows the two behavioural continua of neuroticism and psychoticism running, respectively, from dysthymia to hysteria and from active psychosis to retarded psychosis. The two hypothetical psychophysiological processes assumed to account for these behavioural continua are shown by broken lines. Neuroticism is thus represented as a congruence between the two processes,

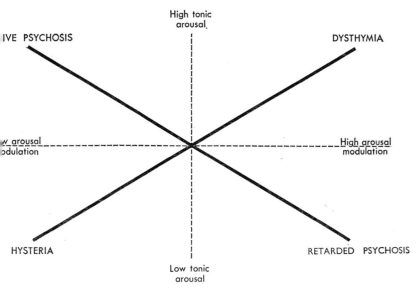

FIG. 8.2. Diagram illustrating the relationship between two causal processes (broken lines) and two behavioural continua (solid lines). Neuroticism is represented as a congruence and psychoticism as a dissociation between tonic arousal and arousal modulation.

variations in tonic arousal being matched by appropriate degrees of modulating inhibition. Both are assumed to be high in dysthymics and low in hysterics.

Conversely, psychoticism is represented as a dissociation between the two underlying causal mechanisms. Weak arousal modulation and high tonic arousal is assumed to be characteristic of the active, emotionally responsive, or paranoid patient shown to have a high sedation threshold, low spiral after-effect, and a greater tendency to overinclusive thinking. The more withdrawn, emotionally retarded psychotic, having a low sedation threshold and long spiral after-effect would be characterized by a low level of tonic arousal and a highly excitable arousal modulating system with its consequently greater inhibitory and facilitatory control over the stimulus input. The assumption in psychosis, therefore, is that the active patient, because of his poor modulation of arousal will tend to make weak orienting responses to a greater range of stimuli than normal. The retarded psychotic, on the other hand, will respond with considerable intensity to an excessively narrow range of stimuli.

This theory may help to resolve the difficulty of deciding whether the psychotic patient is highly or poorly aroused. Both may be said to be true in the sense that both types of psychotic appear to have one component of arousal weighted towards heightened responsiveness and one towards diminished responsiveness. The more important feature of psychosis, however, seems to be the kind of dissociation that occurs between mechanisms concerned with the maintenance of gross arousal and those inhibitory and facilitatory mechanisms concerned with the filtering and integration of environmental stimuli to which discrete attentional responses are made. Normal CNS functioning presumably requires that both of these mechanisms act in unison, so that where, for example, high levels of tonic arousal are present equally strong inhibitory processes are necessary to prevent arousal responses being made to irrelevant stimuli.

This different conception of inhibition constitutes an important departure from the position adopted by Eysenck, who regards inhibition and excitation as being reciprocally related processes. According to the present theory, in cases where the two arousal systems are congruent in activity—i.e. in neurotics—the inhibitory functions of the arousal modulating system will be matched in intensity to the activating functions of the tonic arousal system. The dysthymic, therefore, is presumed to require a high level of inhibition in order to maintain equilibrium with his high degree of tonic arousal. The hysteric, on the other hand, because of his poor tonic arousal, requires less inhibition to maintain homeostasis. In both cases, because the two systems are in equilibrium, albeit at different levels of excitability, normal integration of internal and external stimuli is possible. The present theory would also appear to provide a more adequate explanation of, for example, some of the performance differences between hysterics and dysthymics, especially those found on psychomotor tasks. There, it will be recalled, tonic arousal or drive seemed to be a primary determinant of performance, while inhibition had a mainly homeostatic function.

The theory has the further advantage that it is able to take account of neurosis and psychosis within the same conceptual causal framework, the main difference between these two types of patient lying, it would seem, in the way in which the same psychophysiological processes are organized within the central nervous system. It must be borne in mind, of course, that an important part of the theory relies on empirical data that require considerable investigation, namely the fortuitous finding that the sedation threshold and spiral after-effect correlate in opposite directions in neurotics and psychotics. The postulation of a tonic arousal system clearly rests on a firm empirical foundation and its identification with sedation threshold and related autonomic measures finds support from other psychophysiological and neurophysiological data. This is certainly less true of the arousal modulating system and its identification with the spiral after-effect. The surprising prominence attained by the latter test in the course of the research is even more inexplicable because little, if anything, is known about its neural determinants.[1] Its physiological correlates appear, if anything, to be with EEG indices, particularly alpha index and the alpha blocking response. In this respect it is interesting to recall the view that alpha rhythm may reflect thalamic activity, forming part of the screening mechanisms of the CNS. This accords with the hypothesis proposed here that differences in spiral after-effect are due to variations in the strength of the modulating processes that help to filter input into the nervous system.

Performance on the Archimedes spiral could, of course, reflect some quite superficial aspect of behaviour, such as the ability to fixate or the rate of eye movement. While it seems unlikely that either variable could entirely account for the wide individual differences found on the test, the part they play in determining the duration of the after-effect is not yet fully understood. Both fixation and eye movements have been discussed recently by Holland (1965) as variables requiring further investigation. Prior to that review he

---

[1] One of the few attempts to investigate the neurophysiological correlates of the spiral after-effect has recently been reported by Shagass et al. (1965), who found no correlation between the test and various parameters of the cortical evoked response to flash. The authors unfortunately used a very heterogeneous group of patients and further studies in this area seem to be indicated.

himself (Holland, 1960) described a technique for measuring eye movement based on the frequency with which "flashes", or brief glimpses of a stationary spiral, appear during fixation of a spiral disc rotating at high speed, above the threshold for fusion of the black and white segments. Holland himself found no relationship between this measure and personality, though Franks (1963a) subsequently demonstrated that flash frequency—and therefore presumably eye movement—was greater in extraverts than in introverts. Holland (1965) also quotes some unpublished evidence obtained by Reason that low spiral after-effects tend to be associated with high flash frequency.[1] If such factors as fixation prove to be important determinants of the spiral after-effect, the technique may lose some of its significance as a psychophysiological measure *per se*. On the other hand, its possible dependence on centrally determined attentional factors, having their effect through peripheral mechanisms, could still be contained within the theory presented here and would simply indicate the need for a more detailed investigation of the basic neurophysiological correlates of the spiral after-effect.

The need to propose two causal mechanisms underlying personality has now been recognized formally by Eysenck (1967) in the most recent revision of his theory. Taking more account than hitherto of neurophysiological evidence Eysenck has proposed two separate, but functionally related, neural circuits. The first, which he identifies with introversion–extraversion, involves a reticular-cortical loop. The second, associated with neuroticism or emotionality, is identified with the visceral brain, including the hypothalamus. This theory perhaps implies greater anatomical localization of behavioural personality dimensions than the neurophysiological evidence would now seem to justify, although it is more consistent with the psychological evidence that at least two causal processes determine individual differences in personality. The formulation is very similar to that proposed in an earlier publication by the present

---

[1] In this respect it is interesting to note the views on schizophrenia expressed by Silverman (1964a), whose theory will be discussed in more detail later. Silverman has suggested a scanning hypothesis to account for attention dysfunction in schizophrenia, the paranoid patient being thought of as an excessive scanner of the environment. The poor fixation presumably associated with this might partly account for the low spiral after-effects found in some paranoid patients. This possibility would also be consistent with the somewhat greater extraversion found in active psychotics.

writer and his colleagues (Davies *et al.*, 1963), who suggested two sources of arousal in the nervous system, "sensory arousal" and "autonomic arousal", associated, respectively, with reticular and hypothalamic activation.

Before closing this chapter it is worth commenting briefly on the recent attempt by Gray (1964) to provide an arousal interpretation of the Pavlovian typology, from which, of course, Eysenck's theory is partly derived. As Gray points out, Pavlov considered that both the excitatory and inhibitory processes of the nervous system can vary in strength, though Teplov, on whose writings Gray's arousal model is largely based, has confined himself to variations in the strength of the excitatory process. Gray has identified excitation with reticular activation, suggesting that variations in the strength of this process define a dimension of arousability. Like the present writer, Gray has further proposed a homeostatic feedback loop, involving inhibition, which damps down brainstem arousal at high levels of excitation.

In reinterpreting Russian theory Gray paid little formal attention to Western work on individual differences, though he notes in passing that his dimension of arousability may be a correlate of the personality factors studied by Eysenck. The present evidence suggests that the dimension may coincide with the dysthymia–hysteria continuum postulated here. By concentrating, like Teplov, on excitation as a source of individual differences, Gray was also led to a much simpler theory than the present one, which proposes additional variations in the strength of the inhibitory processes to account for psychosis. This hypothesis is well supported by the early speculations of Pavlov himself, whose views on the pathogenesis of the psychoses have been concisely summarized by Ivanov-Smolensky (1954). This author comments that Pavlov concerned himself particularly with catatonia, which he considered to be a state of heightened cortical inhibition and which, in terms of the present theory, would be identified as retarded psychosis. Perhaps more interesting is Pavlov's suggestion that paranoid psychosis and hypomania are characterized by weakening of the inhibitory processes, in the first case of internal and in the second case of transmarginal inhibition. This heterogeneity of the psychoses, implicitly recognized by Pavlov, is paralleled in more recent Soviet research which has distinguished two major types of schizophrenia characterized, respectively, by hyper- and hyporeactivity of the autonomic nervous system (Lynn, 1963).

In conclusion, the theory proposed here clearly arose out of a combination of Pavlov's ideas on the pathophysiology of mental illness, Eysenck's reinterpretation of the Pavlovian typology applied to neurosis, and current Western views on the neurophysiology of awareness and attention. These different viewpoints are now rapidly converging towards a more unified approach to behaviour in general and to personality in particular. It is therefore against this background, and mainly as a heuristic model for further research, that the present theory can best be judged.

SUMMARY

The theory has been proposed that central nervous arousal depends upon two interacting mechanisms, a system responsible for tonic arousal and an arousal modulating system having two functions: (a) to maintain homeostasis in the CNS through suppressor influences on tonic arousal and (b) to filter sensory input into the nervous system. It has been suggested that these two mechanisms normally operate in equilibrium, though at different levels of excitability. Variations in excitability are assumed to account for the behavioural dimension of dysthymia–hysteria. It is proposed that in psychosis the two mechanisms become dissociated so that normal equilibrium is not maintained. Dissociation may occur in either of two directions: (a) towards a state where there is poor modulation of sensory input and poor inhibitory control over tonic arousal or (b) towards a state where increased excitability of the modulating system leads to excessive inhibition and a reduction in tonic arousal. These two kinds of dissociation are assumed to account for a dimension of psychoticism running from active to retarded psychosis.

CHAPTER 9

THEORETICAL INTEGRATION
II. IMPLICATIONS OF THE THEORY FOR FURTHER RESEARCH

INTRODUCTION

The theory presented in the previous chapter has provided a general explanatory framework for the two major subdivisions of psychiatric illness, neurosis and psychosis. In this final chapter the intention is to consider some of the implications of the theory for further investigation of personality, to draw together some additional data in support of the theory, and to relate the present model to other theoretical viewpoints. Although there will inevitably be some overlap in the discussion, it is convenient to divide the chapter into three parts. The first will be concerned with the normal personality, and in particular to suggest how the theory might account for normal variations in personality. The second part will deal with problems in the study of psychiatric disorder that were not touched upon in the present research. The third will consist of a brief discussion of some of the implications that the theory has for research into the physical methods of treatment in psychiatry. The presentation will inevitably be speculative and will often take the form of suggestions for further experimentation. However, this is as it should be, since, as Professor Eysenck has forcibly pointed out on a number of occasions, a good measure of a vigorous theory is its ability to yield testable hypotheses. The book will have served its main purpose if it stimulates a few of its readers to carry out experimental research along some of the lines suggested here.

THE NORMAL PERSONALITY

It is an assumption of the proposed theory that dysthymics and hysterics, and the two types of psychotic recognized here, form "criterion groups" which define the ends of two continuously variable dimensions of personality. It is thus assumed that these two dimensions and their causal concomitants, run through the non-psychiatric population, accounting for normal variations in personality. The present research was confined largely to the psychiatric patient and extension of the theory to cover normal personality variation must rely on indirect evidence. The theory of normal personality to be suggested is based on an attempt to integrate with it some other personality typologies, particularly those of Jung, Kretschmer, and Eysenck. Before presenting this model of normal personality, some of the relevant evidence will be reviewed.

Review of Evidence

The history of psychology abounds with attempts to provide descriptive classifications of personality, perhaps the most well-known of these being the typologies of Jung and Kretschmer. The former's introversion–extraversion and the latter's schizothymia–cyclothymia dichotomies are clearly similar in some respects and reflect a common theme running through a number of lesser-known typologies, which have distinguished between individuals characterized by inwardly, as compared with outwardly, directed thinking.[1]

Despite their similarities, there are at the same time a number of vital differences between the Jungian and Kretschmerian typologies. Each writer, of course, took a different form of psychiatric disorder as his prototype of personality and Kretschmer's schizothymia–cyclothymia dimension overlaps with Jung's introversion–extraversion mainly with respect to the sociability component they have in common. Otherwise Kretschmer's stress on psychosis led to a description of schizothymia–cyclothymia which naturally emphasized the abortive features of schizophrenic and manic-depressive illnesses. These were mainly affective characteristics, such as the coldness and hypersensitivity of the schizothyme and the emotional fluidity and impulsiveness of the cyclothyme.

Previous attempts to relate the Jungian and Kretschmerian typologies together have not been entirely successful and Eysenck (1953) has discussed some of the theoretical difficulties that this entails. He states, for example, that it would necessitate taking a view of psychiatric illness which regards neurosis and psychosis as

[1] See MacKinnon (1944) and Eysenck (1953) for historical reviews of these typologies.

lying along the same continuum. The evidence, both from his book and from earlier studies (Eysenck, 1952), is against this hypothesis. Another difficulty considered by Eysenck is the inconsistency with which Jung attempted to apply his typology to psychosis and Kretschmer to relate schizothymia–cyclothymia to neurosis. Jung regarded psychasthenia and introversion as characteristic of the schizophrenic, while Kretschmer linked schizophrenia with hysteria. It is hoped to show later how some of these difficulties may be resolved, but first it is necessary to look at some more recent studies of extraversion in normal subjects.

As seen in an earlier chapter, Eysenck's experimental analysis of the Jungian typology of neurosis led him to identify introversion–extraversion as a second-order factor of personality. In recent years there has been some controversy about the unitary nature of extraversion. Carrigan (1960), for example, reviewed a number of questionnaire studies in normal subjects and concluded that two independent factors had frequently appeared which could qualify for the description "extraversion". One of these was sociability and the other a factor of impulsiveness or weak super-ego strength. Carrigan suggested that the former may reflect a well-adjusted type and the latter a maladjusted type of extraversion.

Eysenck and Eysenck (1963) have themselves provided evidence about the dual nature of extraversion. They factor analysed a large number of questionnaire items and demonstrated the two clearly definable components mentioned above, namely, sociability and impulsiveness. They differed from Carrigan, however, in suggesting that these two components were not independent, the correlation between them being about $+0 \cdot 5$. In a replication of this study Sparrow and Ross (1964) confirmed the findings of the Eysencks and reported very high correlations between the equivalent factors extracted in the two experiments.

Adcock (1965) has recently discussed the complex nature of extraversion in comparing the concepts of Eysenck and Cattell. He matched the impulsiveness component with Cattell's objective factor UI 17, described at the introverted end as "general inhibition" and defined in terms of timidity, caution, and restraint. Cattell (1965) himself certainly considers this factor to be quite different from, and independent of, his version of extraversion–introversion, namely, exvia–invia. However, exvia–invia, being considered a second-order factor, is itself multiply determined. It is made up of such traits as surgency, group dependency and, perhaps most interesting of all, affectothymia–sizothymia, the last of these being identified by Cattell with Kretschmer's cyclothymia–schizothymia.

There is clearly a good deal of consistent evidence, despite detailed discrepancies, that various characteristics, forming at least two trait clusters, contribute to a general personality dimension of extraversion or outgoing behaviour, as defined by contemporary psychologists. To the present author it seems that the emergence of these two clusters from recent statistical analyses may confirm in a modern guise the clinical observations of Jung and Kretschmer and may help to account for the difficulty experienced so far in satisfactorily relating their respective typologies to each other. The integration of these varied but similar viewpoints forms the basis of the theoretical model of normal personality to be presented below.

A Model of Personality

The general thesis to be presented here contains two proposals. The first is that the Jungian and Kretschmerian typologies can be roughly matched to the two continua of psychiatric disorder isolated in our own research. Thus, variations in the normal population along the psychoticism continuum would correspond approximately to Kretschmer's cyclothymia–schizothymia dimension. Similarly variations along the neuroticism continuum would be due to some of those characteristics of psychasthenia–hysteria that Jung labelled as introversion–extraversion. The second proposal is that the cluster of traits described by Kretschmer is roughly equivalent to the impulsiveness component present in the modern concept of extraversion. The latter's sociability component is tentatively identified with Jung's introversion–extraversion cluster of traits.

This theoretical model is illustrated diagrammatically in Fig. 9.1, which shows the two behavioural continua described in the previous chapter, running from dysthymia to hysteria and from active to retarded psychosis. As before, the two hypothetical causal processes assumed to account for these behavioural dimensions are also included, shown by broken lines. To represent the normal counterparts of the neuroticism and psychoticism dimensions the respective terms, "schizoid–cycloid" and "obsessoid–hysteroid", have been used. This descriptive terminology is in keeping with current usage and also maintains some link with the Kretschmerian and Jungian typologies.

Also included in Fig. 9.1 are some of the behavioural traits expected to be shown by individuals falling at different points along the two continua. Taking that for psychoticism first, the features characteristic of normal people at the cycloid end (top left-hand quadrant) closely correspond with those traditionally used in describing the cyclothymic personality. They are almost identical,

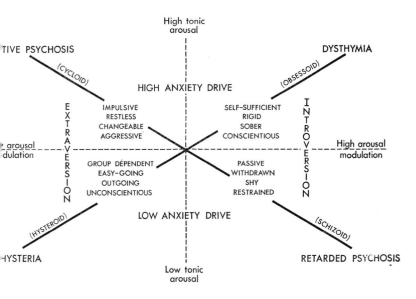

FIG. 9.1. Diagram illustrating descriptive model of personality. Broken lines refer to two underlying causal mechanisms determining two behavioural continua of neuroticism and psychoticism, represented by solid lines. Existing typologies from which the model was derived are also shown, together with some of the descriptive features of normal individuals falling in various positions along the two continua (see text for full explanation).

too, with the questionnaire items found by Eysenck and Eysenck (1963) to load highly on impulsiveness. At the opposite, schizoid, end of the same continuum would be individuals characterized by social withdrawal, emotional restraint, and features having a negative weighting on impulsiveness. The comparable descriptions for the neuroticism continuum contrast the self-sufficient, conscientious individual at the obsessoid end (top right-hand quadrant) with the relaxed, care-free, group-dependent person at the hysteroid end.

It will be seen in Fig. 9.1 that the terms "extraversion" and "introversion" have been retained to describe the composite behaviour of the normal individuals on the left and right sides of the figure, respectively. This usage is consistent with the dual nature of introversion–extraversion and its status as a second-order factor. Thus, general extraversion is seen as a characteristic common to two otherwise quite different types of person: the restless, changeable cyclothyme and the carefree, sociable hysteroid. Similarly, though both personality types can be described as introverted, the obsessoid and schizoid personalities are probably introverts for two quite different reasons; the former because of his self-sufficient lack of need for social stimulation and the latter because of his withdrawal from social intercourse.

An entirely suitable composite description from the personality field does not seem to be available for corresponding variations in a vertical direction in Fig. 9.1. The differentiating characteristics would seem to be those concerned with drive, related causally to tonic arousal. From the evidence reviewed earlier linking it with autonomic arousal, "neuroticism" might seem suitable, if it were not for the fact that this term has already been used in a quite different sense. In any case it has connotations of adjustment that cut across the main dimensions postulated here. We have, therefore, tentatively used the term "anxiety drive" to indicate highly versus poorly driven behaviour. For example, the obsessoid and cycloid personalities may be said to resemble each other in showing a high level of energy or drive, characterized by general anxiety. In contrast, the schizoid and hysteroid have in common a certain degree of inertia, clinically recognizable in the former as a lack of volition and in the latter as a lack of concern or emotional tension.

This theoretical model can thus overcome some of the difficulties mentioned by Eysenck (1953) in trying to reconcile the Jungian and Kretschmerian typologies. It allows neuroticism and psychoticism to be retained as different dimensions but, by linking them at a causal level, makes it possible to recognize the overlap that is apparent in the psychophysiological and behavioural status of various normal personality types. It has the advantage, too, of taking account of some of the evidence from recent studies of introversion–extraversion.

Further Discussion

One problem that arises out of the theory proposed above and one which requires some consideration here is the definition of "normality". This problem is not peculiar to the present theory, though it does carry special difficulties that should be mentioned. Referring back to Fig. 9.1, it can be seen that the assumption has been made that normal individuals can fall at any position in the space defined by the two behavioural continua shown there. This conclusion would be supported by the sedation threshold and spiral after-effect data for the normal group used in the present research. It will be recalled that in normal subjects all combinations of performance on these two tests were found, suggesting that the causal features of both psychosis and neurosis will be represented in a random sample of normal people.

There is one difficulty with this conclusion that will not have escaped the perceptive reader. This concerns the demonstration by Herrington and Claridge (1965) that psychotics who recover show a shift in sedation threshold and spiral after-effect until performance resembles that of neurotics. This suggests that the causal processes underlying these two tests are somehow "normalized" by treatment. It also indicates that the neuroticism continuum might provide an alternative criterion of normality. Indeed, departure from the neurotic regression line relating threshold to spiral after-effect was used as such in the experimental analysis of psychosis. Looked at from a causal viewpoint, one advantage of using dysthymia–hysteria for this purpose is that congruence in the activity of the two psychophysiological mechanisms postulated might seem superficially more "normal" than their dissociation. There are arguments against this, some of which will be considered later, but one of which may be noted here. That is the finding (Claridge *et al.*, 1966) that a few control subjects occupy extreme positions on the psychoticism continuum and even show disturbed conceptual thinking, though they are not overtly ill.

At present it is impossible to reconcile these apparently contradictory results, since no conclusive explanation can be given for the performance shift found in recovered psychotic patients. There are several hypotheses that could be considered, one of which is that the change in spiral/threshold performance was due to some specific effect of physical treatment and only coincidentally related

202 PERSONALITY AND AROUSAL

to the personality change occurring on recovery from psychosis. A more likely possibility is that the post-treatment results reflected a temporary change to a neurotic behaviour pattern as part of the recovery from psychosis. This relationship between neurotic symptomatology and the onset and remission of psychosis has been discussed by Foulds (1965a, 1965b); while it is a common clinical observation that in the early stages of their illness psychotics often go through a phase resembling neurosis, a process that may be reversed during the period of recovery.

Whatever the explanation, it is clearly necessary to recognize that acute shifts in psychophysiological status can occur, either naturally, or as a result of intervention with physical methods of treatment. At the same time it is also true that there are a small number of individuals in the normal population who score highly on tests of psychoticism without showing the clinical signs of psychosis (see also Lovibond, 1963). We can perhaps tentatively conclude that, using a statistical criterion, the normal population would be contained within a circle enclosing the middle portion of Fig. 9.1. Extreme positions on either of the two major dimensions might help to predict the nature of the illness in the event of psychiatric breakdown.

Returning to the theory itself, it is fairly obvious that psychoticism and neuroticism as defined here are not "dimensions" in quite the same sense in which Eysenck has used this term. He has employed factor analysis to isolate test clusters that define dimensions upon which *all* psychotics or *all* neurotics occupy extreme positions. His psychoticism and neuroticism dimensions do not, and are not intended to, differentiate between various kinds of patient falling within each of these two diagnostic groups; nor are the dimensions linked at a causal level. By contrast, the two continua postulated here rely on the existence of a different causal relationship between the same kind of measure. Various patients within each of the two diagnostic groups of neurosis and psychosis have in common only the fact that they occupy extreme positions along their respective dimensions.

The difference in emphasis is presumably due to the level at which the analysis is carried out. Thus, at a certain level in the hierarchy of personality structure it is obviously possible to find gross behavioural measures which, for example, differentiate neurotics as a whole from psychotics as a whole. Psychomotor slowness, for instance, may be characteristic of all psychotics and may, therefore, help to define a general factor of psychoticism which, at that level of behaviour, differentiates such patients from neurotics. However, psychomotor slowness may have a totally different aetiology in different psychotic patients. What the present data appear to reflect is the interrelationship between measures at this more fundamental level of description.

Such an explanation could also account for the lack of correspondence, noted in an earlier chapter (p. 112 ff.), between the MPI N-scores of hysterics and psychopaths and their status on psychophysiological tests. Thus, at a descriptive level neuroticism, as measured by the MPI, may simply reflect social and emotional maladjustment common to all neurosis, even though aetiologically this may be associated with abnormally *high* or abnormally *low* levels of arousability.

At present it can only be regarded as a fortuitous finding, requiring further examination, that the reversal in sign between two measures should have played such a crucial part in causally linking neurosis and psychosis in this way. Two methods could be used to investigate this aspect of the theory further. The first would be a factor analysis, in a randomly selected population, of a battery of tests thought to measure tonic arousal and arousal modulation. This should give rise to two orthogonal factors corresponding to these two causal processes. The second method would be to carry out similar analyses separately on a group of neurotic and a group of psychotic patients. Here the factors extracted would be expected to correlate in opposite directions in the two groups. The results of either of these experiments would be of considerable theoretical interest and may help to elucidate further the causal processes underlying personality.

Turning to the more immediate implications of the theory for normal personality study, a particularly fruitful area for further research lies in the relationship between causal and descriptive measures in non-psychiatric groups. At the beginning of this book it was noted that the results of work carried out so far within Eysenck's theory have been much more equivocal than in the case of experiments using psychiatric patients. Attempts to correlate the MPI and EPI scales with objective measures in normal subjects have often produced conflicting or negative findings, so much so that many psychologists have come to doubt the validity of the theory.

A possible reason for this is suggested by the position adopted here with respect to extraversion, since it has been postulated that the two components of extraversion reflect an interaction, in opposite directions, between two causal processes. Thus, impulsiveness is assumed to represent the normal counterpart of a dissociation between the two processes and to be associated at the cyclothymic end with high tonic arousal. The sociability component, on the other hand, would be associated at the hysteroid end with *low* tonic arousal. It would follow, therefore, that such measures as sedation threshold and sympathetic reactivity would correlate *positively* with impulsiveness but *negatively* with sociability, even though both behavioural components contribute in the same direction to extraversion.

Although at the time of writing the crucial experiments remain to be done there is some indirect evidence which might be taken to support this prediction. Pawlik and Cattell (1965), for example, reported positive correlations between a number of EEG measures of arousal and assertiveness, which may have some overlap with impulsiveness. Of more direct interest, is a series of results already referred to in another context in Chapter 5 (p. 106). This concerns the interaction between extraversion and neuroticism in determining measures such as spiral after-effect, nitrous oxide tolerance, and alpha amplitude. Savage (*op. cit.*), for example, reported that at high levels of extraversion neuroticism tended to reduce the amplitude of the alpha rhythm. It is possible that findings such as these could be explained in terms of a differential weighting on the two extraversion components in high and low N-scorers on the MPI. For example, in their paper referred to earlier Eysenck and Eysenck (1963) reported that impulsiveness was positively correlated with neuroticism, while sociability was negatively correlated with that dimension. They also noted that questionnaire items high on impulsiveness, such as aggressiveness, tended to be more commonly answered in the affirmative by High E/High N scorers, i.e. by those individuals falling, according to the present theory, in the cycloid quadrant.

The possibility that the apparent interaction between E and N may be explained in this way will suggest to the reader a number of experiments that might be undertaken using the many objective techniques already reported on by Eysenck and his colleagues in normal subjects. One conclusion seems inescapable, namely that the use of such global measures as the Maudsley and Eysenck Personality Inventories may dilute or obscure important connections that exist between performance and the two components of extraversion. Since, if the present analysis is correct, these components may cancel each other out at the causal level, re-examination of the problem according to the theory suggested here may help to account for some puzzling contradictions in the results of previous studies. It may also lead to the discovery of more meaningful relationships between causal processes and normal personality traits and in doing so strengthen a part of Eysenck's theory that has hitherto been most open to criticism by psychologists.

PSYCHIATRIC DISORDER

In proposing a theory of psychiatric disorder here little attention has been paid to detailed differences between the discrete subgroups of neurosis and psychosis recognized by clinical psychiatry. Some similarities between the different varieties of dysthymia and hysteria were demonstrated, while a few preliminary findings were described concerning the subdivision of the psychoses. Essentially, however, the theory has confined itself to the two broadest categories of psychiatric nosology, neurosis and psychosis. This has certain advantages since it is here that there is likely to be least disagreement about diagnosis upon which, in the last analysis, the research has been based. Where misdiagnosis did occur it is likely, in any case, to have operated against, rather than in favour of, the theory. This is because, while some early psychotics will almost certainly have been misdiagnosed as neurotics, the presence of florid psychotic symptoms will rarely have been overlooked.

Another limitation of the theory is that the data on which it is based were collected almost exclusively on a somewhat atypical population of psychiatric patients. Some of the advantages and disadvantages of this were discussed in the Introduction to the book and we would simply reiterate here that, on balance, the former are considered to outweigh the latter. Access to the patient material used made it possible to isolate important features of psychiatric illness that might otherwise have been obscured by such crucial variables as age and treatment history which contaminate much experimental work in this field. The general validity of the theory can only be judged from the support it finds in the surrounding body of knowledge concerning personality and from further experimentation on more heterogeneous psychiatric populations. We shall try to suggest here how it may provide a working causal and descriptive framework for further investigation of some problems in psychiatry that could only be briefly touched upon in the present research.

Probably the most controversial topic in current psychiatry, and certainly one of the most difficult diagnostic problems, is that of depression. Arguments continue unabated about the validity of distinguishing between two types of reactive or neurotic and endogenous or psychotic depression. To illustrate the confusion that still exists about the problem it is necessary only to quote two of the most recent communications on the topic, both appearing in the same issue of the same psychiatric journal. Carney *et al.* (1965), after a factor analytic study of depressive symptoms, concluded that it was possible and necessary to separate neurotic from endogenous depression. Mendels (1965), on the other hand, after a similar analysis, stressed what he called the "endo-reactive" nature of most depressive illnesses.[1]

Most of the discussion among clinicians about depression has been carried on at the descriptive, symptomatological level, although the experimental literature provides a rather more consistent picture of this condition. Much of the evidence was reviewed in detail in Chapters 6 and 7 and will only be briefly recapitulated here. With two exceptions, most studies of the sedation threshold have reported low tolerance of barbiturates in psychotic compared with neurotic depressives; while parallel differences in the tolerance of methamphetamine have been found using the complementary technique of "stimulation threshold" (Giberti and Rossi, 1962; Giberti *et al.*, 1962). This very low tonic arousal in psychotic depression would be supported by the poor sympathetic reactivity found on the Mecholyl test and the demonstration by Shagass and Schwartz (1962) that, compared with neurotic cases, endogenous depressives show a lengthening of the recovery cycle of the somatosensory evoked response. Few psychotic patients in the present research carried the diagnosis of depression, but those that did tended to have low sedation thresholds and long spiral after-effects. The latter finding

---

[1] See also subsequent correspondence, *British Journal of Psychiatry*, 1965 and 1966.

would be consistent with the demonstration by Paulson and Gottlieb (1961) that psychotic depressives showed an increased alpha blocking response, a measure found here to correlate with the spiral after-effect.

It seems possible to conclude that psychotic depressives would fall at the retarded end of the psychoticism continuum postulated here. This conclusion would be further supported by the finding of Payne and Hewlett (1960) that such patients resemble some schizophrenics in being high on their factor of retardation. Indeed, on many measures there seem to be few grounds for distinguishing between psychotic depression and a large proportion of patients diagnosed as schizophrenic.

The main difference between psychotic and neurotic depression would therefore be expected on the sedation threshold, since both conditions should be alike on the spiral after-effect. This is because of the similarity between reactive depression and other dysthymic neurotic disorders, in whom long spiral after-effects tend to predominate (see Chapter 4).

Although reactive depressives would on average be expected to have high sedation thresholds, a hypothesis worth further investigation concerns the curvilinear relationship found here in neurotics between sedation threshold and both spiral after-effect and alpha index (see Fig. 4.2, p. 61, and Fig. 3.3, p. 39). It is possible that some chronic cases of neurotic depression occupy the downward part of the curve relating sedation threshold to both of these measures. This would be consistent with the theoretical position adopted here, since it might be expected, even in neurotics, that, once tonic arousal reached a certain critical point, restraining inhibitory processes would lead to a fall in arousal and a relative drop in sedation threshold. This condition of overarousal might, therefore, represent the psychophysiological substrate of neurotic depression. Such a possibility would be consistent with the sedative or fatigue-like symptoms occurring as a result of prolonged anxiety, an effect reviewed at length by Breggin (1964). Breggin notes the similarity between this phenomenon and the evidence, cited in the last chapter, that adrenaline may have paradoxical depressant effects in animals under certain conditions.[1]

Perhaps the most important conclusion to be drawn from this brief review of depression is the need for more experimental research

[1] Further physiological evidence consistent with this view is discussed by Dr. Herrington in the Appendix.

which will define both the causal and the descriptive parameters of this heterogeneous group of conditions. More progress might be made if, for example, precise psychophysiological measures were included in large-scale computer analyses of depressive symptoms, such as that reported by Carney *et al.* (*op. cit.*). It is a source of perplexity to the present writer that this has rarely been done. Indeed, such studies appear to be carried out without any reference to and, it can only be assumed, without any awareness of the evidence about depression in the experimental literature. The inclusion of causal measures, and an attempt to integrate the results with some systematic theory of personality, would considerably enhance the value of what appear at present to be purely empirical analyses of large quantities of subjectively assessed data on the descriptive features of depression.

The other major problem emphasized by the present research is that which Venables (1964) has called "input dysfunction" in schizophrenia. The evidence described in Chapters 6 and 7 has provided considerable support for this newly emerging view of schizophrenia as a dysfunction of the central mechanisms controlling attention and sensory input into the nervous system. Although the "dissociation" hypothesis of psychosis proposed here does not appear to have been considered previously, that part of it concerned with information filtering has, of course, been used to explain a number of features of schizophrenic behaviour, e.g. overinclusive thinking (Payne, 1960). In the most recent literature it has been discussed particularly by Silverman (1964a) who has proposed a scanning-control or cognitive filtering mechanism in the nervous system. This determines two basic "styles" of dealing with environmental stimulation which correspond closely to those postulated here in active and retarded psychotics. According to Silverman, minimal scanning, characteristic of non-paranoid schizophrenics, leads to excessive constriction of the field of awareness. The paranoid patient, on the other hand, is thought to show extreme scanning of the environment, a process forming the basis of delusions.

Like the present author, Silverman (1964b) has extended his theory beyond the problem of schizophrenia itself. He has suggested that the two cognitive styles he describes are distributed throughout the normal population and are not peculiar to psychosis. He reviewed a number of studies of perception, including size constancy, which suggests that extreme scanning behaviour may be characteristic of extraverted or cyclothymic individuals. The special relevance of this hypothesis to work on the spiral after-effect will be recalled from the previous chapter and it is of interest to note that, in a recent study, Levy and Lang (1966) demonstrated that the impulsiveness component of extraversion was associated with a reduction in the duration of the spiral after-effect. Anxiety, on the other hand, tended to lengthen it, the authors concluding that it was necessary to postulate two reciprocally interacting mechanisms of activation and cognitive control to account for performance on the test. The results of this study accord well with the theoretical model of normal personality proposed earlier and the link suggested between introversion–extraversion and psychoticism.

Another interesting suggestion made by Silverman is that creative thinking may depend upon a particular kind of cognitive style, a certain degree of cognitive scanning being essential to this ability. This fact may account for the comparison often made between high degrees of creativity in normal individuals and some stages of psychosis, a view discussed in more detail by McConaghy (1960, 1961). Like Silverman, McConaghy has distinguished two modes of abstract thinking, one of which he calls "allusive thinking" in which the ability to form remote associations is increased. This mode of abstraction is clearly similar to overinclusive thinking and, according to McConaghy, is due to weak levels of inhibition in the central nervous system resulting from a low level of cortical excitability. Review of the literature on creative thinking is beyond the scope of this book, but its re-evaluation within the framework of a psychophysiological theory of personality should prove to be a fruitful area of research.

A quite different line of investigation which promises to throw light on the basic mechanisms underlying attention dysfunction concerns the study of psychotomimetic drugs. A particularly relevant example of this work is that reported by Bradley and his colleagues on the effects of LSD–25 in animals. Key, for instance, has demonstrated that in the cat this drug causes an increase in the amount of generalization occurring during the learning of conditioned responses to both auditory and visual stimuli (Key, 1961, 1964). He concluded that LSD–25 appears to alter the level of significance or meaning of stimuli. Key's finding is of particular interest in view of Mednick's (1958) interpretation of overinclusion in terms of stimulus generalization and Bradley's (1957) suggestion that LSD–25 acts, not on the

brainstem reticular formation directly, but on the afferent collaterals into this system. This may imply some interference, not
with arousal as such, but with the filtering properties of the nervous
system.

It is clear from the foregoing discussion that studies of schizophrenia form only one part of a much broader movement in
research which may help to elucidate some of the psychophysiological
mechanisms of attention. Investigations of the schizophrenic himself
will certainly contribute to this movement, especially with the
adoption of more precise experimental techniques; for example, the
cortical evoked response, as used recently in the measurement of
schizophrenic "set" (Callaway *et al.*, 1965). It is possible that, just as
in neurosis, the various types of psychosis, categorized by means of
objective tests such as those used here, could become "criterion
groups" for studying some of the basic processes underlying normal
behaviour. In turn, feedback of information from areas of research
outside psychiatry may help to throw further light on the aetiology
of the psychoses.

PHYSICAL METHODS OF TREATMENT

An important aim of any scientific theory is to provide a means
of manipulating the phenomena it tries to describe and explain. In
psychiatry this becomes the crucially practical problem of treatment.
Here necessity, and the absence of an adequate theory of abnormal
personality, has led to the adoption of treatment methods having
little scientific rationale for their use. A good example is electro-
convulsive treatment, the therapeutic efficacy of which in certain
conditions is beyond doubt, but the precise mode of action of which
is little understood. It would be impossible in a book of this kind,
and in any case beyond the writer's experience, to attempt a comprehensive critique of the physical methods of treatment in psychiatry. On the other hand, the discussion here would be incomplete
without some brief reference to them. It will be confined to some
general comments arising out of the preceding theoretical analysis of
personality.

In his drug postulate Eysenck (1957a) himself laid some of the
groundwork for a more rational use of pharmacotherapy by suggesting a causal link between natural personality variations and the
influence of drugs, particularly the barbiturates. In the psychiatric

field this has led indirectly to the development of more objective methods of assessing the effects of sedative drugs in anxiety (Wing and Lader, 1965). The pharmacological control of anxiety, of course, is probably the least of the problems facing the clinical psychiatrist, whose main difficulty here is that of choosing between the older, well-established barbiturates and newer drugs claimed to have special anxiolytic properties. More precise comparative bioassay techniques recently reported (Lader and Wing, 1965) promise to put this choice on a more rational basis and open up important areas of research in psychopharmacology. A more fundamental theoretical problem concerns, not anxiety, but that of providing a rationale for the treatment of depressive disorders, on the one hand, and of schizophrenia, on the other. Paralleling the discussion in the previous section, each of these will be considered in turn.

There is little disagreement among clinicians that ECT is most effective in severely endogenously depressed patients. According to the present theory these would be individuals falling at the retarded end of the psychoticism continuum and showing low levels of tonic arousal. It is of some theoretical interest, therefore, that Gellhorn has suggested that electro-shock stimulates the posterior hypothalamus, causing an increase in sympathetic reactivity. He supports this hypothesis with evidence from experimental physiology and from clinical studies using the Mecholyl test (Gellhorn and Loofbourrow, 1963). A decrease in the hypotensive effect of Mecholyl is expected to follow remission after ECT, the Funkenstein test being claimed by its originators as having prognostic value in the treatment of depression (Funkenstein et al., 1948).

Although ECT undoubtedly has widespread effects on the brain as a whole (Ottoson, 1960), a specific influence on the arousal mechanisms does seem to be supported by the results of sedation threshold studies. Increases in the barbiturate tolerance of endogenously depressed patients after ECT have been reported by Shagass and his colleagues, using both the sedation threshold (Shagass et al., 1956) and sleep threshold techniques (Shagass et al., 1959). Shagass and Jones (1958), reporting on a larger group of mixed cases, concluded that as the pre-treatment sedation threshold increased, the chance that a given patient would benefit from ECT diminished. This conclusion was supported in a more recent study by Perris and Brattemo (1963). The relatively poorer response to ECT of patients with high sedation thresholds is consistent with the clinical fact that this form of therapy is not recommended in neurotic depression (Sargant and Slater, 1963). This is because it may result in a worsening of the condition and an increase in anxiety, an observation that accords well with the experimental evidence that neurotic depression is essentially a state of high or even overarousal.

There has been heavy criticism of previous attempts to use procedures like the Mecholyl and sedation threshold tests as prognostic indicators of ECT response. Reviews of studies on the former by Rose (1962) and on both tests by Thorpe (1962) have led to adverse conclusions being reached about the ability of either to predict the outcome of this form of treatment. Thorpe, however, found some of these studies wanting on the grounds of poor experimental technique and scientific reporting, a criticism that is more than usually damaging in a field so complex as psychiatry. On theoretical grounds there would, in fact, appear to be sufficient evidence to encourage further investigation, under precise experimental conditions, of psychophysiological techniques in the selection of depressed patients for electro-convulsive therapy.

The picture with respect to pharmacotherapy in depression is much more confusing because there seems to be no consistent evidence about the two kinds of drug commonly used, viz. imipramine and the monoamine oxidase inhibitors. Pare (1965) commented that it was "generally agreed" that the former is most effective in endogenous and the latter in reactive or atypical cases of depression. This was to some extent confirmed by the results of the recent MRC clinical trial of antidepressant treatments (1965), which demonstrated the superiority of imipramine over phenelzine in a group consisting mainly of severely depressed patients.

The ability of imipramine to relieve endogenous depression might suggest that, like ECT, it does so partly by causing an increase in tonic arousal. There is, however, considerable disagreement about the precise action of imipramine, some authors suggesting that it has an activating effect on central adrenergic mechanisms and others that it depresses the reticular formation (Kalinowsky and Hoch, 1961). The latter authors concluded that the mode of action of the drug probably does not lie merely in arousal or depression of the reticular formation. Himwich (1960), who favours the generally depressant action of imipramine, has speculated that it may share with chlorpromazine the ability to alter the filtering properties of the reticular formation.

Imipramine is, in fact, chemically similar to the phenothiazines and, in one study reported in the Russian literature, Traugott and Balonov (1963) found that it had a two-phase effect in most patients they studied. At one stage during treatment, but depending on the patient's symptomatology, imipramine had effects similar to chlorpromazine. Elsewhere, Lapin (1963) has demonstrated that both imipramine and chlorpromazine may have either tranquillizing or analeptic properties depending on dosage. Thus, imipramine has excitant properties at low doses but depressant properties at high doses. Lapin concluded that small doses of imipramine might be suitable for treating retarded depression but not cases with super-added anxiety or agitation, where the tranquillizing effects of larger doses of the same drug might be more appropriate. The results of this important study may account for some of the inconsistencies in clinical studies of antidepressant drugs. It also opens up a large potential area of research into the relationship between dosage level, therapeutic effect, and the psychophysiological status of the depressed patient.

The treatment problems presented by schizophrenia inevitably overlap considerably with those found in the affective disorders. This is not particularly surprising in view of the difficulty of distinguishing between these conditions both experimentally and clinically. Most of the physical methods of treatment used in other psychiatric illnesses have also been tried in schizophrenia. The convulsive therapies, including ECT and insulin coma therapy, were, of course, introduced initially as specific treatments for schizophrenia. In modern therapeutic practice they are rarely used alone, but rather in combination with some form of pharmacotherapy.

On theoretical grounds it would be expected that ECT would be most effective in the schizophrenic patient with a low sedation threshold. This prediction accords well with the clinical observations of Sargant and Slater (*op. cit.*) who suggest that the schizophrenic symptoms most likely to respond to ECT are affective ones. Their description of the ECT-responsive patient is of a depressed, anergic, apathetic individual of the kind defining the retarded end of the psychoticism continuum postulated here. The same authors, when discussing pharmacotherapy, point out that such patients respond poorly to chlorpromazine, which may produce a greater degree of inertia and depression than ever.

Chlorpromazine is effective, however, in the floridly deluded, hallucinated, and emotionally responsive schizophrenic, an observation which again coincides with theoretical expectation. In this respect it is of interest to note that Key (1961), in his auditory conditioning experiment referred to in the previous section, found that chlorpromazine had the opposite effect to LSD–25 on generalization. That is to say, it *reduced* the range of stimuli to which a response was made. Bradley (1957), in speculating on the action of chlorpromazine, has classified it with LSD–25 as a drug having its effect on the afferent collaterals into the reticular formation. Similarly, Killam and Killam (1957) concluded that chlorpromazine had little effect on the reticular mechanisms of consciousness, but rather enhanced the controlling and filtering properties of the reticular formation. These suggestions would support the clinical efficacy of this phenothiazine in patients presumed here to fall at the active end of the psychoticism continuum and to be characterized by poor modulation of sensory input into the nervous system.

Any conclusions to be drawn from this brief review of psychiatric treatment must inevitably be rather general. The psychoses are still as much a major research problem therapeutically as they are aetiologically and it is probably no mere coincidence that the paradoxical nature of these conditions is paralleled in the contradictory views that have been expressed about the effects of the various techniques used in their treatment. A simple view of drug action is clearly as untenable as a similar explanation of psychosis itself. As Herrington and Claridge (1965) demonstrated, the "normalizing" effect of treatment on the behaviour of psychotics involves a complex shift in psychophysiological status. On the other hand, their study did illustrate the value of carrying out theory-directed, rather than purely empirical research into the effects of treatment. It is hoped that the particular theory presented here may prove of some heuristic value in guiding further investigations and help to carry into a wider field the earlier attempts of Eysenck to provide a more rational basis for psychiatric therapy.

CONCLUDING REMARKS

The orientation of this book has been neither purely physiological nor purely psychological. Instead, personality has been viewed from the standpoint of psychophysiology, a rapidly expanding discipline that occupies a unique position among the sciences contributing to the study of behaviour. Having its theoretical constructs grounded in contemporary neurophysiology, it enables the psychologist, perhaps for the first time, to build a conceptual bridge between the behavioural phenomena he observes and tries to explain and the neural mechanisms underlying them.

Psychophysiology has a long natural history, of course, and it would be less than modest to pretend that the views expressed here represent anything other than an attempt to apply to a selected area of personality concepts that have been slowly emerging in general psychology over many decades. To some readers the results reported here in neurotics, for example, will not appear too unexpected. Terms such as "arousal" have long since passed into the everyday language of experimental psychology. In the abnormal field they have an established place, too, helping to provide some understanding in physiological terms of such personality variables as anxiety. It will not be too surprising either that some integration has been achieved between the arousal concept and Eysenck's excitation–inhibition construct, with its rather different roots in the history of psychology. This integration is merely another example of how different theoretical viewpoints in the behavioural sciences are now beginning to converge. That it was possible is perhaps some measure of the essential correctness of this general approach to personality study.

Further comment is necessary about the results obtained in psychosis, and about their theoretical interpretation. The psychoses have been the subject of many diverse views, although there is still a firm belief, especially in British psychiatry, that an organic aetiology for them will eventually be found. This may well prove to be true in a certain proportion of cases, as, for example, in periodic catatonia (Gjessing, 1938) or in the schizophreniform psychoses associated with temporal lobe epilepsy (Slater *et al.*, 1963). For the most part, however, the psychoses remain an aetiological enigma, in which the biochemical anomalies occasionally described, but rarely confirmed, appear almost as epiphenomena of some more primary disturbance of CNS function.

It may be argued, of course, that the failure so far to demonstrate any consistent organic pathology in most psychoses is due to the fluctuating nature of these illnesses and the gross disregard in many experimental studies of their obvious heterogeneity. This is unlikely in view of the intensive research already undertaken with little success. A more fundamental reason may be that the functional psychoses are, in the literal sense of the word, truly "functional". The results reported here would certainly tend to support this view and more progress might be made in understanding the psychoses if they were conceptualized as neither purely psychological nor purely organic illnesses, but as unusual functional disorders of those psychophysiological mechanisms that underly normal CNS activity. Viewed in this way the psychoses would be regarded as essentially similar to the neuroses in that both seem to involve a disturbance of the same physiological mechanisms controlling emotion, attention, and perception. The psychoses appear to stand out as distinctly different disorders mainly because of the peculiar nature of the dysfunction underlying them. It has been suggested here that this may be due to a dissocation between those functional processes of arousal and attention in the nervous system that are normally congruent in their activity. This hypothesis could account for some of the clinical features of, for example, schizophrenia, where a principal disturbance is the psychological dissociation between affect, on the one hand, and perception, on the other: the schizophrenic either attaches strong and inappropriate emotion to stimuli that are wrongly perceived, or expresses no emotion to psychologically relevant stimuli. A functional rather than disease view of the psychoses might also help to explain the difficulty met in trying to understand a group of conditions which, as a total clinical picture, are perplexingly incongruous, yet which, in some areas of behaviour and at some stages in their development, have certain features in common with normal experience.

Research into personality is, of course, being carried out on a much broader front than that emphasized here and many problems will only be solved by interdisciplinary enquiry. Some attempt has been made, however, to interrelate various levels of investigation; Eysenck's hierarchical approach to personality has been of considerable guidance in this respect, helping to thread through a maze of data representing different strata of behaviour. The integration of physiological and descriptive phenomena is perhaps the most difficult task facing the research worker in this field. The results reported in this book point towards one way in which such an integration might eventually be achieved. In doing so they lead to two inescapable conclusions. The first is that a unified theory of abnormal personality is not only possible but necessary if research in psychiatry is to progress beyond its present stage of empiricism. The second is that psychophysiology, because of its strategic position among the behavioural sciences, promises to play an increasingly vital role in future studies of personality and personality disorder.

THE SEDATION THRESHOLD: PHARMACOLOGICAL CONSIDERATIONS

by R. N. Herrington

SOME GENERAL FACTORS INFLUENCING BARBITURATE ANAESTHESIA

In the analysis of the action of psychoactive drugs, it is widely assumed that their behavioural effects are the result of a direct action of the drug on the central nervous system. Individual differences in susceptibility to such drugs have been held to indicate differences in the strength of certain processes within the brain, and have been used in the construction of typologies (Pavlov, 1927; Shagass, 1954; Eysenck, 1957a). However, barbiturates, which have been most frequently used in this way, particularly in sedation threshold studies, have no especial affinity for the nervous system (Aldridge, 1962), but on the contrary show considerable activity in other tissues. It is therefore possible that individual differences are, at least in part, due to variation in the activity of organs other than the brain. These other tissues may condition the response of the brain to barbiturates, either by controlling the amount of drug available to it through their effect on drug distribution or destruction, or through the barbiturate modification of some aspect of their activity which is important for brain function. Available evidence allows some limited evaluation of these extracerebral mechanisms and offers some guidance in the selection of a test procedure in which their influence is minimal.

Exchange between blood and tissues is, in general, determined by a number of factors, notably blood flow to the tissue (Price, 1963a), physico-chemical characteristics of the substance concerned which govern exchange by simple diffusion (Brodie and Hogben, 1957), and "active transport" mechanisms which allow entry or extrusion of metabolically important substances whose physico-chemical properties are not conducive to rapid passage across cellular membranes. Entry of many substances into the brain is also limited by unknown factors which probably derive from unique metabolic and structural characteristics of the central nervous system (Dobbing, 1961). The totality of processes impeding passage into the central nervous system are collectively known as the "blood–brain barrier". The immense variation in the ease with which different barbiturates penetrate the blood–brain barrier mostly reflects differences in their physico-chemical properties. Active transport and other mechanisms appear not to be involved. Poor ionization and high lipid solubility of the unionized moiety are associated with rapid entry into the brain (Mayer *et al.*, 1959; Rall *et al.*, 1959; Brodie *et al.*, 1960), and there is thus no barrier against thiobarbiturates (Mark *et al.*, 1958).

The encounter between barbiturates and tissue cells involves a number of powerful interactions, some of which outlive the presence of the drug within the tissues. A variety of biochemical activities is disturbed, including those regulating the ionic movements which are the basis of the electrical properties of the neuronal membrane (McIlwain, 1962). At the same time barbiturates are themselves degraded in many tissues, including brain and skeletal muscle, but mostly in the microsomes of the liver. This destruction leads to falling plasma concentrations and barbiturates leave the brain in accordance with the physico-chemical laws governing their entry. Adaptive changes are triggered within the tissues, notably the brain and liver. The brain becomes less sensitive to the barbiturate—the phenomenon of "acute tolerance" (Brodie *et al.*, 1951; Dundee *et al.*, 1956; Maynert and Klingman, 1960; Stumpf and Chiari, 1965; Aston, 1965)—and the activity of enzymes in the liver microsomes is increased (Remmer, 1962; Conney and Burns, 1962; Kato *et al.*, 1964). With repeated drug administrations, these changes are more marked and more stable and are major factors accounting for drug tolerance. Drug distribution is not altered in tolerant animals (Ebert *et al.*, 1964) (see below).

Factors regulating exchange between blood and tissues necessarily regulate absorption of a drug into the blood-stream from its site of administration, such as the gut or muscle. Direct entry into the blood-stream by intravenous injection is preferred in the clinical and experimental studies under consideration here, since variation due to absorption is eliminated. Physico-chemical properties favouring entry into the tissues necessarily also favour entry into the cellular, protein and lipid elements in the blood (Goldbaum and Smith, 1954; Anderson and Magee, 1956; Mayer *et al.*, 1959; Brodie *et al.*, 1960; Yoshikawa and Loehning, 1965). Only drug that is free in the plasma water is therefore immediately available for transfer to the tissues.

The barbiturate group of drugs contains substances with a wide spectrum of physico-chemical and pharmacological properties which alter the relative importance of the processes just described. Access of any drug to the tissues is unequal. This is most readily seen with the "ultra-short acting" thiobarbiturates (thiopentone, kemithal, thiamylal) which, being highly soluble in fat, enter the brain and other tissues so rapidly that differences in tissue uptake probably simply reflect the pattern of blood distribution obtaining at the time of injection. After a rapid intravenous injection of thiopentone (Price 1960a; Price *et al.*, 1960) high concentrations of the drug are quickly attained in the rapidly perfused viscera, especially the brain, and these begin to fall as aqueous tissues with a poorer blood supply, for example muscle, begin to take up the drug. This early loss by the brain to other tissues probably accounts for the brief anaesthesia of thiobarbiturates after rapid administration (Plough *et al.*, 1956; Goldstein and Aranow, 1960; Price, 1960a). Further redistribution of the drug then slowly occurs as it is taken up by poorly perfused depot fat (Brodie *et al.*, 1950). Following a slow intravenous infusion of thiobarbiturates, blood flow is less limiting a factor, tissue concentrations rise more uniformly and the ultra-short action is lost. Drug distribution is then similar to that of oxybarbiturates, such as pentobarbitone or amylobarbitone, whose lower lipid solubility diminishes considerably the advantage of high blood flow. A similarly uniform distribution is seen with barbitone and phenobarbitone whose physico-chemical properties permit slow entry into the tissues where drug distribution is further stabilized by the negligible metabolic degradation of these substances.

Thus, narcosis involves many processes, the relative importance of which varies with time and the drug employed. Conditions may therefore exist in which sensitivity of the central nervous system is a major factor determining individual differences.

SELECTION OF AN INDEX OF CENTRAL SENSITIVITY

Quantification of the course of narcosis is not simple. For a given dose of drug, measurement may be made of the depth of narcosis achieved, the speed with which this is reached, the duration of a particular stage of narcosis, or, in animals, the number of individuals killed. It must be emphasized that *there is no simple, single measure of the narcotic effect* since its various aspects need not be consistently related, either in the same animal on different occasions or under different experimental conditions. It is possible for example, to increase the duration of narcosis thirty-seven times without altering the toxicity (Cook *et al.*, 1954) and to reduce the duration without changing the speed of induction (Major *et al.*, 1959; Tucchi *et al.*, 1949). Even considering the phase of induction alone, indices obtained from different end-points may not be too closely related, the correlation between "sedation" and "sleep" thresholds in man, for example, being only 0·58 (Shagass and Kerenyi, 1958b). These measurements are not determined by a single process and the choice of the most suitable index depends on the aim of the investigation.

The sensitivity of the nervous system is best determined by an end-point occurring early in the sequence of events described above, since most barbiturates penetrate the blood–brain barrier rapidly and disturb cerebral activity before the complications of metabolism, acute tolerance and redistribution are operative. Some measure of the ease with which a given level of narcosis is achieved, such as the sedation threshold, is thus preferable to a measure of its duration. Of the two possibilities, namely determination of the effect of a standard dose of the drug or of the dose of drug necessary to reach a given behavioural or physiological end-point, the latter is preferable since it is easier to measure the amount of drug administered than the degree of narcosis achieved. Whilst the recognition of a defined end-point (electroencephalographic, autonomic, behavioural) is not without difficulty, it was recognized in early animal investigations that a measure of induction of anaesthesia showed consistent differences between individuals and was more reliable than an estimate of the duration of narcosis (Eichler and Smiatek, 1937; Kohn, 1938; Clark and Raventos, 1940). Despite this, sleeping time or an equivalent measure has since been extensively employed in pharmacological studies, even though it is heavily influenced by metabolism of the barbiturate. This, in turn, is affected by such factors as diet (Dixon *et al.*, 1960; Manthei *et al.*, 1964), stress (Driever and Bousquet, 1965) and previous drug administrations (Kato and Chiesara, 1962). It is not surprising, therefore, that measures of sleeping time show a low reliability (Rümke *et al.*, 1963) as well as a marked influence of phenothiazine administration (Brodie, *et al.*, 1955; Dobkin, 1960) and barbiturate tolerance (Green and Koppanyi, 1944; Gruber and Keyser, 1946; Hubbard and Goldbaum, 1949). As a result, changes in sleeping time are difficult (or perhaps too easy!) to interpret (Riley and Spinks, 1958). In contrast, the literature on measures of induction, including the sedation threshold, is small and affords little guidance for human studies, since species differences reduce the applicability of animal data to man (Brodie, 1962).

However, recent work has established the stability of induction measurements and documented some of the effects of chemotherapy. High retest reliabilities have been reported for measures of induction time (Shagass and Naiman, 1956; Shagass *et al.*, 1957; Shagass *et al.*, 1959; Nymgaard, 1959), even though changes in the severity of illness (Shagass *et al.*, 1957) and evanescent effects (Shagass *et al.*, 1959) alter the sedation threshold in man. In a group of psychiatric patients of mixed diagnosis, a product moment correlation of $0 \cdot 96$ between two estimates of the sedation threshold has been obtained when only subjects showing no change in clinical status are studied (Shagass *et al.*, 1957). Less consistency has been found in animal experiments (Eichler and Smiatek, 1937; Kohn, 1938; Clark and Raventos, 1940; Shagass *et al.*, 1962). In one study much smaller correlations were obtained, accounting for a maximum of one-quarter of the variance from test to test (Shagass *et al.*, 1962). Indices of induction are reduced minutes or hours following small doses of chlorpromazine (Bradley and Jeavons, 1957; Major *et al.*, 1959; Shagass *et al.*, 1962; McCance, 1964) and other phenothazines (Dundee *et al.*, 1964). However, they appear not to be affected by more prolonged chemotherapy with phenothiazines (Nymgaard, 1959), repeated thiopentone injections (Tucchi *et al.*, 1949) or addiction to alcohol or drugs, either in animals (Lee *et al.*, 1964) or man (Shagass and Jones, 1957; Moffat and Levine, 1964). On the other hand, Shagass *et al.* (1959), using very high doses of meprobamate in man, found the sedation threshold lowered during administration and raised following its withdrawal. Dundee (1955),

on the contrary, describes increased induction times to thiobarbiturates during the sustained administration to dogs of analgesics,
non-barbiturate sedatives, antihistamines or chlorpromazine, this
effect being absent five days after the cessation of therapy.

PERIPHERAL MECHANISMS

This stability does not indicate that peripheral factors can be
ignored since they may well contribute to differences between
individuals.

The most clearly relevant of these, since they alter drug distribution, are body composition, circulation, and blood–brain barrier
permeability. Induction thresholds are usually expressed as milli-
grams of drug per kilogram body weight, since if the drug is uniformly
distributed within the body, a larger animal will require more of the
drug to attain a given tissue concentration. Distribution within the
body is not uniform, however, particularly during the induction of
anaesthesia. Ideally, since the central aim is the determination of the
sensitivity of the central nervous system of an individual, drugs
should be administered at a steady rate per unit weight of nervous
tissue. Since in adult animals of a given species, organ weights are
not simply related to body weight (Setnikar and Magistretti, 1965),
there is no very accurate way of assessing brain weight.

The greatest source of error in oxybarbiturate thresholds arising
from body composition differences is due to fat and other tissues
with a poor blood supply. If a drug is infused intravenously at a
given rate per unit of body weight, the plasma concentration in fat
animals will remain elevated. This is because the blood supply to
fat is poor and a smaller proportion of the tissues is exposed to the
drug. The brain concentration, which rapidly equilibrates with that
of the plasma, will rise more rapidly and the threshold will be
reached when a smaller amount of drug per unit body weight has
been administered. Such error is eliminated by reference of drug
dosage to lean body mass (Behnke, 1941), an index related to the
active metabolic mass of the body, to plasma volume and to other
pharmacologically important variables (Behnke, 1953). Lean body
mass may be computed from anthropometric data with considerable
accuracy (Allen *et al.*, 1956a; Behnke, 1959, 1961, 1963; Hechter,
1959; Nicholson and Zilva, 1964).

However, no such simple correction seems available for dosage of thiobarbiturates. Their distribution throughout body water at equilibrium is less even than that of oxybarbiturates (Aldridge, 1962) and the role of depot fat and metabolism in the brief action of these drugs remains a matter of controversy (Mark, 1963; Price, 1963b; Saidman and Eger, 1966). Even in the case of sleeping time, where the high avidity of fat for thiobarbiturates should overcome the effect of poor perfusion, data are conflicting. Some studies (Bazett and Erb, 1933; Herman and Wood, 1952) confirm the expectation that fat animals will have shorter sleeping times to thiobarbiturates whilst others do not (Keéri-Szanto, 1960; Feinstein and Hiner, 1963).

These considerations are of importance since comparisons based on lean body mass eliminate error due to the known variation of adiposity and blood volume with age (Brožek, 1952; Behnke, 1963), sex (Edwards, 1951; Allen et al., 1956b) and body build (Gregersen and Nickerson, 1950; Seltzer and Mayer, 1964). Moreover, changes in body composition are described following drugs and physical activity (Pařízková, 1963) and in psychiatric illness (Post, 1956). The latter seems not to be due, however, to the disease process itself but to be secondary to changes in caloric intake (Remenchik and Talso, 1965). The marked weight changes described following phenothiazine treatment (Klett and Caffey, 1960; Caffey, 1961; Amdisen, 1964) are again probably related to increased caloric intake (Mefferd et al., 1958). Hence they are probably a manifestation of increased adiposity, though water retention may also be involved (Supek et al., 1960a, 1960b; Tiwari et al., 1960; Boris and Stevenson, 1964).

Even if body composition is allowed for, there are other peripheral factors affecting distribution which could conceivably account for individual differences in the sedation threshold. For two of these, changes in the circulation and in blood–brain barrier permeability, enough data exist to allow an estimate of their importance.

The pattern of blood distribution is constantly changing with alterations in mental activity, body position, motor activity, alimentary function and so on. Such changes may affect the sedation threshold by altering the cerebral blood flow or the pattern of blood flow to other organs, thereby directing blood into territories which take up more or less of the drug. Cerebral blood flow is reported normal in acute apprehension (Scheinberg and Stead, 1949) and schizophrenic psychosis (Kety et al., 1947; Gordon et al., 1955;

Sokoloff *et al.*, 1957). However, changes are described in other vascular beds. The marked muscle vasodilation accompanying acute anxiety (Brod *et al.*, 1959; Vanderhoof and Clancy, 1962) would undoubtedly increase considerably the capillary surface available for drug exchange (Folkow and Mellander, 1960): blood levels, and hence amount of drug available to the brain, would be reduced and the sedation threshold raised. However, it seems that in chronic anxiety, skeletal muscle changes are not so marked (Harper *et al.*, 1965) and are overshadowed by skin vasoconstriction (Ackner, 1956b) which would probably reduce the sedation threshold. The poor peripheral circulation often reported in schizophrenia (Shattock, 1950; Ackner, 1956a) would also tend to lower the threshold. These changes cannot be too readily interpreted since they are probably accompanied by compensatory adjustments in other vascular beds and may be overridden or enhanced by the circulatory changes occurring early in barbiturate narcosis (Price, 1960b; Acheson, 1963; Strandness *et al.*, 1964; Barlow and Knott, 1964).

Nevertheless, vascular factors affecting drug distribution outside the central nervous system may contribute to the variations in sedation threshold, particularly since the differences in capillary structure (Doust, 1955) and flow (Doust and Melville, 1956) described in psychiatric illness may indicate that exchange between blood and tissues is directly involved.

The blood–brain barrier imposes little delay on the entry of most barbiturates into the central nervous system (Mark *et al.*, 1958), but this may be sufficient to affect the speed of induction of anaesthesia. Blood–brain barrier permeability is generally reported normal in psychiatric illness (Coppen, 1959, 1960; Fotherby *et al.*, 1963; Guerrant *et al.*, 1964) and is variably affected by phenothiazines (Christensen *et al.*, 1958; Quadbeck and Sacsse, 1961; Guerrant *et al.*, 1964). Electroplexy undoubtedly increases the permeability of the barrier for a few hours (see below), though this is probably prevented by anaesthetization during the treatment (Bauer and Leonhardt, 1956; Lee and Olszewski, 1961). It seems unlikely, therefore, that the permeability of the blood–brain barrier is a factor of importance in the sedation threshold.

There are, therefore, many factors outside the brain which could account for differences in barbiturate tolerance. If these differences do reflect the sensitivity of the brain, they may even yet be secondary to differences in the activity of other organs. These may well change during a psychiatric illness, either as part of the natural history of the illness itself, or due to therapeutic procedures. Of many possibilities, there is ample evidence that adrenal function is important. Deficiency of adrenocortical hormones shortens the induction time of barbiturate anaesthesia (Winter and Flataker, 1952; Shibata and Komiya, 1953; Komiya and Shibata, 1956; Cook et al., 1960; Feldman, 1962; Chambers et al., 1963). Administration of corticoids to normal animals lengthens induction time (Komiya and Shibata, 1957). However, in psychiatric illness, no simple relation between sedation threshold and plasma corticoid levels exists, since plasma cortisol is raised in anxiety (Hamburg, 1962) and early psychosis (Bliss et al., 1956; Gibbons and McHugh, 1963). On recovery plasma cortisol falls even though release of these hormones is provoked by electroplexy, insulin coma (Bliss et al., 1954) and phenothiazines (Smith et al., 1963). However, lack of simple correspondence does not necessarily negate a causal relation. The electrolyte changes reported in depressive illness (Coppen and Shaw, 1963; Anderson et al., 1964), which may be due to adrenocortical hyperactivity (Gibbons and McHugh, 1963), may perhaps account for the low sedation thresholds reported in psychotic depression (see Chapters 6 and 9).

Changes in brain sensitivity, unrelated to its therapeutic efficacy, may also be wrought by electroplexy as evidenced by changes in the electroencephalogram (Moriarty and Siemens, 1947; Kennard and Willner, 1948; Roth, 1951), indices of cerebral excitability (Essig et al., 1961, 1964; Pollack et al., 1963) and psychometric tests (Campbell, 1960). Although it has no effect on cerebral blood flow (Wilson et al., 1952), electroshock promotes a short-lived water retention (Russell, 1960) and briefly disrupts the blood–brain barrier (Bjerner et al., 1944; Aird et al., 1958; Bauer and Leonhardt, 1956; Rosenblatt et al., 1960; Lee and Olszewski, 1961; Nair and Roth, 1962; Angel et al., 1965). Most of these changes should lead to a reduction of the sedation threshold, but Shagass et al. (1959) provide evidence that it is raised.

MEASUREMENT OF THE SEDATION THRESHOLD

Clearly, peripheral factors may obscure individual differences in the sensitivity of the nervous system to barbiturates and any change in them accompanying psychiatric disturbance. Interpretation of experimental findings undoubtedly carries some risk, though this is minimized in studies guided by a correct hypothetico-deductive approach (Eysenck, 1960d, 1960f). Nevertheless, identification of and allowance for these peripheral processes can be expected to improve the estimation of central sensitivity, particularly in indicating the experimental precautions to be taken in estimating the sedation threshold and in the choice of the barbiturate to be employed.

A major problem in studies of psychiatric illness is the effect of previous treatment, particularly drugs. The majority of reports (see above) indicate that chronic administration of alcohol, barbiturates, and phenothiazines does not alter the sedation threshold though acute administrations reduce it. It would, however, seem preferable to test patients after at least a brief withdrawal of drugs, but one outlasting withdrawal phenomena that are to be seen even with phenothiazines (Bennett and Kooi, 1961). Following acute or chronic administration, phenothiazines are largely absent from the body after 3 to 5 days (Salzman and Brodie, 1956; Walkenstein and Seifter, 1959; Haynes, 1960; Huang and Kurland, 1961; Emmerson and Miya, 1962; Caffey et al., 1963). On the other hand, psychotropic drugs are known to initiate long-lasting biochemical changes in the brain (Hess et al., 1956; Utena et al., 1959). Both physiological (Oswald and Thacore, 1963) and psychometric (Clark et al., 1963; Ray et al., 1964) manifestations of these changes have been detected. A further complication, minimized in a test of narcosis induction, is the increased metabolism of barbiturates by the liver microsomes beginning 48 hours after the administration of many drugs, including barbiturates and tranquillizers (Kato and Chiesara, 1962; Kato et al., 1964). Changes in sleeping time associated with the development of tolerance disappear within a few days of drug withdrawal (Green and Koppanyi, 1944; Gruber and Keyser, 1946), and Dundee's (1955) study suggests that this is also true for any changes in induction time. However, a recent report (Aston, 1965) records complex changes in induction and sleeping times for 2 weeks following a large single dose of pentobarbitone. Information is lacking regarding the permanence of the rises in threshold attributed to electroplexy (Shagass et al., 1959) but it is probable that they do not persist longer than 2 weeks if we are to judge from changes in the EEG (Moriarty and Siemens, 1947; Kennard and Willner, 1948) and in excitability (Essig *et al.*, 1961, 1964). It would seem, therefore, that the sedation threshold should not be determined until at least 1, preferably 2, weeks following the cessation of therapy. Night sedation should be avoided, since it is known to affect psychological performance the following morning (Kornetsky *et al.*, 1959), though Shagass and Jones (1958) report that the sedation threshold is unaffected.

Situational anxiety is always a problem in studies on conscious animals or man, especially in personality research where it cannot be assumed identical in different experimental groups. It is known to affect the autonomic changes following intravenous sodium amylobarbitone (Martin and Davies, 1965) and therefore probably the sedation threshold (Shagass *et al.*, 1959). Such effects may perhaps be minimized if experimental subjects are familiarized with the experimental procedure and a remote injection procedure employed (Martin and Davies, 1965). However, it is possible that situational anxiety may reinforce the psychological adaptations present in psychiatric illness and maximize differences between groups.

Error in the determination of the sedation threshold can probably be further reduced by attention to other factors in the preparation of the subject. Apart from the effects of circulatory adjustments, a meal may also reduce the sedation threshold, particularly if a thiobarbiturate is employed, either by increasing serum lipids (Foldes and Beecher, 1943; Stavinoha and Davis, 1955; Anderson and Magee, 1956) or by absorption of the barbiturate into fat inside the gut (Winters *et al.*, 1962). On the other hand, a prolonged fast may lead to hypoglycaemia or dehydration, especially in psychiatric patients whose diet may have been disturbed for days. Hydration greatly modifies the duration of narcosis (Borzelleca and Manthei, 1955; Bhide, 1960; Ramwell and Lester, 1961), perhaps by its effect on the blood–brain barrier (Becker and Aird, 1955). Sensitivity to pentobarbitone shows marked diurnal variation in rodents (Davis, 1962; Emlen and Kem, 1963; Pauly and Scheving, 1964; Lindsay and Kullman, 1966). The sedation threshold in man probably also varies, since physiological functions known to influence it, especially adrenal function, show definite circadian periodicity in man (Mills, 1966). In order to minimize the influence of these factors, the present authors have regularly determined the sedation threshold between 10.00 and 12.00 a.m., following a light breakfast at 8.00 a.m. of two slices of buttered toast and two cups of sugared tea.

Following Shagass (1954), the sedation threshold has usually been obtained with sodium amylobarbitone. The use of a shorter-acting drug is clinically desirable, but presents difficulties. The brief action of N-methyl barbiturates (hexobarbitone, methohexital) is due largely to rapid metabolism (Brodie, 1952; Burns, 1963) and the sedation threshold obtained with these drugs may therefore be greatly influenced by factors modifying metabolism. Thiobarbiturates would appear, at first sight, to have the required properties, namely rapid entry into the brain and brief action due to redistribution of the drug. However, such redistribution is seen only with fast injection rates, at which individual differences would be difficult to demonstrate. The brief action of thiobarbiturates, depending largely on redistribution, is lost at the slow rates of injection required in the accurate determination of an end-point. Revived controversy regarding the roles of depot fat (Mark, 1963; Price, 1963b) and metabolism (Saidman and Eger, 1966) in the ultra-short action of thiobarbiturates, and the problem of body composition already discussed, reduce confidence in their use in sedation threshold studies.

INTERPRETATION

Individual differences in tolerance to sedative drugs have often been related to psychological or behavioural variables. Should this interrelation derive from the direct pharmacological action of these substances in the brain, these studies offer the possibility of a link between psychophysiological and neurophysiological conceptions of cerebral activity and perhaps the identification of disturbed physiological mechanisms in mental illness.

However, after thirty years of study, little is definitely known of the distortion of nervous activity produced by barbiturates. They are known to interfere with the ionic movements which are the basis of the electrical properties of nerve cells (McIlwain, 1962). Subsynaptic membrane (Somjen, 1963) and presynaptic nerve terminal (Løyning et al., 1964) appear particularly sensitive. In line with these findings it has been recently shown that a new type of inhibitory synaptic action, "presynaptic inhibition", is greatly strengthened by pentobarbitone (Eccles et al., 1963), though the general significance of this cannot yet be assessed, since the existence of this process outside the spinal cord has been barely investigated.

In the present state of knowledge it is not possible to deduce from these general properties any consequences of barbiturate action in integrated neuronal systems, even in simple spinal reflex arcs, though it does seem that barbiturates have a more global depressant action than other types of central nervous "depressants" (Esplin, 1963).

A more promising lead is given by the ability of barbiturates, in low doses, to curtail the repetitive discharge, so characteristic of central neurons (McIntyre et al., 1956) in the cerebral cortex (Mountcastle et al., 1957; Burns, 1958; Yamamoto and Schaeppi, 1961; Herz and Fuster, 1964) and reticular formation (Schlag, 1956; Yamamoto and Schaeppi, 1961; Scheibel and Scheibel, 1965). Very small doses of barbiturates should therefore disrupt the organized activity of chains of neurons (see Verzeano and Negishi, 1960). Such activities, of which neurophysiological study is just beginning (e.g. Rosner, 1956; Vastola, 1965), would have a slow time course and be more equivalent to processes described by psychologists and known to be affected by small doses of drugs. No close correspondence between the constructs of neuronal physiology and psychology can, however, be expected. It is becoming increasingly clear (Brooks, 1959) that inhibitory checks on excitation are universal, both spatially and with respect to time (together presumably constituting Pavlovian "negative induction"), and are the basis of localization and precision within the nervous system. When such inhibitory influences have been studied by conventional neurophysiological (Mountcastle, 1957; Preston and Whitlock, 1960; Kubota and Takahashi, 1965) or conditioned reflex (Tsobkallo and Kalinina, 1960) techniques, they have proved more susceptible to barbiturate narcosis than excitation. Barbiturates are therefore likely to impair perceptual discriminations and motor co-ordination and thus strengthen "inhibition" as conceived by Eysenck.

That such a vague and general neurophysiological description of the behavioural effects of barbiturates is all that is possible, is exemplified by the failure of an immense literature to localize the action of these drugs to an anatomical site or simple physiological system within the brain, though it does appear that the midbrain reticular formation (Domino, 1962; Killam, 1962) and the septal area (Harvey et al., 1964) are strategic sites regulating the sensitivity of the brain to barbiturates. It is clear that interpretation along the lines of a simple arousal theory is somewhat hazardous.

"Dissociations" between different so-called measures of "arousal" are not infrequent, peripheral autonomic measures may not co-vary in a simple way, and the reticular formation itself shows considerable anatomical, physiological and pharmacological complexity. In particular, it should be noted that the fast cortical activity induced early in barbiturate action, changes in which were the basis of the original sedation threshold concept (Shagass, 1954, 1957a), is probably due to early suppression of the brainstem synchronizing component of the ascending reticular system (Magni *et al.*, 1959) and is a further example of the particular susceptibility of inhibitory mechanisms to barbiturates.

Caution is also necessary in the analysis of the action of barbiturates on peripheral autonomic indices of arousal since these drugs provoke increased sympathetic tone (Barlow and Knott, 1964), block transmission through autonomic ganglia (Exley, 1954) and dilate (oxybarbiturates) or constrict (thiobarbiturates) arterioles by a direct action (Gruber *et al.*, 1952). Autonomic changes during barbiturate anaesthesia cannot, therefore, be taken too readily to indicate drifts in central autonomic regulatory mechanisms.

This susceptibility of certain components of the reticular formation need not necessarily lie in the architecture of neuronal interconnection in these areas, but in some other factor such as vascularity (Barlow *et al.*, 1958) which is known to show considerable individual variation (Nair *et al.*, 1960). The distribution of barbiturates within the brain is not uniform, (Landau *et al.*, 1955; Freygang and Sokoloff, 1958; Sokoloff, 1961; Roth and Barlow, 1961). The pattern also differs with the barbiturate employed, being governed by vascular distribution in the case of thiopentone but not so for phenobarbitone (Domek *et al.*, 1959). In addition, blood flow to different regions of the brain is altered by barbiturates themselves: there is a general reduction in blood flow, but some areas change more than others. Blood flow to the reticular formation changes little (Sokoloff, 1961; Birzis and Tachibana, 1964b). Though capable of many explanations this may mean that this area of the brain would be exposed to high drug concentrations and therefore appear especially susceptible. The pattern of blood flow within the brain changes with the mental state (Sokoloff, 1961; Birzis and Tachibana, 1964a), and it is therefore possible that the correlations between the sedation threshold and personality factors reflect, at least in part, differences in reactivity of the cerebral vasculature.

At the moment, therefore, physiological analysis is barely superior to a molar approach in disclosing the significance of sedation threshold findings. Its chief value lies in the detection of peripheral "artefacts" which are unlikely to be of psychological significance. This may be exemplified by considering the possible effect of adrenaline and noradrenaline on the sedation threshold. These amines have powerful, well-studied peripheral actions which may well prove to be of considerable significance in psychopharmacology. Increased plasma and urinary levels of these substances are reported with mental activity (Frankenhauser and Post, 1962) and accompanying anxiety (Bloom et al., 1963). They rise, too, during psychotic exacerbations in schizophrenia (Gjessing, 1964; Pscheidt et al., 1964), even in association with motor retardation which would itself reduce catecholamine output (Euler and Hellner, 1952; Vendsalu, 1960). Furthermore, marked and stable individual differences in the response of the circulation to these amines have been described in dogs (Lockett, 1950).

These substances do not pass the blood–brain barrier (Weil-Malherbe et al., 1959), but induce behavioural and electrocortical arousal through peripheral mechanisms (Baust and Niemczyk, 1964); hence a rise in sedation threshold would be expected through a secondary central action. Surprisingly, despite cardiovascular, electromyographic and electroencephalographic evidence of high arousal in early schizophrenia (Malmo and Shagass, 1949a; Whatmore and Ellis, 1958; Goldstein et al., 1963, 1965), increased sensitivity to barbiturates in many psychotics is disclosed by sedation threshold (Shagass and Jones, 1958; Herrington and Claridge, 1965) and other (Goldman, 1959; Sila et al., 1962) studies of this condition. It is therefore of interest that systemic administration of adrenaline and noradrenaline has long been known to prolong the sleeping time and reduce induction time to barbiturates (Lamson et al., 1952; Pradhan et al., 1956; Lee et al., 1965). Since neither adrenaline (Fouts, 1962) nor noradrenaline (Dixon et al., 1964) affects the metabolism of barbiturates under the conditions of these experiments, some modification of drug distribution is the likely explanation of their action. This must undoubtedly occur since these amines drastically reduce blood flow to most tissues whilst the cerebral blood flow is unaffected (Green and Kepchar, 1959). (It will be recalled that diminished circulation in the limbs attributable to vasconstriction and normal cerebral blood flow are found in schizophrenia.) Exchange of drug between blood and tissues, apart from the brain (and also the heart), is thus impeded (Berde *et al.*, 1964) and the sedation threshold therefore reduced. The clinical and experimental situations are therefore very similar and implicate peripheral processes in reducing the sedation threshold in psychosis. Yet central mechanisms may be involved. Whilst catecholamines do not affect total blood flow to the brain, they do change its regional distribution (Birzis and Tachibana, 1964a; Haggendal, 1966) and hence the regional availability of barbiturate during the phase of induction. They may also exert a direct action on the central nervous system by gaining access to areas without a blood–brain barrier or by the slow entry into other regions for which evidence now exists (Breggin, 1964, 1965). Their well-known central "depressant" action would presumably lower the sedation threshold. Catecholamines can therefore be expected to influence the sedation threshold through several, often opposing mechanisms, the actual outcome depending on the relative strength of these processes, which are in turn determined by other controlling variables, notably the plasma concentration of the amines themselves.

This example, which illustrates the complexities of the problem, demonstrates the value of physiological analysis. Should powerful peripheral interactions be demonstrated, sedation threshold studies would be of limited value in the analysis of the neurophysiological mechanisms underlying molar constructs such as "arousal" or "excitation–inhibition balance" in health or in functional mental illness. On the other hand, if the correlations between the sedation threshold and behavioural indices reported in this volume derive from altered processes within the brain, study of the sedation threshold may ultimately provide a link between physiological and psychological conceptions. At the present time physiological considerations, at the very least, may eliminate erroneous deductions from the hypotheses under investigation and sharpen the efficiency of their experimental verification or rejection.

BIBLIOGRAPHY

ACHESON, F. (1963) The transient effect on muscle blood flow of thiopental sodium in the cat. *Anesthesiology* **24**, 658–664.

ACKNER, B. (1956a) Emotions and the peripheral vascular system. *J. psychosom. Res.* **1**, 3–20.

ACKNER, B. (1956b) The relationship between anxiety and level of peripheral vasomotor activity: an experimental study. *J. psychosom. Res.* **1**, 21–48.

ACKNER, B. and PAMPIGLIONE, G. (1958) Discussion on physiological measurements of "emotional tension". *Proc. Roy. Soc. Med.* **51**, 76–81.

ACKNER, B. and PAMPIGLIONE, G. (1959) An evaluation of the sedation threshold test. *J. psychosom. Res.* **3**, 271–281.

ADCOCK, C. J. (1965) A comparison of the concepts of Eysenck and Cattell. *Brit. J. educ. Psychol.* **35**, 90–97.

ADEY, W. R., SEGUNDO, J. P. and LIVINGSTON, R. B. (1957) Corticifugal influences on intrinsic brain-stem conduction in cat and monkey. *J. Neurophysiol.* **20**, 1–16.

AGATHON, M. (1964) Effets consécutifs perceptifs et résponses électroencéphalographiques. *Psychologie Française* **9**, 35–46.

AGATHON, M. and LELORD, G. (1961) Etude comparée de phénomènes consécutifs observés à la suite d'une stimulation lumineuse brève et après la présentation de la spirale d'Archimède. *Paper presented at Fifth International Congress of Electroencephalography and Clinical Neurophysiology*, Rome.

AGNEW, N. and AGNEW, MARY. (1963) Drive level effects on tasks of narrow and broad attention. *Quart. J. exp. Psychol.* **15**, 58–62.

AIRD, R. B., STRAIGHT, L. A., PACE, J. W., HRENOFF, M. K. and BOWDITCH, S. C. (1958) Neurophysiologic effects of electrically induced convulsions. *Arch. Neurol. Psychiat. (Chic.)* **79**, 711–715.

ALDRIDGE, W. N. (1962) Action of barbiturates upon respiratory enzymes. In MONGAR, J. L. and DE REUCK, A. V. S. (Eds.) *Enzymes and Drug Action. Ciba Foundation Symposium.* Little, Brown & Co., Boston.

ALEXANDER, L. (1955) Epinephrine-Mecholyl test (Funkenstein test). *Arch. Neurol. Psychiat. (Chic.)* **73**, 496–514.

AL-ISSA, I. (1964) The Eysenck Personality Inventory in chronic schizophrenia. *Brit. J. Psychiat.* **110**, 397–400.

ALLEN, T. H., PENG, M. T., CHEN, K. P., HUANG, T. F., CHANG, C. and FANG, H. S. (1956a) Prediction of blood volume and adiposity in man from body weight and cube of height. *Metabolism* **5**, 328–345.

ALLEN, T. H., PENG, M. T., CHEN, K. P., HUANG, T. F., CHANG, C. and FANG, H. S. (1956b) Prediction of total adiposity from skinfolds and the curvilinear relationship between external and internal adiposity. *Metabolism* **5**, 346–352.

ALTMAN, L. L., PRATT, D. and COTTON, J. M. (1943) Cardio-vascular response to acetyl-beta-methylcholine (Mecholyl) in mental disorders. *J. nerv. ment. Dis.* **97**, 296–309.

ALTSCHULE, M. (1953) *Bodily Physiology in Mental and Emotional Disorders.* Grune and Stratton, New York.

235

AMDISEN, A. (1964) Drug-produced obesity. *Danish Medical Bulletin* 11, 182–189.

AMMONS, C. H. (1955) Task for the study of perceptual learning and performance variables. *Percept. mot. Skills* 5, 11–14.

ANDERSON, E. G. and MAGEE, D. F. (1956) A study of the mechanism of the effect of dietary fat in increasing thiopental sleeping time. *J. Pharmacol. exp. Ther.* 117, 281–286.

ANDERSON, W. M., DAWSON, J. and MARGERISON, J. H. (1964) Serial biochemical, clinical and electroencephalographic studies in affective illness. *Clin. Sci.* 26, 323–336.

ANGEL, C., HARTMAN, A. M., BURKETT, M. L. and ROBERTS, A. J. (1965) Effects of electroshock and trypan red on the blood–brain barrier and response retention in the rat. *J. nerv. ment. Dis.* 140, 405–411.

ASTON, R. (1965) Quantitative aspects of tolerance and post-tolerance hypersensitivity to pentobarbital in the rat. *J. Pharmacol. exp. Ther.* 150, 253–258.

BADDELEY, A. D. (1964) Reduced body temperature and time estimation. *Paper presented to the London Conference of the British Psychological Society.*

BAKAN, P. (1959) Extraversion–introversion and improvement in an auditory vigilance task. *Brit. J. Psychol.* 50, 325–332.

BAKAN, P., BELTON, J. A. and TOTH, J. C. (1963) Extraversion–introversion and decrement in an auditory vigilance task. In BUCKNER, D. N. and McGRATH, J. J. (Eds.) *Vigilance: a Symposium.* McGraw-Hill, New York.

BARLOW, C. F., SCHOOLAR, J. C. and ROTH, L. J. (1958) An autoradiographic demonstration of the relative vascularity of the central nervous system of the cat with iodine 131-labeled serum albumen. *J. Neuropath. exp. Neurol.* 17, 191–198.

BARLOW, G. and KNOTT, D. H. (1964) Hemodynamic alterations after 30 minutes of pentobarbital sodium anesthesia in dogs. *Amer. J. Physiol.* 207, 764–766.

BARTHOLOMEW, A. A. (1959) Extraversion, introversion and neuroticism. *Brit. J. Delinq.* 10, 120–129.

BARTHOLOMEW, A. A. and MARLEY, E. (1959) The temporal reliability of the Maudsley Personality Inventory. *J. ment. Sci.* 105, 238–240.

BAUER, K. F. and LEONHARDT, H. (1956) A contribution to the pathological physiology of the blood–brain barrier. *J. comp. Neurol.* 106, 363–370.

BAUST, W. and NIEMCZYK, H. (1964) Further studies on the action of adrenergic drugs on cortical activity. *Electroenceph. clin. Neurophysiol.* 17, 261–271.

BAZETT, H. C. and ERB, W. H. (1933) Standardisation of the dosage of Nembutal for anaesthesia in cats and dogs. *J. Pharmacol. exp. Ther.* 49, 352–361.

BECKER, R. A. and AIRD, R. B. (1955) Mechanisms influencing the permeability of the blood–brain barrier. *J. cell. comp. Physiol.* 46, 127–141.

BEHNKE, A. R. (1941) Physiologic studies pertaining to deep sea diving and aviation, especially in relation to the fat content and composition of the body. *Harvey Lectures* 37, 198–226.

BEHNKE, A. R. (1953) The relation of lean body weight to metabolism and some congruent systematisations. *Ann. N.Y. Acad. Sci.* 56, 1095–1142.

BEHNKE, A. R. (1959) The estimation of lean body weight from "skeletal" measurements. *Human Biol.* 31, 295–315.

BEHNKE, A. R. (1961) Quantitative assessment of body build. *J. appl. Physiol.* 16, 960–968.

BEHNKE, A. R. (1963) Anthropometric evaluation of body composition throughout life. *Ann. N.Y. Acad. Sci.* 110, 450–464.

BELLAK, L. (Ed) (1958) *Schizophrenia: a Review of the Syndrome.* Logos, New York.

BENJAMIN, L. S. (1963) Statistical treatment of the law of initial values (LIV) in autonomic research: a review and recommendation. *Psychosom. Med.* **25**, 556–566.

BENNETT, J. L. and KOOI, K. A. (1961) Five phenothiazine derivatives. Evaluation and toxicity studies. *Arch. gen. Psychiat.* **4**, 413–418.

BERDE, B., SCHALCH, W. R. and DOEPFNER, W. (1964) Über die lokalvasoconstrictorische Wirkung von Octapressin, Adrenalin und Hypertensin. *Helv. physiol. Acta* **22**, 110–119.

BERLYNE, D. E. (1960) *Conflict, Arousal and Curiosity*. McGraw-Hill, New York.

BHIDE, N. K. (1960) Effect of hydration on hexobarbital-induced sleep in mice. *Nature* **187**, 1030.

BILLS, A. G. (1931) Blocking: a new principle of mental fatigue. *Amer. J. Psychol.* **43**, 230–245.

BILLS, A. G. (1964) A study of blocking and other response variables in psychotic, brain-damaged and personality disturbed patients. *Behav. Res. Ther.* **2**, 99–106.

BIRZIS, L. and TACHIBANA, S. (1964a) Local cerebral impedance and blood flow during sleep and arousal. *Exp. Neurol.* **9**, 269–285.

BIRZIS, L. and TACHIBANA, S. (1964b) The action of stimulant and depressant agents on local cortical impedance and circulation. *Psychopharmacologia (Berl.)* **6**, 256–266.

BJERNER, B. (1950) Alpha depression and lowered pulse rate during delayed actions in a serial reaction test. *Acta psychol. scand.* **19**, Suppl. 65, pp. 93.

BJERNER, B., BROMAN, T. and SWENSSON, A. (1944) Tierexperimentelle Untersuchungen über Schadigungen der Gerfässe mit Permeabilitätsstörungen und Blutungen im Gehirn bei Insulin-, Cardiazol- und Electroshockbehandlung. *Acta psychiat. (Kbh)* **19**, 431–452.

BLISS, E. L., MIGEON, C. J., BRANCH, C. H. H. and SAMUELS, L. T. (1956) Reaction of the adrenal cortex to emotional stress. *Psychosom. med.* **18**,56–76.

BLISS, E. L., MIGEON, C. J., NELSON, D. H., SAMUELS, L. T. and BRANCH, C. H. H. (1954) Influence of ECT and insulin coma on the level of adrenocortical steroids in the peripheral circulation. *Arch. Neurol. Psychiat. (Chic.)* **72**, 352–361.

BLOOM, G., EULER, U. S. VON and FRANKENHAUSER, M. (1963) Catecholamine excretion and personality traits in paratroop trainees. *Acta physiol. scand.* **58**, 77–89.

BONVALLET, M., DELL, P. and HIEBEL, G. (1954) Tonus sympathique et activité électrique corticale. *Electroenceph. clin. Neurophysiol.* **6**, 119–144.

BORIS, A. and STEVENSON, R. H. (1964) Effects of some psychotropic drugs upon urinary water output. *Proc. Soc. exp. Biol. Med. (N. Y.)* **115**, 170–172.

BORZELLECA, J. F. and MANTHEI, R. W. (1955) Factors influencing pentobarbital sleeping time in mice. *Arch. int. Pharmacodyn.* **111**, 296–307.

BOUDREAU, D. (1958) Evaluation of the sedation threshold test. *Arch. Neurol. Psychiat. (Chic.)* **80**, 771–775.

BRADLEY, P. B. (1957) The central action of certain drugs in relation to the reticular formation of the brain. In JASPER, H. H. *et al.* (Eds.) *Reticular Formation of the Brain*. Churchill, London.

BRADLEY, P. B. and JEAVONS, P. M. (1957) The effect of chlorpromazine and reserpine on sedation and convulsive thresholds in schizophrenic patients. *Electroenceph. clin. Neurophysiol.* **9**, 661–672.

BREGGIN, P. R. (1964) The psychophysiology of anxiety with a review of the literature concerning adrenaline. *J. nerv. ment. Dis.* **139**, 558–568.

BREGGIN, P. R. (1965) Sedative-like effect of epinephrine. *Arch. gen. Psychiat. (Chic.)* **12**, 255–259.

BRENGELMANN, J. C. (1959) Abnormal and personality correlates of certainty. *J. ment. Sci.* **105**, 146–162.

BRENGELMANN, J. C. (1960) Extreme response set, drive level and abnormality in questionnaire rigidity. *J. ment. Sci.* **106**, 171–186.

BROADBENT, D. E. (1958) *Perception and Communication.* Pergamon, Oxford.

BROADBENT, D. E. (1963) Possibilities and difficulties in the concept of arousal. In BUCKNER, D. N. and McGRATH, J. J. (Eds.) *Vigilance: a Symposium.* McGraw-Hill, New York.

BROADHURST, P. L. and BROADHURST, A. (1964) An analysis of the pursuit rotor learning of chronic psychotics. *Brit. J. Psychol.* **55**, 321–331.

BROADHURST, P. L. and EYSENCK, H. J. (1965) Emotionality in the rat: a problem of response specificity. In BANKS, C. and BROADHURST, P. L. (Eds.) *Studies in Psychology.* Univ. London Press, London.

BROD, J., FENCL, V., HEJL, Z. and JIRKA, J. (1959) Circulatory changes underlying blood pressure elevation during acute emotional stress (mental arithmetic) in normotensive and hypertensive subjects. *Clin. Sci.* **18**, 269–279.

BRODIE, B. B. (1952) Physiological disposition and chemical fate of thiobarbiturates in the body. *Fed. Proc.* **11**, 632–639.

BRODIE, B. B. (1962) Difficulties in extrapolating data on metabolism of drugs from animals to man. *Clin. Pharmacol. Ther.* **3**, 374–380.

BRODIE, B. B. and HOGBEN, C. A. (1957) Some physico-chemical factors in drug action. *J. Pharm. Pharmacol.* **9**, 345–380.

BRODIE, B. B., KURZ, H. and SCHANKER, L. S. (1960) The importance of dissociation constant and lipid-solubility in influencing the passage of drugs into the cerebrospinal fluid. *J. Pharmacol. exp. Ther.* **130**, 20–25.

BRODIE, B. B., MARK, L. C., LIEF, P. A., BERNSTEIN, E. and PAPPER, E. M. (1951) Acute tolerance to thiopental. *J. Pharmacol. exp. Ther.* **102**, 215–218.

BRODIE, B. B., MARK, L. C., PAPPER, E. M., LIEF, P. A., BERNSTEIN, E. and ROVENSTINE, E. A. (1950) The fate of thiopental in man and a method for its estimation in biological materials. *J. Pharmacol. exp. Ther.* **98**, 85–96.

BRODIE, B. B., SHORE, P. A., SILVER, G. L. and PULVER, R. (1955) Potentiating action of chlorpromazine and reserpine. *Nature* **175**, 1133–1134.

BROOKS, V. B. (1959) Contrast and stability in the nervous system. *Trans. N.Y. Acad. Sci.* **21**, 387–394.

BROWN, G. W. (1960) Length of hospital stay and schizophrenia. *Acta psychiat. et neurol. scand.* **35**, 414–430.

BROŽEK, J. (1952) Changes of body composition in man during maturity and their nutritional implications. *Fed. Proc.* **11**, 784–793.

BUCKNER, D. N. (1963) An individual-difference approach to explaining vigilance performance. In BUCKNER, D. N. and McGRATH, J. J. (Eds.) *Vigilance: a Symposium.* McGraw-Hill, New York.

BURCH, N. R. and GREINER, T. H. (1960) A bioelectric scale of human alertness: concurrent recordings of the EEG and GSR. *Psychiat. Res. Rep. Amer. psychiat. Ass.* **12**, 183–193.

BURNS, B. D. (1958) *The Mammalian Cerebral Cortex.* Edward Arnold, London.

BURNS, J. J. (1963) Role of biotransformation. In PAPPER, E. M. and KITZ, R. J. (Eds.) *Uptake and Distribution of Anesthetic Agents.* McGraw-Hill, New York.

CAFFEY, E. M. (1961) Experiences with large scale interhospital cooperative research in chemotherapy. *Amer. J. Psychiat.* **117**, 713–719.

CAFFEY, E. M., FORREST, I. S., FRANK, T. V. and KLETT, C. J. (1963) Phenothiazine excretion in chronic schizophrenics. *Amer. J. Psychiat.* **120**, 578–582.

CAINE, T. M. and HOPE, K. (1964) Validation of the Maudsley Personality Inventory E scale. *Brit. J. Psychol.* **55**, 447–452.

CALLAWAY, E. (1959) The influence of amobarbital (amylobarbitone) and methamphetamine on the focus of attention. *J. ment. Sci.* **105**, 382–392.

CALLAWAY, E. III and DEMBO, E. (1958) Narrowed attention: a psychological phenomenon that accompanies a certain physiological change. *Arch. Neurol. Psychiat. (Chic.)* **79**, 74–90.

CALLAWAY, E. III, JONES, R. T. and LAYNE, R. S. (1965) Evoked responses and segmental set of schizophrenia. *Arch. gen. Psychiat. (Chic.)* **12**, 83–89.

CAMERON, N. (1938) A study of thinking in senile deterioration and schizophrenic disorganization. *Amer. J. Psychol.* **51**, 650–665.

CAMERON, N. (1944) The functional psychoses. In HUNT, J. McV. (Ed.) *Personality and the Behaviour Disorders*. Ronald, New York.

CAMPBELL, D. (1960) The psychological effects of cerebral electroshock. In EYSENCK, H. J. (Ed.) *Handbook of Abnormal Psychology*. Pitman, London.

CANNON, W. B. (1929) *Bodily Changes in Pain, Hunger, Fear and Rage*. Branford, Boston.

CARNEY, M. W. P., ROTH, M. and GARSIDE, R. F. (1965) The diagnosis of depressive syndromes and the prediction of ECT response. *Brit. J. Psychiat.* **111**, 659–674.

CARRIGAN, P. M. (1960) Extraversion–introversion as a dimension of personality: a re-appraisal. *Psychol. Bull.* **57**, 329–360.

CATTELL, R. B. (1965) *The Scientific Analysis of Personality*. Penguin, London.

CHAMBERS, W. F., FREEDMAN, S. L. and SAWYER, C. H. (1963) The effect of adrenal steroids on evoked reticular responses. *Exp. Neurol.* **8**, 458–469.

CHRISTENSEN, J., FENG, Y. S. L., POLLEY, E. and WASE, A. W. (1958) Influence of chlorpromazine on the transport of ions into cerebral tissues. *Fed. Proc.* **17**, 358.

CLARIDGE, G. S. (1960) The excitation–inhibition balance in neurotics. In EYSENCK, H. J. (Ed.) *Experiments in Personality*. Routledge & Kegan Paul, London.

CLARIDGE, G. S. (1961a) Arousal and inhibition as determinants of the performance of neurotics. *Brit. J. Psychol.* **52**, 53–63.

CLARIDGE, G. S. (1961b) Individual differences in the tolerance of depressant drugs. *Paper presented to British Association Annual Meeting*, Norwich.

CLARIDGE, G. S., BURNS, B. H. and FOSTER, A. R. (1964) Sedation threshold and Archimedes spiral after-effect: a follow-up of their use with civilian psychiatric patients. *Behav. Res. Ther.* **1**, 363–370.

CLARIDGE, G. S. and HERRINGTON, R. N. (1960) Sedation threshold, personality and the theory of neurosis. *J. ment. Sci.* **106**, 1568–1583.

CLARIDGE, G. S. and HERRINGTON, R. N. (1963a) An EEG correlate of the Archimedes spiral after-effect and its relationship with personality. *Behav. Res. Ther.* **1**, 217–229.

CLARIDGE, G. S. and HERRINGTON, R. N. (1963b) Excitation–inhibition and the theory of neurosis: a study of the sedation threshold. In EYSENCK, H. J. (Ed.) *Experiments with Drugs*. Pergamon, Oxford.

CLARIDGE, G. S., WAWMAN, R. J. and DAVIES, M. H. (1963) Sedation threshold, autonomic lability and the excitation–inhibition theory of personality. I. The Cold Pressor Test. *Brit. J. Psychiat.* **109**, 548–552.

CLARIDGE, G. S., WAWMAN, R. J., DAVIES, M. H. and BURNS, B. H. (1966) Sedation threshold, spiral after-effect and overinclusion. *Brit. J. soc. clin. Psychol.* **5**, 63–70.

CLARK, A. J. and RAVENTOS, J. (1940) Dynamic variation in response to barbiturates. *Quart. J. exp. Physiol.* **30**, 187–194.

CLARK, M. L., RAY, T. S. and RAGLAND, R. E. (1963) Chlorpromazine in chronic schizophrenic women: rate of onset and rate of dissipation of drug effects. *Psychosom. Med.* **25**, 212–217.

CONNEY, A. H. and BURNS, J. J. (1962) Factors influencing drug metabolism. *Advances in Pharmacology* **1**, 31–58.

COOK, L., TONER, J. J. and FELLOWS, E. J. (1954) The effect of β-diethylamino-ethylphenyl propyl acetate hydrochloride (SKF 525 A) on hexobarbital. *J. Pharmacol. exp. Ther.* **111**, 131–141.

COOK, S., MAVOR, H. and CHAMBERS, W. F. (1960) Effects of reticular stimulation in altered adrenal states. *Electroenceph. clin. Neurophysiol.* **12**, 601–608.

COPPEN, A. J. (1959) Blood-CSF bromide ratios in mental patients. *J. Neurol. Neurosurg. Psychiat.* **22**, 61–64.

COPPEN, A. J. (1960) Abnormality of the blood-CSF barrier of patients suffering from depressive illness. *J. Neurol. Neurosurg. Psychiat.* **23**, 156–161.

COPPEN, A. J. and METCALFE, M. (1965) Effect of a depressive illness on MPI scores. *Brit. J. Psychiat.* **111**, 236–239.

COPPEN, A. J. and SHAW, D. M. (1963) Mineral metabolism in melancholia. *Brit. med. J.* **ii,** 1439–1444.

CORCORAN, D. W. J. (1964) Changes in heart rate and performance as a result of loss of sleep. *Brit. J. Psychol.* **55**, 307–314.

CYVIN, K., JÖRSTAD, J. and RETTERSTÖL, N. (1956) Sympathomimetics as diagnostic tests in psychiatry. *Acta psychiat. et neurol. scand.* **106**, 206–220.

DARROW, C. W., PATHMAN, J. and KRONENBERG, G. (1946) Level of autonomic activity and electroencephalogram. *J. exp. Psychol.* **36**, 355–365.

DAVIES, M. H., CLARIDGE, G. S. and WAWMAN, R. J. (1963) Sedation threshold, autonomic lability and the excitation–inhibition theory of personality. III. The blood pressure response to an adrenaline antagonist as a measure of autonomic lability. *Brit. J. Psychiat.* **109**, 558–567.

DAVIS, W. M. (1962) Day–night periodicity in pentobarbital response of mice and the influence of socio-psychological conditions. *Experientia* **18**, 235–237.

DELL, P. C. (1957a) General discussion, page 204. In JASPER, H. H. *et al.* (Eds.) *Reticular Formation of the Brain.* Churchill, London.

DELL, P. C. (1957b) Humoral effects on the brainstem reticular formation. In JASPER, H. H. *et al.* (Eds.) *Reticular Formation of the Brain.* Churchill, London.

DELL, P. C. (1958) Some basic mechanisms of the translation of bodily needs into behaviour. In WOLSTENHOLME, G. E. W. and O'CONNOR, C. M. (Eds.) *Neurological Basis of Behaviour. Ciba Foundation Symposium.* Churchill, London.

DELL, P. C., BONVALLET, M. and HUGELIN, A. (1961) Mechanisms of reticular deactivation. In WOLSTENHOLME, G. E. W. and O'CONNOR, M. (Eds.) *The Nature of Sleep. Ciba Foundation Symposium.* Churchill, London.

DIAMOND, S., BALVIN, R. S. and DIAMOND, F. R. (1963) *Inhibition and Choice.* Harper & Row, New York.

DIXON, R. L., ROGERS, L. A. and FOUTS, J. R. (1964) The effects of norepinephrine treatment on drug metabolism of liver microsomes from rats. *Biochem. Pharmacol.* **13**, 623–631.

DIXON, R. L., SHULTICE, R. W. and FOUTS, J. R. (1960) Factors affecting drug metabolism by liver microsomes. IV. Starvation. *Proc. Soc. exp. Biol. Med. (N.Y.)* **103**, 333–335.

DOBBING, J. (1961) The blood–brain barrier. *Physiol. Rev.* **41**, 130–188.

DOBKIN, A. B. (1960) Potentiation of pentothal anaesthesia by derivatives and analogues of phenothiazine. *Anesthesiology* **21**, 292–296.

DOMEK, N. S., BARLOW, C. F. and ROTH, L. J. (1959) C^{14}-phenobarbital and S^{35} pentothal in the CNS of adult cats. *Fed. Proc.* **18**, 384.

DOMINO, E. (1962) The site of action of some nervous depressants. *Ann. Rev. Pharmacol.* **2**, 215–251.

DOUST, J. W. L. (1955) The capillary system in patients with psychiatric disorder: the autogenetic structural determination of the nailfold capillaries as observed by photomicroscopy. *J. nerv. ment. Dis.* **121**, 516–526.

DOUST, J. W. L. and MELVILLE, P. M. (1956) Capillary blood flow in psychiatric patients and its modification by stress. *Canad. med. Ass. J.* **75**, 742–746.

DREW, G. C., COLQUHOUN, W. P. and LONG, H. A. (1958) Effect of small doses of alcohol on a skill resembling driving. *Brit. Med. J.* **ii**, 993–999.

DRIEVER, C. W. and BOUSQUET, W. F. (1965) Stress stimulation of drug metabolism in the rat. *Psychopharmacologist* **6**, 207.

DUFFY, E. (1934) Emotion: an example of the need for reorientation in psychology. *Psychol. Rev.* **41**, 239–243.

DUFFY, E. (1962) *Activation and Behaviour*. Wiley, New York.

DUNDEE, J. W. (1955) Acquired tolerance to intravenous thiobarbiturates in animals. *Brit. J. Anaesth.* **27**, 165–170.

DUNDEE, J. W., NICHOLL, R. M. and MOORE, J. (1964) Clinical studies of induction agents. X. The effect of phenothiazine premedication on thiopentone anaesthesia. *Brit. J. Anaesth.* **36**, 106–109.

DUNDEE, J. W., PRICE, H. L. and DRIPPS, R. D. (1956) Acute tolerance to thiopentone in man. *Brit. J. Anaesth.* **28**, 344–352.

EARLE, A. and EARLE, B. V. (1955) The blood pressure response to pain and emotion in schizophrenia. *J. nerv. ment. Dis.* **121**, 132–139.

EASTERBROOK, J. A. (1959) The effect of emotion on cue utilization and the organization of behaviour. *Psychol. Rev.* **66**, 183–201.

EBERT, A. G., YIM, G. K. W. and MIYA, T. S. (1964) Distribution and metabolism of barbital-C^{14} in tolerant and non-tolerant rats. *Biochem. Pharmacol.* **13**, 1267–1274.

ECCLES, J. C., SCHMIDT, R. and WILLIS, W. D. (1963) Pharmacological studies on presynaptic inhibition. *J. Physiol. (Lond.)* **168**, 500–530.

EDWARDS, D. A. W. (1951) Differences in the distribution of subcutaneous fat with sex and maturity. *Clin. Sci.* **10**, 305–315.

EICHLER, O. and SMIATEK, A. (1937) Uber die Beziehungen der Empfindlichkeit für Chloroform, Avertin und Eunarkon untereinander. *Arch. exp. Path. Pharmak.* **186**, 702–720.

EMLEN, S. T. and KEM, W. (1963) Activity rhythm in Peromyscus: its influence on rates of recovery from Nembutal. *Science* **142**, 1682–1683.

EMMERSON, J. L. and MIYA, T. S. (1962) Metabolism of S^{35} chlorpromazine by the rat. *Fed. Proc.* **21**, 181.

ESPLIN, D. W. (1963) Criteria for assessing effects of depressant drugs on spinal cord synaptic transmission with examples of drug selectivity. *Arch. int. Pharmacodyn.* **143**, 479–497.

ESSIG, C. F. and FLANARY, H. G. (1964) Repeated electroconvulsion: elevation of threshold proximal and distal to origin. *Exp. Neurol.* **9**, 31–35.

ESSIG, C. F., GROCE, M. E. and WILLIAMSON, E. L. (1961) Reversible elevation of electroconvulsive threshold and occurrence of spontaneous convulsions upon repeated electrical stimulation of the cat brain. *Exp. Neurol.* **4**, 37–47.

EULER, U. S. VON and HELLNER, S. (1952) Excretion of noradrenaline and adrenaline in muscular work. *Acta physiol. scand.* **26**, 183–191.

EXLEY, K. A. (1954) Depression of autonomic ganglia by barbiturates. *Brit. J. Pharmacol.* **9**, 170–181.

EYSENCK, H. J. (1947) *Dimensions of Personality*. Kegan Paul, London.

EYSENCK, H. J. (1952) *The Scientific Study of Personality*. Routledge & Kegan Paul, London.

EYSENCK, H. J. (1953) *The Structure of Human Personality*. Methuen, London.

EYSENCK, H. J. (1955a) A dynamic theory of anxiety and hysteria. *J. ment. Sci.* **101,** 28–51.

EYSENCK, H. J. (1955b) Cortical inhibition, figural after-effect, and the theory of personality. *J. abnorm. soc. Psychol.* **51,** 94–106.

EYSENCK, H. J. (1956a) Reminiscence, drive and personality theory. *J. abnorm. soc. Psychol.* **53,** 328–333.

EYSENCK, H. J. (1956b) The questionnaire measurement of neuroticism and extraversion. *Riv. di Psicologia* **50,** 113–140.

EYSENCK, H. J. (1956c) "Warm up" in pursuit rotor learning as a function of the extinction of conditioned inhibition. *Acta psychol.* **12,** 349–370.

EYSENCK, H. J. (1957a) Drugs and personality. I. Theory and methodology. *J. ment. Sci.* **103,** 119–131.

EYSENCK, H. J. (1957b) *Dynamics of Anxiety and Hysteria.* Routledge & Kegan Paul, London.

EYSENCK, H. J. (1958) Hysterics and dysthymics as criterion groups in the measure of introversion–extraversion: a reply. *J. abnorm. soc. Psychol.* **57,** 250–252.

EYSENCK, H. J. (1959a) *Manual of the Maudsley Personality Inventory.* Univ. London Press, London.

EYSENCK, H. J. (1959b) Personality and the estimation of time. *Percept. mot. Skills* **9,** 405–406.

EYSENCK, H. J. (1959c) Some recent criticisms of the dimensional analysis of personality. *J. ment. Sci.* **105,** 220–223.

EYSENCK, H. J. (1960a) Classification and the problem of diagnosis. In EYSENCK, H. J. (Ed.) *Handbook of Abnormal Psychology.* Pitman, London.

EYSENCK, H. J. (Ed.) (1960b) *Experiments in Personality.* Routledge & Kegan Paul, London.

EYSENCK, H. J. (1960c) Levels of personality, constitutional factors, and social influences: an experimental approach. *Int. J. soc. Psychiat.* **6,** 12–24.

EYSENCK, H. J. (1960d) Objective psychological tests and the assessment of drug effects. *Int. Rev. Neurobiol.* **2,** 333–384.

EYSENCK, H. J. (1960e) Reminiscence, extraversion and neuroticism. *Percept. mot. Skills,* **11,** 21–22.

EYSENCK, H. J. (1960f) The place of theory in psychology. In EYSENCK, H. J. (Ed.) *Experiments in Personality.* Routledge & Kegan Paul, London.

EYSENCK, H. J. (1961) Psychosis, drive and inhibition: a theoretical and experimental account. *Amer. J. Psychiat.* **118,** 198–204.

EYSENCK, H. J. (1962a) Conditioning and personality. *Brit. J. Psychol.* **53,** 299–305.

EYSENCK, H. J. (1962b) Correspondence. *Brit. J. Psychol.* **53,** 455–459.

EYSENCK, H. J. (1962c) Reminiscence, drive and personality—revision and extension of a theory. *Brit. J. soc. clin. Psychol.* **1,** 127–140.

EYSENCK, H. J. (1963) Biological basis of personality. *Nature* **199,** 1031–1034.

EYSENCK, H. J. (1964a) An experimental test of the "inhibition" and "consolidation" theories of reminiscence. *Life Sciences* **3,** 175–188.

EYSENCK, H. J. (Ed.) (1964b) *Experiments in Motivation.* Pergamon, Oxford.

EYSENCK, H. J. (1964c) Personality and reminiscence—an experimental study of the "reactive inhibition" and "conditioned inhibition" theories. *Life Sciences* **3,** 189–198.

EYSENCK, H. J. (1965) Extraversion and the acquisition of eyeblink and GSR conditioned responses. *Psychol. Bull.* **63,** 258–270.

EYSENCK, H. J. (1967) *The Biological Basis of Personality.* Charles C. Thomas, Springfield, Ill.

EYSENCK, H. J. and CLARIDGE, G. S. (1962) The position of hysterics and dysthymics in a two-dimensional framework of personality description. *J. abnorm. soc. Psychol.* **64,** 46–55.

EYSENCK, H. J. and EYSENCK, S. B. G. (1960) Reminiscence on the spiral after-effect as a function of length of rest and number of pre-rest trials. *Percept. mot. Skills*, **10**, 93–94.

EYSENCK, H. J. and EYSENCK, S. B. G. (1963) On the dual nature of extraversion. *Brit. J. soc. clin. Psychol.* **2**, 46–55.

EYSENCK, H. J. and EYSENCK, S. B. G. (1964) *Manual to the Eysenck Personality Inventory*. Univ. London Press, London.

EYSENCK, H. J. and MAXWELL, A. E. (1961) Reminiscence as a function of drive. *Brit. J. Psychol.* **52**, 43–52.

EYSENCK, H. J. and WARWICK, K. M. (1964a) Situationally determined drive and the concept of "arousal". In EYSENCK, H. J. (Ed.) *Experiments in Motivation*. Pergamon, Oxford.

EYSENCK, H. J. and WARWICK, K. M. (1964b) The effects of drive level on a multiple-choice reaction task. In EYSENCK, H. J. (Ed.) *Experiments in Motivation*. Pergamon, Oxford.

EYSENCK, H. J. and WILLETT, R. A. (1962a) Cue utilization as a function of drive: an experimental study. *Percept. mot. Skills*, **15**, 229–230.

EYSENCK, H. J. and WILLETT, R. A. (1962b) Performance and reminiscence on a symbol substitution task as a function of drive. *Percept. mot. Skills*, **15**, 389–390.

EYSENCK, S. B. G. (1956) Neurosis and psychosis: an experimental analysis. *J. ment. Sci.* **102**, 517–529.

FAHRENBERG, J. and DELIUS, L. (1963) Eine Faktorenanalyse psychischer und vegetativer Regulationsdaten. *Der Nervenarzt*, **34**, 437–443.

FEINBERG, I. (1958) Current status of the Funkenstein Test. A review of the literature through December 1957. *Arch. Neurol. Psychiat. (Chic.)* **80**, 488–501.

FEINSTEIN, L. and HINER, R. L. (1963) Anesthesia and its relationship to body composition. *Ann. N. Y. Acad. Sci.* **110**, 661–674.

FELDBERG, W. S. (1964) Depressant effects of intraventricular adrenaline. In STEINBERG, H. (Ed.) *Animal Behaviour and Drug Action. Ciba Foundation Symposium*. Churchill, London.

FELDMAN, M. P. (1964) Motivation and task performance: a review of the literature. In EYSENCK, H. J. (Ed.) *Experiments in Motivation*. Pergamon, Oxford.

FELDMAN, S. (1962) Electrophysiological alterations in adrenalectomy. *Arch. Neurol. (Chic.)* **7**, 460–470.

FINK, M. (1958) Lateral gaze nystagmus as an index of the sedation threshold. *Electroenceph. clin. Neurophysiol.* **10**, 162–163.

FISH, F. A. (1961) A neurophysiological theory of schizophrenia. *J. ment. Sci.* **107**, 828–838.

FOLDES, F. F. and BEECHER, H. K. (1943) The effect of cholesterol administration on anesthesia. *J. Pharmacol. exp. Ther.* **78**, 276–281.

FOLKOW, B. and MELLANDER, S. (1960) Aspects of the nervous control of the precapillary sphinctus with regard to the capillary exchange. *Acta physiol. scand.* **50**, Suppl. 175, 52–54.

FOTHERBY, K., ASHCROFT, G. W., AFFLECK, J. W. and FORREST, A. D. (1963) Studies on sodium transfer and 5-hydroxyindoles in depressive illness. *J. Neurol. Neurosurg. Psychiat.* **26**, 69–73.

FOULDS, G. A. (1961) The logical impossibility of using hysterics and dysthymics as criterion groups in the study of introversion and extraversion. *Brit. J. Psychol.* **52**, 385–387.

FOULDS, G. A. (1965a) *Personality and Personal Illness*. Tavistock, London.

FOULDS, G. A. (1965b) The significance of intra-individual diagnostic levels. *Brit. J. Psychiat.* **111**, 761–768.

K

FOULDS, G. A. and DIXON, P. (1962a) The nature of intellectual deficit in schizophrenia. Part I. A comparison of schizophrenics and neurotics. *Brit. J. soc. clin. Psychol.* **1**, 7–19.

FOULDS, G. A. and DIXON, P. (1962b) The nature of intellectual deficit in schizophrenia. Part III. A longitudinal study of the sub-groups. *Brit. J. soc. clin. Psychol.* **1**, 199–207.

FOULDS, G. A., DIXON, P., MCCLELLAND, M. and MCCLELLAND, W. J. (1962) The nature of intellectual deficit in schizophrenia. Part II. A cross-sectional study of paranoid, catatonic, hebephrenic and simple schizophrenics. *Brit. J. soc. clin. Psychol.* **1**, 141–149.

FOUTS, J. R. (1962) Interaction of drugs and hepatic microsomes. *Fed. Proc.* **21**, 1107–1111.

FRANKENHAUSER, M. and POST, B. (1962) Catecholamine excretion during mental work as modified by centrally acting drugs. *Acta physiol. scand.* **55**, 74–81.

FRANKS, C. M. (1956) Conditioning and personality: a study of normal and neurotic subjects. *J. abnorm. soc. Psychol.* **52**, 143–150.

FRANKS, C. M. (1957) Personality factors and the rate of conditioning. *Brit. J. Psychol.* **48**, 119–126.

FRANKS, C. M. (1963a) Ocular movements and spontaneous blink rate as functions of personality. *Percept. mot. Skills* **16**, 178.

FRANKS, C. M. (1963b) Personality and eyeblink conditioning seven years later. *Acta Psychol. (Amst.)* **21**, 295–312.

FREEMAN, G. L. and KATZOFF, E. T. (1942) Methodological evaluation of the galvanic skin response, with special reference to the formula for R.Q. (Recovery Quotient). *J. exp. Psychol.* **31**, 239–248.

FRENCH, J. D. (1960) The reticular formation. In FIELD, J. *et al.* (Eds.) *Handbook of Physiology. Section I: Neurophysiology*, 1281–1305. American Physiological Society, Washington.

FRENCH, J. D., HERNÁNDEZ-PÉON, R. and LIVINGSTON, R. B. (1955) Projections from cortex to cephalic brain stem (reticular formation) in monkey. *J. Neurophysiol.* **18**, 74–95.

FREYGANG, W. H. and SOKOLOFF, L. (1958) Quantitative measurement of regional circulation in the central nervous system by the use of radioactive inert gas. *Advances Biol. Med. Phys.* **6**, 263–279.

FULTON, J. F. (1949) *Physiology of the Nervous System.* Oxford Univ. Press, London.

FUNKENSTEIN, D. H., GREENBLATT, M., and SOLOMON, H. C. (1948) Autonomic nervous system changes following electric shock treatment, *J. nerv. ment. Dis.* **108**, 409–422.

FUNKENSTEIN, D. H., GREENBLATT, M. and SOLOMON, H. C. (1949) Psychophysiological study of mentally ill patients. I. The status of the peripheral autonomic nervous system as determined by the reaction to epinephrine and mecholyl. *Amer. J. Psychiat.* **106**, 16–28.

GALAMBOS, R. (1956) Suppression of auditory nerve activity by stimulation of efferent fibres to cochlea. *J. Neurophysiol.* **19**, 424–437.

GELLHORN, E. (1953) *Physiological Foundations of Neurology and Psychiatry.* Univ. Minnesota Press, Minneapolis.

GELLHORN, E. and LOOFBOURROW, G. N. (1963) *Emotions and Emotional Disorders.* Harper, New York.

GIBBONS, J. L. and MCHUGH, P. (1963) Plasma cortisol levels in depressive illness. *J. psychiat. Res.* **1**, 162–171.

GIBERTI, F. and ROSSI, R. (1962) Proposal of a psychopharmacological test ("stimulation threshold") for differentiating neurotic from psychotic depressions. *Psychopharmacologia (Berl.)* **3**, 128–131.

GIBERTI, F., ROSSI, R. and DE CAROLIS, V. (1962) La "soglia di stimolazione" alla metilanfetamina mediante weckanalisi frazionata. *Riv. sper. Freniat.* **86,** 814–829.

GIBERTI, F., ROSSI, R., DE CAROLIS, G. and ROCCATAGLIATA, L. V. (1965) La C.D. "weckanalisi frazionata" negli psiconevrotici. *Riv. Neurobiol.* **11,** 132–148.

GIFFORD, R. W., ROTH, G. M. and KVALE, W. F. (1951) The evaluation of use of Regitine (C7337) as a new pharmacologic test for phaeochromocytoma. *J. lab. clin. Med.* **38,** 812.

GJESSING, L. R. (1964) Studies of periodic catatonia. ii. The urinary excretion of phenolic amines and acids with and without loads of different drugs. *J. psychiat. Res.* **2,** 149–162.

GJESSING, R. (1938) Disturbances of somatic functions in catatonia with periodic course and their compensation. *J. ment. Sci.* **84,** 608–621.

GLASER, G. H. (1952) The effects of frontal topectomy on autonomic nervous system stability in schizophrenia. *J. nerv. ment. Dis.* **115,** 189–202.

GOLD, L. (1943) Autonomic balance in patients treated with insulin shock as measured by mecholyl chloride. *Arch. Neurol. Psychiat. (Chic.)* **50,** 311–317.

GOLDBAUM, L. R. and SMITH, P. K. (1954) The interaction of barbiturates with serum albumin and its possible relation to their disposition and pharmacological actions. *J. Pharmacol. exp. Ther.* **111,** 197–209.

GOLDMAN, D. (1959) Specific electroencephalographic changes with pentothal activation in psychotic states. *Electroenceph. clin. Neurophysiol.* **11,** 657–667.

GOLDSTEIN, A. and ARANOW, L. (1960) The duration of action of thiopental and pentobarbital. *J. Pharmacol. exp. Ther.* **128,** 1–6.

GOLDSTEIN, K. and SCHEERER, M. (1941) Abstract and concrete behaviour: an experimental study with special tests. *Psychol. Monogr.* **53,** No. 2.

GOLDSTEIN, L., MURPHREE, H. B., SUGARMAN, A. A., PFEIFFER, C. C. and JENNEY, E. H. (1963) Quantitative electroencephalographic analysis of naturally occurring (schizophrenic) and drug-induced psychotic states in human males. *Clin. Pharmacol. Ther.* **4,** 10–21.

GOLDSTEIN, L., SUGARMAN, A. A., STOLBERG, H., MURPHREE, H. B. and PFEIFFER, C. C. (1965) Electro-cerebral activity in schizophrenics and non-psychotic subjects: quantitative EEG amplitude analysis. *Electroenceph. clin. Neurophysiol.* **19,** 350–361.

GOODMAN, L. S. and GILMAN, A. (1955) *The Pharmacological Basis of Therapeutics.* Macmillan, New York.

GORDON, G. S., ESTESS, F. M., ADAMS, J. E., BOWMAN, F. M. and SIMON, A. (1955) Cerebral oxygen uptake in chronic schizophrenic reaction. *Arch. Neurol. Psychiat. (Chic.)* **73,** 544–545

GRANIT, R. (1955) Centrifugal and antidromic effects on ganglion cells of retina *J. Neurophysiol.* **18,** 388–411.

GRAY, J. A. (1964) *Pavlov's Typology.* Pergamon, Oxford.

GREEN, H. D. and KEPCHAR, J. H. (1959) Control of peripheral resistance in major systemic vascular beds. *Physiol. Rev.* **39,** 617–686.

GREEN, J. D. (1957) The rhinencephalon: aspects of its relation to behaviour and the reticular activating system. In JASPER, H. H. *et al.* (Eds.) *Reticular Formation of the Brain.* Churchill, London.

GREEN, M. W. and KOPPANYI, T. (1944) Studies on barbiturates. XXVII. Tolerance and cross tolerance to barbiturates. *Anesthesiology* **5,** 329–340.

GREENBLATT, M. and SOLOMON, H. C. (Eds.) (1953) *Frontal lobes and Schizophrenia.* Springer, New York.

GREGERSEN, M. I. and NICKERSON, J. L. (1950) Relation of blood volume and cardiac output to body type. *J. appl. Physiol.* **3,** 329–341.

GRUBER, C. M., GRUBER, C. M., Jr. and LEE, K. S. (1952) A study of the effect of the thiobarbiturates on the cardiovascular system. *Arch. int. Pharmacodyn.* **91**, 461–468.

GRUBER, C. M. and KEYSER, G. F. (1946) A study on the development of tolerance and cross tolerance to barbiturates in experimental animals. *J. Pharmacol. exp. Ther.* **86**, 186–196.

GUERRANT, J., BECKER, R. A., ANDERSON, W. W. and AIRD, R. B. (1964) The blood-cerebrospinal fluid barrier in chronic schizophrenia and after trifluoperazine treatment. *J. nerv. ment. Dis.* **139**, 222–231.

HAGGENDAL, E. (1966) Effects of some vasoactive drugs on the vessels of cerebral grey matter in the dog. *Acta physiol. scand.* Suppl. 258, 55–79.

HALL, K. R. L. (1953) Studies of cutaneous pain: a survey of research since 1940. *Brit. J. Psychol.* **44**, 279–294.

HAMBURG, D. A. (1962) Plasma and urinary corticosteroid levels in naturally occurring psychologic stresses. *Res. Publ. Ass. nerv. ment. Dis.* **40**, 406–413.

HAMILTON, M. (1959a) The assessment of anxiety states by rating. *Brit. J. med. Psychol.* **32**, 50–55.

HAMILTON, V. (1959b) Eysenck's theories of anxiety and hysteria—a methodological critique. *Brit. J. Psychol.* **50**, 48–63.

HARPER, M., GURNEY, C., SAVAGE, R. D. and ROTH, M. (1965) Forearm blood flow in normal subjects and patients with phobic anxiety states. *Brit. J. Psychiat.* **111**, 723–731.

HARVEY, J. A., HELLER, A., MOORE, R. Y., HUNT, H. F. and ROTH, L. J. (1964) Effect of central nervous system lesions on barbiturate sleeping time in the rat. *J. Pharmacol. exp. Ther.* **144**, 24–36.

HAWKES, G. R., JOY, R. T. J. and EVANS, W. O. (1961) Autonomic effects on estimates of time: evidence for a physiological correlate of temporal experience. *USA Med. Res. Lab. Report* No. 509, 9 pp.

HAYNES, E. E. (1960) Urinary excretion of chlorpromazine in man. *J. lab. clin. Med.* **56**, 570–575.

HEATH, H. A. and OKEN, D. (1962) Change scores as related to initial and final levels. *Ann. N.Y. Acad. Sci.* **98**, 1242–1256.

HEBB, D. O. (1955) Drives and the CNS (conceptual nervous system). *Psychol. Rev.* **62**, 243–254.

HEBB, D. O. (1958) *A Textbook of Psychology.* Saunders, Philadelphia.

HECHTER, H. (1959) The relationship between weight and some anthropometric measurements in adult males. *Human Biol.* **31**, 235–243.

HEINZEL, F., MATTHES, K., MECHELKE, K. and NUSSER, E. (1952) Die Kreislaufwirkung des Regitin beim gesunden Menschen. *Cardiologia (Basel)* **21**, 743–756.

HEMPHILL, R. E., HALL, K. R. L. and CROOKES, T. G. (1952) A preliminary report on fatigue and pain tolerance in depressive and psychoneurotic patients. *J. ment. Sci.* **98**, 433–440.

HENDRICKSON, A. E. and WHITE, P. O. (1964) Promax: a quick method for rotation to oblique simple structure. *Brit. J. stat. Psychol.* **17**, 65–70.

HENDRICKSON, A. E. and WHITE, P. O. (1966) A method for rotating higher order factors. *Brit. J. stat. Psychol.* (in press).

HERMAN, G. and WOOD, H. C. (1952) Influence of body fat on the duration of thiopental anaesthesia. *Proc. Soc. exp. Biol. Med. (N.Y.)* **30**, 318–319.

HERNÁNDEZ-PÉON, R. (1961) Reticular mechanisms of sensory control. In ROSENBLITH, W. A. (Ed.) *Sensory Communication.* Wiley, New York.

HERNÁNDEZ-PÉON, R., SCHERRER, H. and JOUVET, M. (1956) Modification of electrical activity in cochlear nucleus during "attention" in unanaesthetized cat. *Science* **123**, 331–332.

HERRINGTON, R. N. and CLARIDGE, G. S. (1965) Sedation threshold and Archimedes' spiral after-effect in early psychosis. *J. psychiat. Res.* **3,** 159–170.

HERZ, A. and FUSTER, J. (1964) Uber die Wirkung von Barbituraten und Amphetamin auf die Eutladungstatigkeit corticaler Neurone. *Arch. exp. Path. Pharmak.* **249,** 146–161.

HESS, S. M., SHORE, P. A. and BRODIE, B. B. (1956) Persistence of reserpine action after the disappearance of drug from the brain: effect on serotonin. *J. Pharmacol. exp. Ther.* **118,** 84–89.

HESS, W. R. (1954) The diencephalic sleep centre. In DELAFRESNAYE, J. F. (Ed.) *Brain Mechanisms and Consciousness.* Blackwell, Oxford.

HIGGINS, J. (1964) The concept of process–reactive schizophrenia: criteria and related research. *J. nerv. ment. Dis.* **138,** 9–25.

HILDEBRAND, H. P. (1953) *A Factorial Study of Introversion–Extraversion by Means of Objective Tests.* Ph.D.Thesis, Univ. London.

HIMWICH, H. E. (1960) Biochemical and neurophysiological action of psychoactive drugs. In UHR, L. and MILLER, J. G. (Eds.) *Drugs and Behaviour.* Wiley, New York.

HINES, E. A. and BROWN, G. E. (1936) The cold pressor test for measuring the reactibility of the blood pressure: data concerning 571 normal and hypertensive subjects. *Amer. Heart J.* **11,** 1–9.

HOAGLAND, H. (1933) The physiological control of judgments of duration: evidence for a chemical clock. *J. gen. Psychol.* **9,** 267–287.

HOLLAND, H. C. (1960) Measures of perceptual functions. In EYSENCK, H. J. (Ed.) *Experiments in Personality.* Routledge & Kegan Paul, London.

HOLLAND, H. C. (1962) The spiral after-effect and extraversion. *Acta Psychol. (Amst.)* **20,** 29–35.

HOLLAND, H. C. (1965) *The Spiral After-effect.* Pergamon, Oxford.

HOLLAND, H. C. and BEECH, H. R. (1958) The spiral after-effect as a test of brain damage. *J. ment. Sci.* **104,** 466–471.

HUANG, C. L. and KURLAND, A. A. (1961) Chlorpromazine blood levels in psychotic patients. *Arch. gen. Psychiat. (Chic.)* **5,** 509–513.

HUBBARD, T. F. and GOLDBAUM, L. R. (1949) The mechanism of tolerance to thiopental in mice. *J. Pharmacol. exp. Ther.* **97,** 488–491.

HUGELIN, A. and BONVALLET, M. (1958) Effets moteurs et corticaux d'origine réticulaire au cours des stimulations somesthésiques. Rôle des interactions cortico-réticulaires dans le déterminisme du réveil. *J. Physiol.* **50,** 951–977.

HULL, C. L. (1943) *Principles of Behavior.* Appleton–Century, New York.

HUME, W. I. and CLARIDGE, G. S. (1965) A comparison of two measures of "arousal" in normal subjects. *Life Sciences* **4,** 545–553.

HUNT, J. McV. and COFER, C. N. (1944) Psychological deficit. In HUNT, J. McV. (Ed.) *Personality and the Behaviour Disorders.* Ronald, New York.

IGERSHEIMER, W. W. (1953) Cold pressor test in functional psychiatric syndromes. *Arch. Neurol. Psychiat. (Chic.)* **70,** 794–801.

INGHAM, J. G. and ROBINSON, J. O. (1964) Personality in the diagnosis of hysteria. *Brit. J. Psychol.* **55,** 276–284.

INGRAM, C. G. and BROVINS, W. G. (1966) The reproducibility of the Mecholyl test. *Brit. J. Psychiat.* **112,** 167–171.

INGRAM, W. R. (1960) Central autonomic mechanisms. In FIELD, J. *et al.* (Eds.) *Handbook of Physiology.* Section I: *Neurophysiology,* 951–978. American Physiological Society, Washington.

IVANOV-SMOLENSKY, A. G. (1954) *Essays on the Patho-physiology of the Higher Nervous Activity.* Foreign Languages Publishing House, Moscow.

IWAWAKI, S. (1960) Studies on the relationship between time estimation and personality. *Psychological papers to commemorate the 35th anniversary of Dr. Y. Ohwaki's professorship.*

JACKSON, D. D. (Ed.) (1960) *The Aetiology of Schizophrenia.* Basic Books, New York.

JASPER, H. H. (1949) Diffuse projection systems: the integrative action of the thalamic reticular system. *Electroenceph. clin. Neurophysiol.* **1**, 406–419.

JASPER, H. H. (1954) Functional properties of the thalamic reticular system. In DELAFRESNAYE, J. F. (Ed.) *Brain Mechanisms and Consciousness.* Blackwell, Oxford.

JASPER, H. H. (1957) Recent advances in our understanding of the ascending activities of the reticular system. In JASPER, H. H. *et al.* (Eds.) *Reticular Formation of the Brain.* Churchill, London.

JASPER, H. H. (1960) Unspecific thalamocortical relations. In FIELD, J. *et al.* (Eds.) *Handbook of Physiology. Section I: Neurophysiology*, 1307–1321. American Physiological Society, Washington.

JASPER, H. H., NAQUET, R. and KING, E. E. (1955) Thalamocortical recruiting responses in sensory receiving areas in the cat. *Electroenceph. clin. Neurophysiol.* **7**, 99–114.

JENSEN, A. R. (1958) The Maudsley Personality Inventory. *Acta Psychol. (Amst.)* **14**, 314–325.

JENSEN, A. R. and ROHWER, W. D. (1966) The Stroop Colour-word test: a review. *Acta Psychol. (Amst.)* **25**, 39–93.

JONES, C. H. (1956) The Funkenstein test in selecting methods of psychiatric treatment. *Dis. nerv. Syst.* **17**, 37–43.

JUNG, C. G. (1921) *Psychologische Typen.* Rascher & Cie, Zürich.

JUST, O. (1952) Appréciation du degré anesthésique par le réflexe psycho-galvanique. *Anesth. et Analg.* **9**, 17–19.

KALINOWSKY, L. B. and HOCH, P. H. (1961) *Somatic Treatments in Psychiatry.* Grune & Stratton, New York.

KASANIN, J. and HANFMANN, E. (1938) Disturbances in concept formation in schizophrenia. *Arch. Neurol. Psychiat. (Chic.)* **40**, 1276–1282.

KATO, R. and CHIESARA, E. (1962) Increase of pentobarbital metabolism induced in rats pretreated with some centrally acting compounds. *Brit. J. Pharmacol.* **18**, 29–38.

KATO, R., CHIESARA, E. and VASSANELLI, P. (1964) Further studies on the inhibition and stimulation of microsomal drug-metabolizing enzymes of rat liver by various compounds. *Biochem. Pharmacol.* **13**, 69–83.

KAWI, A. A. (1958) The sedation threshold: its concept and use for comparative studies on drug-induced phenomena. *Arch. Neurol. Psychiat. (Chic.)* **80**, 232–236.

KEELE, C. A. and NEIL, E. (1961) *Samson Wright's Applied Physiology.* Oxford Univ. Press, London.

KEÉRI-SZANTO, M. (1960) Drug consumption during thiopentone-nitrous oxide-relaxant anaesthesia: the preparation and interpretation of time-dose curves. *Brit. J. Anaesth.* **32**, 415–423.

KENNARD, M. A. and WILLNER, M. D. (1948) Significance of changes in the electroencephalogram which result from shock therapy. *Amer. J. Psychiat.* **105**, 40–45.

KETY, S. S. (1960) Recent biochemical theories of schizophrenia. In JACKSON, D. D. (Ed.) *The Aetiology of Schizophrenia.* Basic Books, New York.

KETY, S. S., WOODFORD, S. R. B., HARMEL, M. H., FREYHAN, F. A., APPEL, K. E. and SCHMIDT, C. F. (1947) Cerebral blood flow and metabolism in schizophrenia. The effects of barbiturate semi-narcosis, insulin coma and electro-shock. *Amer. J. Psychiat.* **104,** 765–770.

KEY, B. J. (1961) The effect of drugs on discrimination and sensory generalization of auditory stimuli in cats. *Psychopharmacologia (Berl.)* **2,** 352–363.

KEY, B. J. (1964) Alterations in the generalization of visual stimuli induced by lysergic acid diethylamide in cats. *Psychopharmacologia (Berl.)* **6,** 327–337.

KILLAM, E. K. (1962) Drug action on the brainstem reticular formation. *Pharmacol. Rev.* **14,** 175–223.

KILLAM, K. F. and KILLAM, E. K. (1957) Drug action on pathways involving the reticular formation. In JASPER, H. H. *et al.* (Eds.) *Reticular Formation of the Brain.* Churchill, London.

KIMBLE, G. A. (1949) An experimental test of a two-factor theory of inhibition. *J. exp. Psychol.* **39,** 15–23.

KING, G. F. (1958) Differential autonomic responsiveness in the process–reactive classification of schizophrenia. *J. abnorm. soc. Psychol.* **56,** 160–164.

KLETT, C. J. and CAFFEY, E. M. (1960) Weight changes during treatment with phenothiazine derivatives. *J. Neuropsychiat.* **2,** 102–108.

KNOWLES, J. B. (1960) The temporal stability of MPI scores in normal and psychiatric populations. *J. consult. Psychol.* **24,** 278.

KNOWLES, J. B. and KRASNER, L. (to appear) Extraversion and the duration of the Archimedes spiral after-effect. *Percept. mot. Skills.*

KNOWLES, J. B. and KREITMAN, N. (1965) The Eysenck Personality Inventory. *Brit. J. Psychiat.* **111,** 755–759.

KOHN, R. (1938) Studies on barbiturates with reference to individual susceptibility. *Anesth. and Analg.* **17,** 218–222.

KOMIYA, A. and SHIBATA, K. (1956) Effect of adrenalectomy and replacement with adrenocortical steroids on barbital anaesthesia in mice. *J. Pharmacol. exp. Ther.* **116,** 98–106.

KOMIYA, A. and SHIBATA, K. (1957) Effect of adrenocortical steroids and ACTH administration on barbital anaesthesia in normal mice. *J. Pharmacol. exp. Ther.* **117,** 68–74.

KORNETSKY, C., VATES, T. S. and KESSLER, E. K. (1959) A comparison of hypnotic and residual psychological effects of single doses of chlorpromazine and secobarbital in man. *J. Pharmacol. exp. Ther.* **127,** 51–54.

KRISHNAMOORTI, S. R. and SHAGASS, C. (1964) Some psychological test correlates of sedation threshold. In WORTIS, J. (Ed.) *Recent Advances in Biological Psychiatry,* Vol. VI. Plenum, New York.

KUBOTA, K. and TAKAHASHI, K. (1965) Recurrent facilitatory pathway of the pyramidal tract cell. *Proc. Japan. Acad.* **41,** 191–194.

LACEY, J. I. (1950) Individual differences in somatic response patterns. *J. comp. physiol. Psychol.* **43,** 338–350.

LACEY, J. I. (1956) The evaluation of autonomic responses: toward a general solution. *Ann. N.Y. Acad. Sci.* **67,** 125–164.

LACEY, J. I., BATEMAN, D. E. and VAN LEHN, R. (1953) Autonomic response specificity. An experimental study. *Psychosom. Med.* **15,** 8–21.

LACEY, J. I. and LACEY, B. C. (1958) Verification and extension of the principle of autonomic response stereotype. *Amer. J. Psychol.* **71,** 50–73.

LADER, M. H. (1964) The effect of cyclobarbitone on the habituation of the psycho-galvanic reflex. *Brain* **87,** 321–340.

LADER, M. H. and WING, L. (1964) Habituation of the psychogalvanic reflex in patients with anxiety states and in normal subjects. *J. Neurol. Neurosurg. Psychiat.* **27,** 210–218.

LADER, M. H. and WING, L. (1965) Comparative bioassay of chlordiazepoxide and amylobarbitone sodium therapies in patients with anxiety states using physiological and clinical measures. *J. Neurol. Neurosurg. Psychiat.* **28**, 414–425.

LAMSON, P. D., GREIG, M. E., and WILLIAMS, L. (1952) Potentiation by epinephrine of the anaesthetic effect of chloral and barbiturate anaesthesia. *J. Pharmacol. exp. Ther.* **106**, 219–225.

LANDAU, W. H., FREYGANG, W. H., ROWLAND, L. P., SOKOLOFF, L. and KETY, S. S. (1955) The local circulation of the living brain: values in the unanaesthetized and anaesthetized cat. *Trans. Amer. neurol. Assoc.* **80**, 125–129.

LAPIN, I. P. (1963) Comparison of imipramine and chlorpromazine effects on behaviour of amphetamine-excited animals. In VOTAVA, Z. *et al.* (Eds.) *Psychopharmacological Methods.* Macmillan, New York.

LAVERTY, S. G. (1958) Sodium amytal and extraversion. *J. Neurol. Neurosurg. Psychiat.* **21**, 50–54.

LEE, J. C. and OLSZEWSKI, J. (1961) Increased cerebrovascular permeability after repeated electro-shocks. *Neurology (Minneap.)* **11**, 515–519.

LEE, P. K. Y., CHO, M. H., DOBKIN, A. B. and CURTIS, D. A. (1964) Effects of alcoholism, morphinism and barbiturate resistance on induction and maintenance of general anaesthesia. *Canad. Anaesth. Soc. J.* **11**, 354–381.

LEE, P. K. Y., CHO, M. H., and DOBKIN, A. B. (1965). Effect of catecholamine precursors and phenylethylamines on spontaneous activity and on the response to methohexital anaesthesia. *Canad. Anaesth. Soc. J.* **12**, 137–153.

LEVY, P. and LANG, P. J. (1966) Activation, control, and the spiral aftermovement. *J. Pers. soc. Psychol.* **3**, 105–112.

LINDSAY, H. A. and KULLMAN, V. S. (1966) Pentobarbital sodium: variation in toxicity. *Science* **151**, 576–577.

LINDSLEY, D. B. (1951) Emotion. In STEVENS, S. S. (Ed.) *Handbook of Experimental Psychology.* Chapman & Hall, London.

LINDSLEY, D. B. (1960) Attention, consciousness, sleep and wakefulness. In FIELD, J. *et al.* (Eds.) *Handbook of Physiology. Section I: Neurophysiology,* 1553–1593. American Physiological Society, Washington.

LIVINGSTON, R. B. (1957) Central control of afferent activity. In JASPER, H. H. *et al.* (Eds.) *Reticular Formation of the Brain.* Churchill, London.

LLEWELLYN-THOMAS, E. (1959) Successive time estimation during automatic positive feedback. *Percept. mot. Skills* **9**, 219–224.

LOCKETT, M. (1950) The responses of the heart rate and the systolic blood pressure to sympathomimetic amines in the unanaesthetized, atropinized bitch. *J. Physiol. (Lond.)* **111**, 18–42.

LOVIBOND, S. H. (1963) Conceptual thinking, personality and conditioning. *Brit. J. soc. clin. Psychol.* **2**, 100–111.

LØYNING, Y., OSHIMA, T. and YOKOTA, T. (1964) Site of action of thiamylal sodium on the monosynaptic spinal reflex pathway in cats. *J. Neurophysiol.* **27**, 408–428.

LYNN, R. (1961) Introversion–extraversion differences in judgments of time. *J. abnorm. soc. Psychol.* **63**, 457–458.

LYNN, R. (1963) Russian theory and research on schizophrenia. *Psychol. Bull.* **60**, 486–498.

MCCANCE, I. (1964) Studies of potentiation of hexobarbitone infused intravenously. *Arch. int. Pharmacodyn.* **148**, 270–286.

MCCONAGHY, N. (1960) Modes of abstract thinking and psychosis. *Amer. J. Psychiat.* **117**, 106–110.

MCCONAGHY, N. (1961) The measurement of inhibitory processes in human higher nervous activity: its relation to allusive thinking and fatigue. *Amer. J. Psychiat.* **118**, 125–132.

McDONOUGH, J. M. (1960) Critical flicker frequency and the spiral after-effect with process and reactive schizophrenics. *J. consult. Psychol.* **24,** 150–155.

McDOUGALL, W. (1929) The chemical theory of temperament applied to introversion and extraversion. *J. abnorm. soc. Psychol.* **24,** 293–309.

McGEOCH, J. A. and IRION, A. L. (1952) *The Psychology of Human Learning.* Longmans, New York.

McGHIE, A. and CHAPMAN, J. S. (1961) Disorders of attention and perception in early schizophrenia. *Brit. J. med. Psychol.* **34,** 103–116.

McGUIRE, R. J., MOWBRAY, R. M. and VALLANCE, R. C. (1963) The Maudsley Personality Inventory used with psychiatric inpatients. *Brit. J. Psychol.* **54,** 157–166.

McILWAIN, H. (1962) Appraising enzymic actions of central depressants by examining cerebral tissues. In MONGAR, J. L. and DE REUCK, A. V. S., (Eds.) *Enzymes and Drug Action. Ciba Foundation Symposium.* Little, Brown & Co., Boston.

McINTYRE, A. K., MARK, R. F. and STEINER, J. (1956) Multiple firing at cerebral synapses. *Nature* **178,** 302–304.

MacKINNON, D. W. (1944) The structure of personality. In HUNT, J. McV. (Ed.) *Personality and the Behaviour Disorders.* Ronald, New York.

McLENNAN, H. (1961) Inhibitory transmitters—a review. In FLOREY, E. (Ed.) *Nervous Inhibition.* Pergamon, Oxford.

MACKWORTH, N. H. (1950) Researches in the measurement of human performance. *MRC Special Report* No. 268. H.M.S.O., London.

MAGNI, F., MORUZZI, G., ROSS, G. F. and ZANCHETTI, A. (1959) EEG arousal following inactivation of the lower brainstem by selective injection of barbiturate into the vertebral circulation. *Arch. ital. Biol.* **97,** 33–46.

MAGOUN, H. V. and RHINES, R. (1946) An inhibitory mechanism in the bulbar reticular formation. *J. Neurophysiol.* **9,** 165–171.

MAJOR, R. T., HESS, H-J and STONE, C. A. (1959) Hydroxylamine analogues of pheninamine. *J. med. pharm. Chem.* **1,** 381–390.

MALMO, R. B. (1957) Anxiety and behavioural arousal. *Psychol. Rev.* **64,** 276–287.

MALMO, R. B. (1958) Measurement of drive: an unsolved problem in psychology. In JONES, M. R. (Ed.) *Nebraska Symposium on Motivation.* Univ. of Nebraska Press, Lincoln.

MALMO, R. B. (1959) Activation: a neuropsychological dimension. *Psychol. Rev.* **66,** 367–386.

MALMO, R. B. and SHAGASS, C. (1949a) Physiologic studies of reaction to stress in anxiety and early schizophrenia. *Psychosom. Med.* **11,** 9–24.

MALMO, R. B. and SHAGASS, C. (1949b) Physiologic study of symptom mechanisms in psychiatric patients under stress. *Psychosom. Med.* **11,** 25–29.

MALMO, R. B. and SHAGASS, C. (1952) Studies of blood pressure in psychiatric patients under stress. *Psychosom. Med.* **14,** 82–93.

MALMO, R. B., SHAGASS, C. and DAVIS, J. F. (1951) Electromyographic studies of muscular tension in psychiatric patients under stress. *J. clin. exp. Psychopath.* **12,** 45–66.

MALMO, R. B. and SMITH, A. A. (1955) Forehead tension and motor irregularities in psychoneurotic patients under stress. *J. Personality* **23,** 391–406.

MANTHEI, R. W., HORN, R. S. and LEE, N. H. (1964) Altered hexobarbital activity in response to dietary stress. *Pharmacologist* **6,** 207.

MARK, L. C. (1963) Thiobarbiturates. In PAPPER, E. M. and KITZ, R. J. (Eds.) *Uptake and Distribution of Anesthetic Agents.* McGraw-Hill, New York.

MARK, L. C., BURNS, J. J., BRAND, L., CAMPOMANES, C. I., TROUSOF, N., PAPPER, E. M. and BRODIE, B. B. (1958) The passage of thiobarbiturates and their oxygen analogues into brain. *J. Pharmacol. exp. Ther.* **123,** 70–73.

MARTIN, I. and DAVIES, B. M. (1962) Sleep thresholds in depression. *J. ment. Sci.* **108,** 466–473.

MARTIN, I. and DAVIES, B. M. (1965) The effect of sodium amytal on autonomic and muscle activity in patients with depressive illness. *Brit. J. Psychiat.* **111,** 168–175.

MASON, C. F. (1956) Pre-illness intelligence of mental hospital patients. *J. consult. Psychol.* **20,** 297–300.

MAYER, S., MAICKEL, R. P. and BRODIE, B. B. (1959) Kinetics of penetration of drugs and other foreign compounds into cerebrospinal fluid and brain. *J. Pharmacol. exp. Ther.* **127,** 205–211.

MAYNERT, E. W. and KLINGMAN, G. I. (1960) Acute tolerance to intravenous anaesthetics in dogs. *J. Pharmacol. exp. Ther.* **128,** 192–200.

MEADOW, A. and FUNKENSTEIN, D. H. (1952) The relationship of abstract thinking to the autonomic nervous system in schizophrenia. In HOCH, P. H. and ZUBIN, J. (Eds.) *Relation of Psychological Tests to Psychiatry.* Grune & Stratton, New York.

MEADOW, A., GREENBLATT, M., FUNKENSTEIN, D. H. and SOLOMON, H. C. (1953) Relationship between capacity for abstraction in schizophrenia and physiologic response to autonomic drugs. *J. nerv. ment. Dis.* **118,** 332–338.

MEDICAL RESEARCH COUNCIL CLINICAL PSYCHIATRY COMMITTEE. (1965) Clinical trial of the treatment of depressive illness. *Brit. med. J.* **1,** 881–886.

MEDNICK, S. A. (1955) Distortions in the gradient of stimulus generalization related to cortical brain damage and schizophrenia. *J. abnorm. soc. Psychol.* **51,** 536–542.

MEDNICK, S. A. (1958) A learning theory approach to research in schizophrenia. *Psychol. Bull.* **55,** 316–327.

MEFFERD, R. B., LABROSSE, E. H., GAWIENOWSKI, A. M. and WILLIAMS, R. (1958) Influence of chlorpromazine on certain biochemical variables of chronic male schizophrenics. *J. nerv. ment. Dis.* **127,** 167–179.

MENDELS, J. (1965) Electroconvulsive therapy and depression. II. Significance of endogenous and reactive syndromes. *Brit. J. Psychiat.* **111,** 682–686.

MEZEY, A. G., COHEN, S. I. and KNIGHT, E. J. (1963) Personality assessment under varying physiological and psychological conditions. *J. psychosom. Res.* **7,** 237–240.

MILLS, J. N. (1966) Human circadian rhythms. *Physiol. Rev.* **46,** 128–171.

MOFFAT, J. and LEVINE, S. (1964) The sedation threshold of psychoneurotic and alcoholic patients. *Brit. J. med. Psychol.* **37,** 313–317.

MONROE, R. R., HEATH, R. G., HEAD, R. G., STONE, R. L. and RITTER, K. A. (1961) A comparison of hypertensive and hypotensive schizophrenics. *Psychosom. Med.* **23,** 508–519.

MORIARTY, J. D. and SIEMENS, J. C. (1947) Electroencephalographic study of electric shock therapy. *Arch. Neurol. Psychiat (Chic.)* **57,** 712–718.

MORUZZI, G. (1960) Synchronizing influences of the brain stem and the inhibitory mechanisms underlying the production of sleep by sensory stimulation. In JASPER, H. H. and SMIRNOV, G. D. (Eds.) *The Moscow Colloquium on Electroencephalography of Higher Nervous Activity. Electroenceph. clin. Neurophysiol.,* Suppl. 13.

MORUZZI, G. and MAGOUN, H. W. (1949) Brainstem reticular formation and activation of the EEG. *Electroenceph. clin. Neurophysiol.* **1,** 455–473.

MOUNTCASTLE, V. B. (1957) Modality and topographic properties of single neurons of cat's somatic sensory cortex. *J. Neurophysiol.* **20,** 408–434.

MOUNTCASTLE, V. B., DAVIES, P. W. and BERMAN, A. L. (1957) Response properties of neurons of cat's somatic sensory cortex to peripheral stimuli. *J. Neurophysiol.* **20,** 374–407.

MYERSAN, A., LOMAN, J. and DAMESHEK, W. (1937) Physiologic effects of acetyl-beta-methylcholine (mecholyl) and its relationship to other drugs affecting the autonomic nervous system. *Amer. J. med. Sci.* **193**, 198–214.

NAIR, V., PALM, D. and ROTH, L. J. (1960) Relative vascularity of certain anatomical areas of the brain and other organs of the rat. *Nature* **188**, 497–498.

NAIR, V. and ROTH, L. J. (1962) Studies on permeability of blood–brain barrier to I^{131} Risa and S^{35} sulphate following x-irradiation or metrazol. *Fed. Proc.* **21**, 422.

NAUTA, W. J. H. and KUYPERS, H. G. J. M. (1957) Some ascending pathways in the brainstem reticular formation. In JASPER, H. H. *et al.* (Eds.) *Reticular Formation of the Brain.* Churchill, London.

NELSON, R. and GELLHORN, E. (1957) The action of autonomic drugs on normal persons and neuropsychiatric patients. The role of age. *Psychosom. Med.* **19**, 486–494.

NELSON, R. and GELLHORN, E. (1958) The influence of age and functional neuropsychiatric disorders on sympathetic and parasympathetic functions. *J. psychosom. Res.* **3**, 12–26.

NICHOLSON, J. P. and ZILVA, J. F. (1964) Body constituents and functions in relation to height and weight. *Clin. Sci.* **27**, 97–109.

NYMAN, G. E. and SMITH, G. J. W. (1960) An attempt at describing operationally the effects of psychiatric therapy. *Psychiat. et Neurol. (Basel)* **140**, 258–280.

NYMGAARD, K. (1959) Studies on the sedation threshold. A. Reproducibility and effect of drugs. B. Sedation threshold in neurotic and psychotic depression. *Arch. gen. Psychiat. (Chic.)* **1**, 530–536.

ORME, J. E. (1962) Time estimation and personality. *J. ment. Sci.* **108**, 213–216.

OSTFELD, A. M. and ARUGUETE, ALAYNE (1962) Central nervous system effects of hyoscine in man. *J. Pharm. exp. Ther.* **137**, 133–139.

OSWALD, I. and THACORE, V. R. (1963) Amphetamine and phenmetrazine addiction. *Brit. med. J.* **ii**. 427–431.

OTTOSSON, J-O. (1960) Experimental studies of the mode of action of electroconvulsive therapy. *Acta psychiat. neurol. scand.* **35**, Suppl. 145, pp. 141.

PAPEZ, J. W. (1937) A proposed mechanism of emotion. *Arch. Neurol. Psychiat. (Chic.)* **38**, 725–743.

PARE, C. M. B. (1965) Treatment of depression. *Lancet* **1**, 923–925.

PAŘÍZKOVÁ, J. (1963) Impact of age, diet, and exercise on man's body composition. *Ann. N.Y. Acad. Sci.* **110**, 661–674.

PAULSON, G. W. and GOTTLIEB, G. (1961) A longitudinal study of the electroencephalographic arousal response in depressed patients. *J. nerv. ment. Dis.* **133**, 524–528.

PAULY, J. E. and SCHEVING, L. E. (1964) Temporal variations in the susceptibility of white rats to pentobarbital sodium and tremorine. *Int. J. Neuropharmacol.* **3**, 651–658.

PAVLOV, I. P. (1927) *Conditioned Reflexes.* Translated by G. V. ANREP. Oxford Univ. Press, London.

PAVLOV, I. P. (1934) Experimental pathology of the higher nervous activity. In *Selected Works.* Translated by S. BELSKY (1955). Foreign Languages Publishing House, Moscow.

PAVLOV, I. P. (1941) *Lectures on Conditioned Reflexes.* Vol. II. *Conditioned Reflexes and Psychiatry.* Translated and edited by W. H. GANTT. International Publishers, New York.

PAWLIK, K. and CATTELL, R. B. (1965) The relationship between certain personality factors and measures of cortical arousal. *Neuropsychologia* **3**, 129–151.

PAYNE, R. W. (1960) Cognitive abnormalities. In EYSENCK, H. J. (Ed.) *Handbook of Abnormal Psychology.* Pitman, London.

PAYNE, R. W. (1962) An object classification test as a measure of overinclusive thinking in schizophrenic patients. *Brit. J. soc. clin. Psychol.* 1, 213–221.

PAYNE, R. W. and HEWLETT, J. H. G. (1960) Thought disorder in psychotic patients. In EYSENCK, H. J. (Ed.) *Experiments in Personality.* Routledge & Kegan Paul, London.

PAYNE, R. W., MATTUSSEK, P. and GEORGE, E. I. (1959) An experimental study of schizophrenic thought disorder. *J. ment. Sci.* 105, 627–652.

PEREZ-REYES, M. and COCHRANE, C. C. (1964) Elucidation of some of the neurophysiological factors underlying psychiatric depression. *Paper presented at American Psychiatric Association Annual Meeting*, Los Angeles, California.

EREZ-REYES, M., SHANDS, H. C. and JOHNSON, G. (1962) Galvanic skin reflex inhibition threshold: a new psychophysiologic technique. *Psychosom. Med.* 24, 274–277.

PERRIS, C. and BRATTEMO, C-E. (1963) The sedation threshold as a method of evaluating anti-depressive treatments. *Acta psychiat. scand.* 39, Suppl. 169, 111–119.

PHILLIPS, L. (1953) Case history data and prognosis in schizophrenia. *J. nerv. ment. Dis.* 117, 515–525.

PLOUGH, I. C., WALDSTEIN, S. S., BARILA, T. G. and GOLDBAUM, L. R. (1956) Rate of disappearance of thiopental from plasma in dog and in man. *J. Pharmacol. exp. Ther.* 116, 486–489.

POLLACK, M., ROSENTHAL, F. and MACEY, R. (1963) Changes in electroshock convulsive response with repeated seizures. *Exp. Neurol.* 7, 98–106.

POST, F. (1956) Body-weight changes in psychiatric illness. A critical survey of the literature. *J. psychosom. Res.* 1, 219–226.

PRADHAN, S. N., ACHINSTEIN, B. and SHEAR, M. J. (1956) Potentiation of urethan anesthesia by epinephrine. *Proc. Soc. exp. Biol. Med. (N. Y.)* 92, 146–149.

PRESTON, J. B. and WHITLOCK, D. G. (1960) Precentral facilitation and inhibition of spinal motoneurons. *J. Neurophysiol.* 23, 154–170.

PRICE, A. C. and DEABLER, H. L. (1955) Diagnosis of organicity by means of spiral after-effect. *J. consult. Psychol.* 19, 299–302.

PRICE, H. L. (1960a) A dynamic concept of the distribution of thiopental in the human body. *Anesthesiology* 21, 40–45.

PRICE, H. L. (1960b) General anesthesia and circulatory homeostasis. *Physiol. Rev.* 40, 187–218.

PRICE, H. L. (1963a) Circulation. General considerations. In PAPPER, E. M. and KITZ, R. J. (Eds.) *Uptake and Distribution of Anesthetic Agents.* McGraw-Hill, New York.

PRICE, H. L. (1963b) Discussion (p. 298). In PAPPER, E. M. and KITZ, R. J. (Eds.) *Uptake and Distribution of Anesthetic Agents.* McGraw-Hill, New York.

PRICE, H. J., KOVNAT, P. J., SAFER, J. N., CONNER, E. H. and PRICE, M. L. (1960) The uptake of thiopental by body tissues and its relation to the duration of narcosis. *Clin. Pharmacol. Ther.* 1, 16–22.

PSCHEIDT, G. R., BERLET, H. H., BULL, C., SPAIDE, J. and HIMWICH, H. E. (1964) Excretion of catecholamines and exacerbation of symptoms of schizophrenic patients. *J. psychiat. Res.* 2, 163–168.

QUADBECK, G. and SACSSE, W. (1961) Beeinflussung der Blut–Hirnschranke durch Neuroleptica in Dauerversuch. *Arch. Psychiat. Nervenkr.* 201, 580–592.

QUARTON, G. C. and TALLAND, G. A. (1962) The effects of methamphetamine and pentobarbital on two measures of attention. *Psychopharmacologia (Berl.)* 3, 66–71.

RACHMAN, S. (1963) Inhibition and disinhibition in schizophrenics. *Arch. gen. Psychiat. (Chic.)* 8, 91–98.

RALL, D. P., STABENAU, J. R. and ZUBROD, C. G. (1959) Distribution of drugs between blood and cerebrospinal fluid: general methodology and the effect of pH gradients. *J. Pharmacol. exp. Ther.* **125**, 185–193.

RAMWELL, P. W. and LESTER, I. H. (1961) A potential source of error in hexobarbitone sleeping time test in mice. *Nature* **190**, 640.

RAY, T. S., RAGLAND, R. E. and CLARK, M. L. (1964) Chlorpromazine in chronic schizophrenic women: comparison of differential effects on various psychological modalities during and after treatment. *J. nerv. ment. Dis.* **138**, 348–353.

REMENCHIK, A. P. and TALSO, P. J. (1965) Body composition of schizophrenics. *Arch. gen. Psychiat. (Chic.)* **13**, 444–446.

REMMER, H. (1962) Drug tolerance. In MONGAR, J. L. and DE REUCK, A. V. S. (Eds.) *Enzymes and Drug Action. Ciba Foundation Symposium.* Little, Brown & Co., Boston.

RICHTER, C. P. (1928) The electrical skin resistance. Diurnal and daily variations in psychopathic and in normal persons. *Arch. Neurol. Psychiat. (Chic.)* **19**, 488–508.

RILEY, H. and SPINKS, A. (1958) Biological assessment of tranquillizers. *J. Pharm. Pharmacol.* **10**, 657–671.

RODNICK, E. H. and SHAKOW, D. (1940) Set in the schizophrenic as measured by a composite reaction time index. *Amer. J. Psychiat.* **97**, 214–225.

RODNIGHT, E. and GOOCH, R. N. (1963) A new method for the determination of individual differences in susceptibility to a depressant drug. In EYSENCK, H. J. (Ed.) *Experiments with Drugs.* Pergamon, Oxford.

ROSE, J. T. (1962) The Funkenstein Test—a review of the literature. *Acta psychiat. scand.* **38**, 124–153.

ROSENBLATT, S., CHANLEY, J. D., SOBOTKA, H. and KAUFMAN, M. R. (1960) Interrelationships between electroshock, the blood–brain barrier and catecholamines. *J. Neurochem.* **5**, 172–176.

ROSNER, B. S. (1956) Effects of repetitive peripheral stimuli on evoked potentials of somatosensory cortex. *Amer. J. Physiol.* **187**, 175–179.

ROSS, S., DARDANO, J. and HACKMAN, R. C. (1959) Conductance levels during vigilance task performance. *J. appl. Psychol.* **43**, 65–69.

ROTH, L. J. and BARLOW, C. F. (1961) Drugs in the brain. *Science* **134**, 22–31.

ROTH, M. (1951) Changes in the electroencephalogram under barbiturate anaesthesia produced by electro-convulsive treatment and their significance for the theory of ECT action. *Electroenceph. clin. Neurophysiol.* **3**, 261–280.

ROTHBALLER, A. B. (1956) Studies on the adrenaline-sensitive component of the reticular activating system. *Electroenceph. clin. Neurophysiol.* **8**, 603–621.

RUBIN, L. S. (1960) Pupillary reactivity as a measure of adrenergic-cholinergic mechanisms in the study of psychotic behaviour. *J. nerv. ment. Dis.* **130**, 386–400.

RUBIN, L. S. (1962) Patterns of adrenergic-cholinergic imbalance in the functional psychoses. *Psychol. Rev.* **69**, 501–519.

RUBIN, L. S. (1964) Autonomic dysfunction as a concomitant of neurotic behaviour. *J. nerv. ment. Dis.* **138**, 558–574.

RÜMKE, C. L., STRIK, R. VAN, JONGE, H. DE and DELVER, A. (1963) Experiments on the duration of hexobarbital narcosis in mice. *Arch. int. Pharmacodyn.* **146**, 10–26.

RUSSELL, G. F. M. (1960) Body weight and balance of water, sodium and potassium in depressed patients given electroconvulsive treatment. *Clin. Sci.* **19**, 327–336.

SAIDMAN, L. J. and EGER, E. I. (1966) The effect of thiopental metabolism on duration of anesthesia. *Anesthesiology* **27**, 118–126.

SALZMAN, N. P. and BRODIE, B. B. (1956) Physiological disposition and fate of chlorpromazine, and a method for its estimation in biological material. *J. Pharmacol. exp. Ther.* **118**, 46–54.

SAMUEL, I. (1959) Reticular mechanisms and behavior. *Psychol. Bull.* **56**, 1–25.

SARGANT, W. and SLATER, E. (1963) *An Introduction to Physical Methods of Treatment in Psychiatry.* Livingstone, Edinburgh.

SAVAGE, R. D. (1964) Electro-cerebral activity, extraversion and neuroticism. *Brit. J. Psychiat.* **110**, 98–100.

SCHEIBEL, M. E. and SCHEIBEL, A. B. (1965) The response of reticular units to repetitive stimuli. *Arch. ital. Biol.* **103**, 279–299.

SCHEINBERG, P. and STEAD, E. A. (1949) The cerebral blood flow in male subjects as measured by nitrous oxide technique. Normal values for blood flow, oxygen utilization, glucose utilization, and peripheral resistance with observations on the effect of tilting and anxiety. *J. clin. Invest.* **28**, 1163–1171.

SCHLAG, J. (1956) A study of the action of nembutal on diencephalic and mesencephalic unit activity. *Arch. int. Physiol.* **64**, 470–488.

SEAGER, C. P. (1960a) *A Clinical Evaluation of the Sedation Threshold in Psychiatry.* M.D. Thesis, Univ. Wales.

SEAGER, C. P. (1960b) Problems of technique concerning the sedation threshold. *Electroenceph. clin. Neurophysiol.* **12**, 910–913.

SEGUNDO, J. P., NAQUET, R. and BUSER, P. (1955) Effects of cortical stimulation on electrocortical activity in monkeys. *J. Neurophysiol.* **18**, 236–245.

SEIDEL, C. (1960) The relationship between Klopfer's Rorschach Prognostic Rating Scale and Phillip's Case History Prognostic Rating Scale. *J. consult. Psychol.* **24**, 46–49.

SELTZER, C. C. and MAYER, J. (1964) Body build and obesity—who are the obese? *J. Amer. med. Ass.* **189**, 677–684.

SETNIKAR, I. and MAGISTRETTI, M. J. (1965) Relationships between organ weight and body weight in the male rat. *Arzneimittel–Forschung* **15**, 1042–1047.

SHAGASS, C. (1954) The sedation threshold. A method for estimating tension in psychiatric patients. *Electroenceph. clin. Neurophysiol.* **6**, 221–233.

SHAGASS, C. (1957a) A measurable neurophysiological factor of psychiatric significance. *Electroenceph. clin. Neurophysiol.* **9**, 101–108.

SHAGASS, C. (1957b) A neurophysiological study of schizophrenia. *Congress report of the IInd International Congress for Psychiatry, Zurich.* Vol. II, 248–254.

SHAGASS, C., AZIMA, H. and SANGOWICZ, J. (1959) Effect of meprobamate in sustained high dosage on the electroencephalogram and sedation threshold. *Electroenceph. clin. Neurophysiol.* **11**, 275–283.

SHAGASS, C., BITTLE, R. M., KEASLING, H. H. and SCHWARTZ, M. (1962) "Barbiturate thresholds" in the rabbit. *Psychopharmacologia (Berl.)* **3**, 204–211.

SHAGASS, C. and JONES, A. L. (1957) A neurophysiological study of psychiatric patients with alcoholism. *Quart. J. Stud. Alcohol* **18**, 171–182.

SHAGASS, C. and JONES, A. L. (1958) A neurophysiological test for psychiatric diagnosis: results in 750 patients. *Amer. J. Psychiat.* **114**, 1002–1009.

SHAGASS, C. and KERENYI, A. B. (1958a) Neurophysiologic studies of personality. *J. nerv. ment. Dis.* **126**, 141–147.

SHAGASS, C. and KERENYI, A. B. (1958b) The "sleep" threshold. A simple form of the sedation threshold for clinical use. *Canad. psychiat. J.* **1**, 101–109.

SHAGASS, C. and KERENYI, A. B. (1959) "Sleep" threshold techniques. *Psychiat. Res. Rep. Amer. psychiat. Ass.* **11**, 59–65.

SHAGASS, C., MIHALIK, J. and JONES, A. L. (1957) Clinical psychiatric studies using the sedation threshold. *J. psychosom. Res.* **2**, 45–55.

SHAGASS, C., MULLER, K. and ACOSTA, H. B. (1959) The Pentothal "sleep" threshold as an indicator of affective change. *J. psychosom. Res.* **3**, 253–270.

SHAGASS, C. and NAIMAN, J. (1955) The sedation threshold, manifest anxiety and some aspects of ego function. *Arch. Neurol. Psychiat. (Chic.)* **74**, 397–406.

SHAGASS, C. and NAIMAN, J. (1956) The sedation threshold as an objective index of manifest anxiety in psychoneurosis. *J. psychosom. Res.* **1**, 49–57.

SHAGASS, C., NAIMAN, J. and MIHALIK, J. (1956) An objective test which differentiates between neurotic and psychotic depression. *Arch. Neurol. Psychiat. (Chic.)* **75**, 461–471.

SHAGASS, C. and SCHWARTZ, M. (1962) Excitability of the cerebral cortex in psychiatric disorders. In ROESSLER, R. and GREENFIELD, N. S. (Eds.) *Physiological Correlates of Psychological Disorder.* Univ. Wisconsin Press, Madiso n.

SHAGASS, C., SCHWARTZ, M. and KRISHNAMOORTI, S. R. (1965) Some psychologic correlates of cerebral responses evoked by light flash. *J. psychosom. Res.* **9**, 223–231.

SHAKOW, D. (1962) Segmental set. *Arch. gen. Psychiat. (Chic.)* **6**, 1–17.

SHATTOCK, F. M. (1950) The somatic manifestations of schizophrenia. *J. ment. Sci.* **96**, 32–142.

SHELDON, W. H. and STEVENS, S. S. (1942) *The Varieties of Temperament: a Psychology of Constitutional Difference.* Harper, New York.

SHIBATA, K. and KOMIYA, A. (1953) Effect of adreno-cortical steroids on duration of pentothal anesthesia in adrenalectomized mice. *Proc. Soc. exp. Biol. Med. (N.Y.)* **84**, 308–310.

SIGAL, J. J., STAR, K. H. and FRANKS, C. M. (1958a) Hysterics and dysthymics as criterion groups in the study of introversion–extraversion. *J. abnorm. soc. Psychol.* **57**, 143–148.

SIGAL, J. J., STAR, K. H. and FRANKS, C. M. (1958b) Hysterics and dysthymics as criterion groups in the measure of introversion–extraversion: a rejoinder to Eysenck's reply. *J. abnorm. soc. Psychol.* **57**, 381–382.

SILA, B., MOWRER, M., ULETT, G. and JOHNSON, M. (1962) The differentiation of psychiatric patients by EEG changes after sodium pentothal. In WORTIS, J. (Ed.) *Recent Advances in Biological Psychiatry*, Vol IV. Plenum, New York.

SILVERMAN, J. (1964a) Scanning-control mechanism and "cognitive filtering" in paranoid and non-paranoid schizophrenia. *J. consult. Psychol.* **28**, 385–393.

SILVERMAN, J. (1964b) The problem of attention in research and theory in schizophrenia. *Psychol. Rev.* **71**, 352–379.

SLATER, E., BEARD, A. W. and GLITHERO, E. (1963) The schizophrenia-like psychoses of epilepsy. *Brit. J. Psychiat.* **109**, 95–129.

SLATER, P. (1960) A re-examination of some data collected by H. P. Hildebrand. In EYSENCK, H. J. (Ed.) *Experiments in Personality.* Routledge & Kegan Paul, London.

SLOANE, R. B., LEWIS, J. D. and SLATER, P. (1957) Diagnostic value of blood pressure responses in psychiatric patients. *Arch. Neurol. Psychiat. (Chic.)* **77**, 540–542.

SMITH, G. J. W. and NYMAN, G. E. (1962) The serial colour-word test: a summary of results. *Psychol. Res. Bull. Lund University, Sweden* **2**, No. 6.

SMYTHIES, J. R. (1966) *The Neurological Foundations of Psychiatry.* Blackwell, Oxford.

SMITH, R. L., MAICKEL, R. P. and BRODIE, B. B. (1963) ACTH hypersecretion induced by phenothiazine tranquillizers. *J. Pharmacol. exp. Ther.* **139**, 185–190.

SOKOLOFF, L. (1961) Aspects of cerebral circulatory physiology of relevance to cerebrovascular disease. *Neurology (Minneap.)* **11**, 34–40.

258 BIBLIOGRAPHY

SOKOLOFF, L., PERLIN, S., KORNETSKY, S. and KETY, S. S. (1957) The effect of d-lysergic diethylamide on cerebral circulation and over-all metabolism. *Ann. N.Y. Acad. Sci.* **66**, 468–477.

SOMJEN, G. G. (1963) Effects of ether and thiopental on spinal presynaptic terminals. *J. Pharmacol. exp. Ther.* **140**, 396–402.

SPARROW, N. H. and ROSS, J. (1964) The dual nature of extraversion: a replication. *Austral. J. Psychol.* **16**, 214–218.

SPENCE, K. W. (1956) *Behavior Theory and Conditioning.* Yale Univ. Press, New Haven.

SPENCE, K. W. and TAYLOR, J. A. (1951) Anxiety and the strength of the UCS as determinants of the amount of eyelid conditioning. *J. exp. Psychol.* **42**, 183–188.

SPINACK, G. and LEVINE, M. (1959) Spiral after-effect and measures of satiation in brain-injured subjects. *J. Personality* **27**, 211–227.

STAR, K. (1957) *An Experimental Study of "Reactive Inhibition" and its Relation to Certain Personality Traits.* Ph.D. Thesis, Univ. London.

STAVINOHA, W. D. and DAVIS, J. E. (1955) Effect of prior fat feeding on duration of thiamylal anaesthesia. *Fed. Proc.* **14**, 388.

STENNETT, R. G. (1957) The relationship of alpha amplitude to the level of palmar conductance. *Electroenceph. clin. Neurophysiol.* **9**, 131–138.

STERN, J. A. and McDONALD, D. G. (1965) Physiological correlates of mental disorder. *Ann. Rev. Psychol.* **16**, 225–264.

STERNBACH, R. A. (1960) Two independent indices of activation. *Electroenceph. clin. Neurophysiol.* **12**, 609–611.

STORMS, L. H. (1958) Discrepancies between factor analysis and multivariate discrimination among groups as applied to personality theory. *J. ment. Sci.* **104**, 713–721.

STORMS, L. H. and SIGAL, J. J. (1958) Eysenck's personality theory with special reference to "The Dynamics of Anxiety and Hysteria". *Brit. J. med. Psychol.* **31**, 228–246.

STRANDNESS, D. E., PARRISH, D., DICKSON, A. H. and BELL, J. W. (1964) Effects of depth of anaesthesia on peripheral vascular dynamics. *Angiology* **15**, 479–484.

STROOP, J. R. (1935) Studies of interference in serial verbal reaction. *J. exp. Psychol.* **18**, 643–662.

STUMPF, C. and CHIARI, I. (1965) Echte Gewöhnung an Hexobarbital. *Arch. exp. Path. Pharmak.* **251**, 275–287.

SUPEK, Z., KEČKEŠ, S. and VOJVODIĆ, S. (1960a) The action of chlorpromazine on water and chloride excretion in rats. *Arch. int. Pharmacodyn.* **123**, 253–259.

SUPEK, Z., KEČKEŠ, S. and VOJVODIĆ, S. (1960b) The influence of chlorpromazine on antidiuretic and chloruretic effects of nicotine and post-pituitary extract. *Arch. int. Pharmacodyn.* **123**, 260–263.

SURWILLO, W. W. and QUILTER, R. E. (1965) The relation of frequency of spontaneous skin potential responses to vigilance and to age. *Psychophysiology* **1**, 272–276.

SYZ, H. C. (1926) Psychogalvanic studies in schizophrenia. *Arch. Neurol. Psychiat. (Chic.)* **16**, 747–760.

SYZ, H. C. and KINDER, E. F. (1928) Electrical resistance in normal and in psychotic subjects. *Arch. Neurol. Psychiat. (Chic.)* **19**, 1026–1035.

TAYLOR, J. A. (1951) The relationship of anxiety to the conditioned eyelid response. *J. exp. Psychol.* **41**, 81–92.

TAYLOR, J. A. (1953) A personality scale of manifest anxiety. *J. abnorm. soc. Psychol.* **48**, 285–290.

TEPLOV, B. M. (1964) Problems in the study of general types of higher nervous activity in man and animals. In GRAY, J. A. (Ed.) *Pavlov's Typology*. Pergamon, Oxford.

THERON, P. A. (1948) Peripheral vasomotor reactions as indices of basic emotional tension and lability. *Psychosom. Med.* **10**, 335–346.

THORPE, J. G. (1962) The current status of prognostic test indicators for electro-convulsive therapy. *Psychosom. Med.* **24**, 554–568.

THORPE, J. G. and BARKER, J. C. (1957) Objectivity of the sedation threshold. *Arch. Neurol. Psychiat. (Chic.)* **78**, 194–196.

TISSOT, R. and MOUNIER, M. (1959) On the dualism of the thalamic recruiting system (antagonism between the thalamic recruiting system and the ascending reticular system). *Electroenceph. clin. Neurophysiol.* **11**, 675–680.

TIWARI, N. M., JINDAL, M. N. and JAISWAL, C. L. (1960) Effect of tranquillizing agents on water and saline induced diuresis in rats. *Arch. int. Pharmacodyn.* **128**, 383–390.

TRAUGOTT, N. N. and BALONOV, L. (1963) Neurophysiological analysis of the anti-depressive action of Tofranil. *Zh. Nevropat. Psikhiat.* **63**, 552–563.

TROUTON, D. S. and EYSENCK, H. J. (1960) The effects of drugs on behaviour. In EYSENCK, H. J. (Ed.) *Handbook of Abnormal Psychology*. Pitman, London.

TROUTON, D. S. and MAXWELL, A. E. (1956) The relation between neurosis and psychosis: an analysis of symptoms and past history of 819 psychotics and neurotics. *J. ment. Sci.* **102**, 1–21.

TSOBKALLO, G. I. and KALINANA, M. K. (1960) Effect of barbamyl, nembutal and thiopental on the higher nervous activity of rabbits. *Pavlov J. Higher Nervous Activity* **10**, 644–645.

TUCCHI, J. H., BRAZIER, M. A. B., MILES, H. H. W. and FINESINGER, J. E. (1949) A study of pentothal sodium anaesthesia and a critical investigation of the use of succinate as an antidote. *Anesthesiology* **10**, 25–39.

UTENA, H., EZOE, T., KATO, N. and HADA, H. (1959) Effects of chronic administration of methamphetamine in enzymic patterns in brain tissue. *J. Neurochem.* **4**, 161–169.

VANDERHOOF, E. and CLANCY, J. (1962) Peripheral blood flow as an indicator of emotional reaction. *J. appl. Physiol.* **17**, 67–70.

VAN DER MERWE, A. B. (1948) The diagnostic value of peripheral vasomotor reactions in the psychoneuroses. *Psychosom. Med.* **10**, 347–354.

VASTOLA, E. F. (1965) Analysis for dependence between sequential responses evoked in visual cortex. *Amer. J. Physiol.* **208**, 861–866.

VENABLES, P. H. (1957) A short scale for rating "activity–withdrawal" in schizophrenics. *J. ment. Sci.* **103**, 197–199.

VENABLES, P. H. (1959) Factors in the motor behaviour of functional psychotics. *J. abnorm. soc. Psychol.* **58**, 153–156.

VENABLES, P. H. (1960) The effect of auditory and visual stimulation on the skin potential response of schizophrenics. *Brain* **83**, 77–92.

VENABLES, P. H. (1963a) Selectivity of attention, withdrawal, and cortical activation. *Arch. gen. Psychiat.* **9**, 74–78.

VENABLES, P. H. (1963b) The relationship between level of skin potential and fusion of paired light flashes in schizophrenic and normal subjects. *J. psychiat. Res.* **1**, 279–287.

VENABLES, P. H. (1964) Input dysfunction in schizophrenia. In MAHER, B. A. (Ed.) *Progress in Experimental Personality Research*. Academic Press. New York.

VENABLES, P. H. and TIZARD, J. (1956) Performance of functional psychotics on a repetitive task. *J. abnorm. soc. Psychol.* **53**, 23–26.

VENABLES, P. H. and WING, J. K. (1962) Level of arousal and the subclassification of schizophrenia. *Arch. gen. Psychiat. (Chic.)* **7**, 114–119.

VENDSALU, A. (1960) Studies on adrenaline and noradrenaline in human plasma. *Acta physiol. scand.* **49**, Suppl. 173.

VERZEANO, M. and NEGISHI, K. (1960) Neuronal activity in wakefulness and in sleep. In WOLSTENHOLME, G. and O'CONNOR, M. (Eds.) *The Nature of Sleep. Ciba Foundation Symposium.* Churchill, London.

WALKENSTEIN, S. S. and SEIFTER, J. (1959) The fate and distribution and excretion of S^{35} promazine. *J. Pharmacol. exp. Ther.* **125**, 283–286.

WALTER, W. GREY (1953) *The Living Brain.* Duckworth, London.

WAWMAN, R. J., CLARIDGE, G. S. and DAVIES, M. H. (1963) Sedation threshold, autonomic lability and the excitation–inhibition theory of personality. II The Mecholyl Test. *Brit. J. Psychiat.* **109**, 553–557.

WECKOWICZ, T. E. (1958) Autonomic activity as measured by the mecholyl test and size constancy in schizophrenic patients. *Psychosom. Med.* **20**, 66–71.

WEIL-MALHERBE, H., AXELROD, J. and TOMCHICK, R. (1959) Blood–brain barrier for adrenaline. *Science* **129**, 1226.

WENGER, M. A. (1948) Studies of autonomic balance in Army Air Force personnel. *Comp. Psychol. Monogr.* **19**, 1–111.

WHATMORE, G. B. and ELLIS, R. M. (1958) Some motor aspects of schizophrenia: an EMG study. *Amer. J. Psychiat.* **114**, 882–889.

WILDER, J. (1957) The law of initial values in neurology and psychiatry. *J. nerv. ment. Dis.* **125**, 73–86.

WILLETT, R. A. (1964) Experimentally induced drive and performance on a five-choice serial reaction task. In EYSENCK, H. J. (Ed.) *Experiments in Motivation.* Pergamon, Oxford.

WILLETT, R. A. and EYSENCK, H. J. (1962) An experimental study of human motivation. *Life Sciences* **1**, 119–127.

WILSON, W. P., SCHIEVE, J. F. and SCHEINBERG, P. (1952) Effect of series of electric shock treatments on cerebral blood flow and metabolism. *Arch. Neurol. Psychiat. (Chic.)* **68**, 651–654.

WING, L. and LADER, M. H. (1965) Physiological and clinical effects of amylobarbitone sodium therapy in patients with anxiety states. *J. Neurol. Neurosurg. Psychiat.* **28**, 78–87.

WINTER, C. A. and FLATAKER, L. (1952) The effect of cortisone, desoxycorticosterone, adrenocorticotrophic hormone and diphenhydramine upon the response of albino mice to general anaesthetics. *J. Pharmacol. exp. Ther.* **105**, 358–364.

WINTERS, W. D., CONRAD, A., LENARTZ, H. F. and BLASKOVICS, J. B. (1962) Influence of corn-oil, heparin and albumin on thiopental action in rats. *Anesthesiology* **23**, 27–31.

WOLFF, H. H. (1951) The mechanism and significance of the cold pressor response. *Quart. J. Med.* **20**, 261–273.

YAMAMOTO, S. and SCHAEPPI, U. (1961) Effects of pentothal on neural activity in somatosensory cortex and brainstem in cat. *Electroenceph. clin. Neurophysiol.* **13**, 248–256.

YERKES, R. M. and DODSON, J. D. (1908) The relation of strength of stimulus to rapidity of habit formation. *J. comp. neurol. Psychol.* **18**, 459–482.

YOSHIKAWA, K. and LOEHNING, R. W. (1965) Thiopental binding to serum albumin. *Experientia (Basel)* **21**, 376–377.

ZUCKERMAN, M. and GROSZ, H. J. (1959) Contradictory results using the mecholyl test to differentiate process and reactive schizophrenia. *J. abnorm. soc. Psychol.* **59**, 145–146.

AUTHOR INDEX

Figures in italics refer to entries in Bibliography

SUBJECT INDEX

269